My Father's Ghost

My Father's Ghost

*The Return of My Old Man
and Other Second Chances*

· A MEMOIR ·

Suzy McKee Charnas

JEREMY P. TARCHER/PUTNAM
a member of Penguin Putnam Inc.
New York

Most Tarcher/Putnam books are available at special quantity discounts for bulk purchases for sales promotions, premiums, fund-raising, and educational needs. Special books or book excerpts also can be created to fit specific needs. For details, write Putnam Special Markets, 375 Hudson Street, New York, NY 10014.

Jeremy P. Tarcher/Putnam
a member of
Penguin Putnam Inc.
375 Hudson Street
New York, NY 10014
www.penguinputnam.com

Permission to print letter to Robin McKee from Albert Einstein dated 1936 granted by The Albert Einstein Archives, The Hebrew University of Jerusalem, Israel.

Library of Congress Cataloging-in-Publication Data

Charnas, Suzy McKee.
My father's ghost : a memoir / Suzy McKee Charnas.
p.   cm.
ISBN 1-58542-185-5
I. Charnas, Suzy McKee—Family.   2. Authors, American—20th century—Family relationships.
3. Fathers and daughters—United States.   I. Title.
PS3553.H325Z466   2002   2002025371
813'.54—dc21

Printed in the United States of America
1   3   5   7   9   10   8   6   4   2

This book is printed on acid-free paper. ♾

BOOK DESIGN BY AMANDA DEWEY
FRONTISPIECE PHOTOGRAPH BY STEVE CHARNAS

This account is as true as I can make it. I have, however, disguised the identities of some of the people involved, to safeguard their privacy. Similarly, there are no retirement or nursing homes in Albuquerque named Vista Linda or Gracious Gardens. But you get the idea.

Thanks are due to many members of my family, to friends who have read this book for me in manuscript, and to my agent and publisher for their support. And, of course, thanks to my dad, who seems to have left me something after all.

You know?—when we croak, what we'd like?—to be a ghost. We're mostly one now, so why not be one altogether. . . . A simple ambition. To be a ghost. Since a ghost, by one definition, is a human spirit that doesn't know it's dead, such an extension of our "life" would be perfect, for we don't—so far—know that we are alive.

To be a ghost. Lovely.

ROBINSON MCKEE, JOURNALS, 1969

Contents

B O O K   T W O · *Falling   Off   the   Cliff   as   He*
Fled   from   the   Tiger,   the   Man   Saw   a   Flower
Growing   on   the   Cliff   Face   and   Thought,
"How   Lovely!"

Wine and Ashes

*Death is the resumption of two dimensions,
from volume back to plane.*

FROM ROBIN'S JOURNALS, 1933–45

One cool and sunny March morning in 1993 my half-brother Ian and I drove out to the old place on North Fourth Street, in Albuquerque, where our dad had lived next door to me in a little adobe farmhouse a backyard's length from my own place for the first half of his time in New Mexico, about ten years out of nearly twenty. The two Fourth Street houses, the square farmhouse with the peaked roof covered in galvanized tin and the low, flat-roofed cottage set back behind it, had both been rented out for some years now.

But that was where Dad had lived most independently during his years with my husband and me, and where I felt he might like to return for good.

I'd chosen a weekday on purpose (the tenants were out, at their jobs) so that Ian and I could do what we had come to do without interruptions or witnesses. Ian is my elder by six years, but because Pop had lived his last years with me, here, it had fallen to me to take charge of all the sad necessities connected with our father's death.

We parked in the yard between the two buildings, in the shade of a craggy Russian olive tree and a decrepit Chinese elm, and walked to the back of the small property, the southeast corner of a scant acre of flat valley sand and clay. A sagging wire fence and more scrawny elm trees screened the big field beyond the back fence-line; that field had once grown alfalfa in summer and served as horse-pasture in winter. There had been snow back then, and the view from my kitchen window on crisp mornings of the dark horses cavorting over the white ground against the backdrop of the mountains never failed to raise my spirits. In summer the successive alfalfa crops of the long growing season had cooled the air around our place and made it an island of comfort in the furnace of Southwest heat.

But that was over twenty years ago, when we had first moved in. Now, this early spring day, the back field was rough with neglect. You could still see faint ruts marking the orderly rows of the plowing once done each spring. The ground was covered with an early crop of the weeds that had eventually driven my husband and me from the Valley because of my allergies. But above the weeds, beyond the line of elms down at the end of the field, the plateau of the city's Heights still tipped upward to the crumbling knees of the Sandias, the mountains that rose raw and grainy into the clear blue eastern sky.

"Well," I said, "there it is, the mountain he was going to paint but never did."

"He didn't even make any sketches?" Ian said wistfully. A slighter version of our dad, with the same strong Scots face, my half-brother lived in Phoenix and sold computer chips. This work took him to Sandia Labs and up to Los Alamos from time to time, so he had often come to see Pop and us here in Albuquerque over the past years. "I thought he was drawing, at least."

"I haven't found anything but some old stuff he brought out here with him," I said, and left it at that. I had been the one to suggest to Pop that the mountain was there for him to paint it, following in the footsteps of the great French painter Paul Cézanne, whom he had idolized. Now that I thought about it, Pop had never actually agreed to this program, so it was a little ridiculous for me to complain about him for not having gone along with it.

I set down the brown-paper shopping bag I had brought from the car, took out the small white cardboard box, opened it, and set it on the ground between us. Ian and I sat on the stumps of elms cut down years ago and toasted the old man's ashes, and his unpainted mountain, in good red wine.

Then I upended the box and dumped out the coarse gray grit onto the ground. Together we scooped dirt over the spot to keep everything from being messed with by stray animals or curious human visitors; though who would wander down to the end of that brushy, unused plot, or why, I can't now imagine.

Just the two of us; I have a sister whose father was also Robin, but her life was falling apart at the time. Her disintegrating marriage and her resultant state of chronic emotional and financial meltdown, plus the exigencies of providing for various dependent animals, had kept her stuck in L.A. for some time. My father had so thoroughly cut his ties with everyone back east, friend, colleague, or relative, that I had no idea who else to inform that he was dead, let alone invite to our little free-form service. The obituary notice that I had run in the *New York Times*, just in case, had drawn no response.

Ian and I were Robin's funeral, hunched in our coats because a chilly breeze was blowing; but the sun, that southwestern light that has inspired generations of regional painters out here (but *not* my father), was clear and bright.

So that was that; we poured a little wine on the ground, returned to the car (talking mildly about our memories of the old man), and drove back into the city and down to the house on Cedar Street, with its "mother-in-law quarters" where Pop had finished out his two decades, nearly, with my husband and me.

In the silent studio apartment he had lived in (where the radio used to play all day, tuned to the area's one classical music station), Ian helped me bring down some canvases and boxes of papers from the storage space up under the skylight. He wanted a painting or two to remember the old man by; our sister had asked for some, too.

There was no clutter in the room, apart from Pop's skinny, nearly toothless cat, which wound itself around and around Ian's ankles, purring and meowing in manic excitement. What Pop had left behind was the detritus of failure, a poor man's meager hoard: some beat-up old books on the narrow shelves flanking the fireplace, where they had sat untouched for years gathering dust; a couple of drawers' worth of jeans, long-sleeved shirts, underwear, and socks; a bright red down vest left over from days of winter cold out on Fourth Street, a blue blazer, one pair of barely worn shiny black shoes, and a huge old tweed coat that looked as if Sherlock Holmes would have been at home in it; and a painting-box full of dried up color-tubes and brushes, with a heavily encrusted palette tucked up into the lid.

There were also some paintings: a few small examples of old work that he had brought with him from New York and some abstract watercolor sketches on heavy paper. We looked through them, not saying much. Ian set aside a couple of slashing abstracts done in an electric blue on black paper to take home with him.

He sighed. "It's not much, is it?"

It sure wasn't; not for an eighty-two-year-old man who, so far as we both knew, had devoted the better part of a lifetime to painting pictures that he couldn't sell.

That was when Ian told me about the bonfire Pop had made of a vast pile of his own work back in the mid-sixties, when the slumlord who owned the Canal Street loft he had been renting had evicted him in order to modernize the place and raise the rent. Pop had had to retreat for a time to a tiny apartment in the East Village.

"He told me he had no room for the stuff," Ian said. "Hell, if he'd said something beforehand, I'd have stored those pictures for him! But I only found out about it when it was all over."

That certainly fit our dad: not finding out about things till it was all over.

Then there were the notebooks, ranks of them left standing and leaning in the lower bookshelves. These were actually sketchbooks, the black-bound, blank-paged kind still sold at Sam Flax Art Supplies. Ian picked up one and flicked through it. Dust flew, and ancient, crumbling magazine clippings and postmarked envelopes floated from between the pages and fanned out over the rust-colored carpeting.

"Can you read any of this?" Ian said, peering at the straight but minuscule lines of cramped printing that filled every facing page.

I shrugged and leaned down to retrieve the scattered papers. "Kind of, if I use a magnifying glass and don't spend too long at it at a time. He told me once there was an entire novel in there someplace, but I wouldn't even know where to start looking for it."

He put the book back, eyeing the rows and dusty stacks of similar volumes. "How many are there? Have you counted?"

I had counted: there were forty.

Ian whistled. "Wow! What the heck do you think is *in* them?"

From what I had gathered, skimming through some of the pages, it seemed to be mostly left-wing political ranting and long disquisitions on painting, painters (particularly his ideal and saint, Paul Cézanne), and, well, paint. And, I added, the occasional wisecrack.

"What are you going to do with them?" Ian said, dusting his hands together.

I said I thought I'd try to decipher a few of them, when I had a gap in my own work and some time to spare. As a writer by profession, I thought that there might be something in there I could use in some kind of book about Pop, though frankly I was more doubtful than not.

"Great," Ian said. "Let me know what you find, will you?"

I said I would, and the two of us went back into my house to get some newspaper and string to wrap up the pictures he had chosen to take home with him.

Does this sound cold to you? Do you miss the tears of the dead man's children, the sighs of loss, the fond recollections laid out for mutual solace? Pop was not a demonstrative man, and—not surprisingly, perhaps—we are not particularly demonstrative children in that way, and there are other reasons . . . and, I have discovered, other ways to acknowledge the impact of a parent's death than tears.

A WRITING LIFE is no longer a slow and quiet one, if it ever truly was; abandoned by publishers (who now merely produce and fling out like birdseed the books writers labor to create), all but best-selling authors must be their own publicists, accountants, travel agents, and general career managers. It was over five years and a couple of published novels later before I found myself with the time, and the will, to turn seriously to the task of reading Pop's notebooks.

I had at last completed a sizable writing project of my own, a series of four novels set in a stripped-down, brutalized future where men and women find their way, through bitter gender warfare and fateful alliances and loves, to the prospect of a better life for themselves and their children. I had started this futurist, feminist epic unintentionally with my first novel (*Walk to the End of the World*) in 1974, and only now, as the century drew toward its close, had I completed the saga, along with a good batch of other books and stories published in between.

But this, the final polish and launching of the last volume of that tumultuous fictional saga, felt like some sort of defining moment for me. I was facing the crossing of a border between that long period of one vast, sustained fiction full of willful, passionate people, and—whatever would come next. It was a pretty nervous-making prospect, to tell the truth.

It's a curious fact that whenever I complete a book, I sink into a period of some months of semiparalytic depression. I am told that this is by no means uncommon among writers, which is no help at all. Some writers work on two projects at a time, or start a new novel while completing an old one, and they seem to have less of a problem. For me, unfortunately, each work is discrete, and discretely absorbing, and I'm just not free to think about other possibilities until I've finished the one in hand; and then there are bad dreams that bring me awake in a sweat of anxiety and discomfort every morning, and days of pottling about like a zombie while lists of things prepared for when I would have time to do them lie gathering dust on my desk. I can joke about it, but this is a very uncomfortable part of the writing process for me.

This time I was winding up not a book so much as a thirty-year fictional epic in which the characters in the story had aged just as I did, in real time. What was going to happen now? Catatonia? A wild descent into crazy ravings and bingeing on Twinkies?

I sat thinking about this in my studio one chilly autumn morning in 1998, staring gloomily at the stack of five hundred pages comprising the final draft of Book Four, *The Conqueror's Child*.

And when I turned about restlessly in my swivel chair, I spotted Pop's notebooks, three stacks of them on different bookshelves, with their spines out. Their years were written on them—by me, during a cursory glance through them after he had died, in garish silver lettering, using a fancy blunt-nosed marking pen.

Now, there was Something Completely Different: the job of transcribing Pop's journals into a readable text, or anyway part of them. That was so far from the immersion in a fictional world that I was just beginning to shake off that maybe, just maybe, it offered a hope of really effective distraction. Maybe this could be a way around the hellish bout of discontented uselessness that I glumly foresaw for myself once the novel's manuscript went off in the mail and became the responsibility of other people.

I had no idea what I might find in Pop's notebooks or whether it would be of any significance; but whatever it was, I wouldn't have to flog myself into *inventing* it, would I? Not that invention is a chore, far from it; but it has no appeal when I'm in the miserable throes of letting go of a vivid, fully realized imaginary world that it's time for me to leave behind.

On the level of listening to my own inner promptings, well, there was something going on there too. The books had been important to Robin, or he wouldn't have lugged them out West with him when he came to live with us. By keeping them when we'd moved to our new house down the hill after his death, hadn't I in a way committed myself to at least making a stab at doing something with them? Indicated a willingness, however grudging and uninterested?

It seemed like a pleasingly perverse task, too, for nothing useful was likely to come of it. It's not as if Robin was someone famous whose journals would interest the world at large. Anticipating no particular payoff, I felt nothing enticing about the prospect of dipping into those pages, no whiff of initiatory excitement like that tingling that floats around the start of a fiction-writing project. In my current morose state of tapering-off, as it were, I would have turned away in disgust from anything as delicious as that.

In fact the morbid element in opening those books exactly suited my sense of myself as poised at what looked like a natural terminus of my writing career. I mean, what the hell was I going to write about *now*? There wasn't an idea in my head, not one; I felt completely wrung out. And I was close to crossing the threshold of my own sixtieth year besides, facing in a very definite and unarguable way the downward slope we all must travel toward oblivion.

How could I decline this worthless, unrewarding, pointless task? I didn't have the energy to resist, although not quite the energy to begin right away, either.

The next day I sent off the novel. I spent the rest of the afternoon sitting on the floor in my studio surrounded by teetering stacks of Rob's lumpy black notebooks and sneezing mightily from the dust that drifted up from the pages as I turned them.

The earliest volume was no bigger than the old hardbacks of the Everyman classics series, which had been designed to fit into the side pocket of a man's overcoat. Some of Pop's later notebooks were in a larger format, with pages about the size of a sheet of typing paper. All the books were covered in heavy black paper treated to look like leather, with a once shiny, nubbly texture.

In the one I had picked up, some of the entries had been squeezed in at the bottoms of the pages at a later date. (An economizing move, as I realized later—why buy a new notebook, when all that marginal space sat there blank and unused?) One whole set of comments ran in the same green ink from the bottom of one page to the bottom of the next, one footnote-style rumination after another on Cézanne's rejection of the mysticism of some of his contemporary painters.

The inscription on the flyleaf surprised a chuckle out of me:

Gossip Books, volume 1, 1930
Notebooks of Robinson McKee
Axioms, Apothegms, Aphorisms,
Epigrams, Wisecracks, Humor,
Philosophy, Phrases, Dialogue,
Bilge, Baloney, and Bunk,—
Meant for the confusion of those who
Expect an explanation for everything,
From painting to the song of a bird;
Meant, in a word,
For those who want to be confused.

1930 was nine years before I was born. I wondered how many of these volumes he thought, when he began this one, that he would eventually fill.

The page following the flyleaf is also inscribed:

Malediction to Be Read Aloud
In order to testify to the truth of what I say, I lay myself open to trial by jury according to due process of law, and before all living witnesses and other accusers, before I die, or in Heaven after; and likewise, may the dentist's drill in your teeth one day slip; may your vitamin pills carcinomize your duodenum; may your stocks become worthless and your bonds taxable; may the combustion of your cigarettes, pipes, and cigars ignite your nicotinized flesh and bones by way of your breath; may your coffee keep you ulcerously awake even in hell; may your flatulence become jet propulsion and your sole means of locomotion; may your creams, ointments, astringents, soaps, salves and muds choke, clog and seal up your pores and mummify you before senility does; may your beers, wines, whiskeys, brandys, rums, cordials, cocktails and neat keep you in a perpetual pickle-rot; may your douche-bones eviscerate you; may your promiscuous syszgies fuse and condemn you to the rather limited life of a sexual siamese twin; and may you be regarded as a Communist! In case you do not believe absolutely all that I shall dish out to you in this present chronicle ironical . . ."

What an odd, deliberately antique, spitefully humorous paragraph! And effective, too: the old man had caught my attention.

The last notebook of all was dated 1969, five years before he'd come to live with us. Disappointingly, I found no notes at all for the period of Rob's life in New Mexico. On reflection, however, I had to admit that perhaps this was actually a Very Good Thing.

Skimming gingerly through the pages (I mean, what if there were horrible secrets, gothic revelations, feelthy pictures, dead—or living—spiders?), I found this:

I am locked in the house
of myself. There is no

*Door, no key. I cannot
leave the place that I inhabit,
Until I am dispossessed.
This house can never be a home,
for here none may enter,
none may leave.
I can only sit by the window
and watch, and watch
life that sometimes watches me,
a peeping Tom.*

I was hooked—by the voice: an odd, secretive, thoughtful voice. He himself had never, in all the years I'd known him, spoken like this—freely, even boisterously indulging the dark, quirky, astringent mind that I had only glimpsed in him from time to time.

I'd seen the tip of the iceberg, of course, but here, in these books, I might find the whole underwater mountain of ice, glinting with the hoarded light of his personality. The prospect was irresistible, if daunting; it was going to be a hell of a job, decoding all of this. Thank God the old man only wrote on one side of each page!

In preparation, I went through all the books and set aside the many letters he had read, refolded, returned to their end-slitted envelopes, and tucked away in his notebooks' pages. The vast preponderance of the letters were prosaic notes from his older brother, Irving, who had been an English professor in Sacramento, California.

But there was one startling find among the hundred or so of these documents. It's in faded typing on embossed stationery, and it's written in what turns out to be slightly ungrammatical German. I had it translated, and it goes like this:

A. Einstein
112 Mercer Street,
Princeton,
New Jersey, U.S.A.

February 10, 1938

Mr. Robinson McKee
New Rochelle N.Y.

Dear Sir:

Due to being overburdened by my own productive work it is impossible for me to involve myself with matters which lie outside of my special knowledge. For that reason I am also unable to address purely philosophical questions of a nature such as they are explained in your letter. It would be more proper for you to get in touch with someone who is primarily occupied with philosophy. By the way, the imparted maxims are not understandable to me.

Very truly yours,
A. Einstein

I've found no copy of Pop's letter to Einstein.

Robin was born in February of 1911. At the age of twenty-seven my dad wrote to Einstein and got an answer. I don't know about you, but *I* was impressed.

And my appetite was whetted: who was the man of active mind and playful language who had lived hidden inside my grouchy, lazy, cynical old dad all those years? Who had he left here in these books for me to discover after his death? I remembered him saying to me when I asked what was in the notebooks, "Ah, never mind. Read 'em after I'm dead."

So I did.

FROM ROBIN'S JOURNALS, 1945:

In one's Will one would like to specify that one's remains be cremated and the ashes put to work in an hourglass.

He should have told me sooner.

BOOK ONE

The Second Chance

Going Blind

In the autumn of 1973 my sister Liza called to tell me that she had moved to another part of L.A. and to give me her new phone number. Both of us, Manhattanites by birth and childhood, had done a lot of moving around since our mother died in 1969. I was now settled, with my husband Steve, in New Mexico, where we had moved shortly after my mother's death.

Robin still lived in New York—in Greenwich Village in fact, like any serious painter. I called him up (Liz was shy about doing that—"I never know what to say to him"), told him about Lizzie's change of address, and gave him her new phone number. "Okay, got all that? Why don't you read it back to me."

My father's rough bass voice said, "I didn't get it."

"Eight-one-eight—"

"I can't see to write it down."

"Pop," I said, "turn on the light."

"There's light," he said. "It's still afternoon here, Suzy. But I'm having trouble."

"What kind of trouble?"

"Trouble seeing things."

"Things. Like, what things?"

"Print. Writing."

I got a sinking feeling. My father was living in a loft on Canal Street in lower Manhattan. I now lived in an adobe house in Albuquerque. My husband and I were launching new careers, Steve with a local law firm, me working on a novel. Steve was paying hefty alimony and child support to his ex-wife, and a lawyer's pay in New Mexico was a lot less than back East. There was no money to spare for flying back and forth to New York.

"What *can* you read?" I said. "Newspapers?"

"Nah, that print is so small—"

"Book print?"

"If I hold it close. But it's hard."

"Street signs?"

"Yeah. I can read street signs, if I'm not too far away."

Jangle of serious interior alarm bells: New York City street signs were big and clear (mental image of black background, white lettering and edging, "42nd Street," outside the New York Public Library, where I used to hang out to escape from my mom bugging me at home). "What does your doctor say?"

A pause. I knew what it meant before he answered: "I haven't seen a doctor."

"Good!" I cried with ferocious enthusiasm. "You're an artist. You're going blind. And you haven't seen a doctor."

I was scared, so I waxed sarcastic. As an adult, and a distant adult at that, I had with him at that time what in anthropology textbooks is sometimes called a "joking relationship," as between young spouse and mother-in-law, maybe. Ours was not your garden-variety father-daughter bond.

At least I didn't think it was. I had no other father-daughter bond to measure it against, except in fiction; and it wasn't like any of those that I had ever come across.

He said angrily, "Doctors cost money."

All right, Pop was a Scot by background, or anyway Scots-English, but this was not about Scottish frugality. It was about reality, and we both knew it. After all these years Pop was still an unknown painter. For eating-money he had for many years worked in the kitchen of a West Village pub called the Lion's Head, under the longtime owner he had liked, Leon, and now under Leon's heirs, whom he didn't.

The Lion's Head was a basement joint when I saw it, very English in a wood-paneled sort of way, on the north side of Sheridan Square. Pop lived a few blocks from "the Head" (as he liked to put it, having a lifelong love of gross jokes, locutions, and puns) in a huge, cold loft into which black New York grit ceaselessly sifted through the grimy, tar-spattered panes of a rectangular skylight.

This was at the top of a venerable industrial building with neither elevator nor hot water. The pay for being the "salad man," dishwasher, and garbage-hauler at the Head was enough to buy him that one vast room, with a deep porcelain work-sink fixed to the wall in one corner, next to an unspeakably grimy and questionably functional toilet, behind a screen. He slept on an army cot pushed against the wall.

But first you had to climb those stairs. He said they kept him in good condition, and certainly he had always been a lean man.

"You must have seen a doctor that time you fell down the

stairs," I said into the phone; I knew about this because I had visited him shortly afterward and had asked about the bruises on his face. He had admitted that he'd been drunk but added that being drunk was, for him, a rare occurrence (which, so far as I had ever observed, was true).

But that had been years ago. Now, on the phone with me, he said that he no longer had any contact with the doctor he had seen then. Several minutes of exasperated haranguing later, he reluctantly volunteered the information that there was a clinic nearby that he sometimes went to. I more or less commanded him to go there next day and have his eyes examined. He said he would.

There was a small silence while I considered the idea of my father the painter going blind, and he thought Robin thoughts, whatever they were.

"So how's everything?" he said.

This meant, How's your cat? Pop did not have, or at least did not customarily express, any great interest in the people in my life—husband, stepchildren, editors, colleagues—although when he said, "What's new with the mob?" he was asking for some word about my sister Liza. A brief bulletin always seemed to suffice.

The cat was different. When he asked about the cat, he really wanted to know.

He had, unofficially, a cat of his own. This was the cat at the Head's kitchen, Ketzela (so named by my Wasp, presumably Presbyterian-raised father). According to the health code no cat should have lived in the restaurant kitchen. I pointed out the illegality once, being something of a goody-goody and inclined to follow rules because then people left me in peace to read books, which I did instead of almost everything else. In this—the reading, not the rule-following—I was my father's daughter, as my mother had always (rather bitterly) remarked when she found me sprawled on my bed with a book. Also, like any intelligent child, I picked and chose the rules I obeyed, if you see what I mean.

It was okay, Pop said, about Ketzela; they had mice at the Head, and so the cat was a working cat, which made the code inapplicable. (Having cats myself, I was skeptical of the concept "working cat," but let it ride.)

Now, asked for cat news from New Mexico, I told Robin that Flakey, an apartment-raised cat who had come west with us, was slowly getting used to the terrifying unfamiliarity of actual earth underfoot and no longer went about lifting his feet up almost to shoulder level in a vain effort not to step on the grass. Robin approved, and we parted on amicable terms.

He called me back a few days later to report the results of his visit to the clinic. "The doctor says it's ocular degeneration."

Great; I could have come up with that myself. "From what, though? What's causing it?"

A pause. Then he said, "He thinks it might be alcohol poisoning."

I hugged the phone closer, astonished. "*Alcohol* poisoning? In your *eyes?*"

"Yeah, something like that," he mumbled. I could tell he was embarrassed, and I could see why: my dad, such a drunk that he was losing his sight to it? This was impossible for me to imagine.

One thing that had eased the way for Robin to accept my husband Steve as a son-in-law was that Steve appreciated single-malt whiskey, which was all that Robin would willingly drink in company. I saw this as a bow by Robin to his own Scots ancestry, and a gesture toward being a man of quality despite his poverty. Rob's favorite was "the Glenlivet," which even then was comparatively expensive. I suspect that he was able to cultivate such refined taste only because the bartenders at the Head indulged him in it.

So though he sometimes talked about drinking, I thought he was too much of a liquor snob to be a real drunk—he couldn't be, not on Glenlivet, not with his salary.

"I thought you weren't a drinker," I said, trying to sound light and casual, not accusatory; but it was hard. My stepfather, my mother's second and infinitely worse choice of mates after Robin, had been a heavy drinker. He had left me with no love for alcohol addiction in any of its stages or guises.

"I don't drink liquor, Suzy," Robin said testily. "Not for years now. I hate the taste of booze. But I have to drink half a bottle of wine to get to sleep at night."

I had never thought of him as an insomniac either, and said so.

"I don't have insomnia," he snapped. "When did I ever complain about insomnia? It's working the late shift at the Head. I don't get home till two, three in the morning, and by the time I lie down to sleep the trucks are roaring down Canal Street. You know, the big ones that bring in produce and meat to the wholesale markets. They run from a little after midnight to six a.m., hell of a racket. You hear it all over the neighborhood, it never stops. So I take some wine, and then it doesn't bother me."

This I could understand; I slept then and sleep now with a white-noise machine by my bed because I'm cursed with exceptionally keen hearing (inherited from Guess Who). I know that deafness is a terrible burden, but in this cacophonic modern world better-than-average hearing brings problems of its own.

My brain started cranking again. I asked if the doctor had said whether the eye condition was reversible, and Robin said Yes, maybe; but so what? He couldn't afford to move to a quieter neighborhood—as a longtime tenant he had a special rent break from his current slumlord—or to quit his job to look for another one with better hours.

Okay, I thought; okay. I saw a fairly breathtaking but unavoidable solution. It scared and exhilarated me.

I asked how old he was.

"Sixty-two, almost," he said truculently. "Why d'ya want to know?"

I took a deep breath and turned to look out of my French doors to the crooked little brick patio behind our house, and the sun-blinding half-acre beyond, and then the rising plateau of the developing city, and finally the roots of the mountains. Not lively, art-center Manhattan, but hey, there was a mountain; Pop had always spoken worshipfully of Cézanne, and if Cézanne had his Mont Sainte-Victoire, couldn't Robin paint the Sandias?

And what other choices did we have? Mom had been dead for four years, killed in her late fifties by a broken hip followed by a pulmonary embolism. My cousins who were still in New York had their hands full taking care of their own aging parents. My half-sister, Patty, was still living there but had an intense artistic life of her own going on, and she had no ties to Robin; she barely knew him.

Steve, on the other hand, understood and seriously honored family connections, even weird and heavily compromised ones. His relentless struggle to maintain good, vital relations with his two kids from his first marriage against implacable hostility from their mother demonstrated that pretty clearly.

So, acting on the promptings of my natural impatience (which in its better manifestations takes the form of decisiveness or even impetuosity), I took the plunge. "You're almost old enough to retire, Pop. I want you to quit your job and move out here as soon as you turn sixty-two." That was only a couple of months away.

Quiet. Then he said, "It wouldn't work, Suzy. I'm used to my own place. How can I live with you two in that little apartment out there?"

"No, Pop, that was just somewhere to stay till we figured out where in Albuquerque we wanted to buy a place of our own. We moved out of the apartment on Monte Vista, remember? We've been living in an old adobe house in the North Valley for two years now. I think you'd like it here. This used to be all farms, and it's still pretty rural. A guy built our house for himself and his family when he married the daughter of the farmhouse up in front, which we're also buying."

"What happened to him?" he said, inquisitive as always; only it wasn't what most of us think of as curiosity. He was always alert to pursue odd facts that would bolster one or another of his theories about how viciously and corruptly the world really works, did we fools but know it. "The guy who built the house."

"Oh," I said, "he's still around, but he lives up in the Heights now. People say that he came home drunk one night, threw a rock at his brother-in-law out in the back yard, and killed him. So he had to leave the neighborhood."

Robin snickered appreciatively. He loved stories like that, savage bizarreries that proved what a dim, ruthless, uncouth lot humans are.

"Bill, the old guy who's been living in the front house, has moved to Florida to be near his daughter," I said, "so we're buying his place now, too, for next to nothing. We were thinking of renting it out, but I'd sure rather have you there than some stranger." I had to stop a minute to listen to that: Robin, the father who had left our family when I was eight to become a hermit of the West Village, more familiar than some stranger? Hardly.

But he *could* be familiar; he *would* be. I would make it happen.

I'm not sure I recognized it then, but I sure do now: I saw a golden opportunity to get my lost dad back at last, and I grabbed it.

"You'll start drawing Social Security as soon as you retire," I said, "so you can even pay me a little bit of rent, if that's okay, to help cover my payments on the front place."

"I wouldn't mind retiring," he said tentatively.

"Tell the guys at the restaurant that you're going to quit, and then you pack up your things—"

"Aw, Suzy, that's a big job. You don't know how much stuff I've got here—"

I did know. I'd visited the loft infrequently in the years closely preceding our move out West, but often enough to know that there was practically nothing in it: the cot with a couple of smelly old army blankets (smellier because Pop didn't bother with sheets), a dozen rusted coffee cans with gray bouquets of splayed paintbrushes stuck into them, trays and boxes of oil paints in tubes and glass jars full of dry pigment, cans of varnish and turpentine, rags, canvases, stretchers, and some clothes stuffed into crate shelving or hung from the ceiling pipes and reeking powerfully of tobacco, strong deodorant, and unwashed old man.

It was not a lot of stuff, there were just many individual pieces of it. I overrode him without compunction.

"Look, it's ideal; you'll have your own place here, a separate *house*. There's even a mountain you can see from the back yard. We'll get you some kind of wheels. Have you got a little money saved up? Could you pay for a secondhand car? A down payment, anyway; we could help with the rest."

"Yeah, I've got a little money," Robin said cautiously.

"I'll call Patty and ask her to help you pack up what you need to have sent out here, and maybe she can take you to the plane, too. I'll get you a ticket and mail it to you. Just bring what you need, leave the rest, and we'll fill in the gaps when you get here."

Pause. I listened to the ringing silence of my own amazement at what I was doing.

He said, "What about the painting?"

Ah, The Painting; I didn't have to ask what he meant. This was the huge canvas spread out on the floor of the loft, his major project, which he had been working on for years. This painting, partly modeled on at least the idea of the Navajo sand-paintings I now saw out West, was unlike anything else of Robin's that I had ever seen.

Even in that dirtied light, it glowed with a deep brick-red and black ground, threaded with turquoise and pale yellow and ethereal green ganglia. The pigments, which he ground himself with mortar and pestle, were sprinkled on dry, gradually accreting to such thickness that they made a rough relief of painstakingly built-up layers, small peaks and valleys and humpbacked ranges of hills.

He called it a "dry painting," working with raw pigments trickled from between the fingers of one hand and set on the canvas with plastic fixative. I used to smell the stink of that plastic spray hanging in the air when I visited. The canvas, which occupied a space on the center of the floor under the skylight, measured approximately six by ten feet and probably would have been larger, except that Pop had to be able to kneel and reach to the middle of it with his powdered paint. The edges were stapled to the worn floorboards, and when I walked into that big, gloomy room, this huge, glowing rectangle on the floor was all I could see until my eyes adjusted.

How it could glow I never knew; there was a lamp by the one chair in a corner but no other source of illumination except a row of small windows high up along the ceiling, and of course the skylight directly above the canvas. The skylight had a big curtain of plastic taped under it to catch the dirt and soot that sifted through and to keep them off the painting below. I don't know how I even saw the colors, the light was so murky, what with the filthy skylight panes and the plastic dust-sheet like a tattered shroud. But I knew he had been working on that huge, gem-bright piece for a long, long time.

"Bring it with you, of course," I said.

"I can't, Suzy," he protested. "How'm I going to get it out of here? It's too big to fit through the doorway, let alone down the stairs."

"Well, how were you planning to get it to a gallery, then? If you got it up there, you can get it down again."

"It's fragile. It would never survive a trip across country in a moving van."

"We'll think of something. Talk it over with Patty. She's an artist too, she'll help you figure it out. Anyway, a painting is not a reason to stay in New York and go blind, is it?"

Pause.

"What if the guys at the Head don't want me to quit?"

"You're not quitting. You're retiring. A person who's worked all his damn life has a right to retire, Robin."

He said, "Are you sure about this?"

I wasn't. I felt little flutters of panic. I was a thirty-two-year-old woman about to import the father I barely knew into a life my husband and I had only recently begun in a part of the country new to all of us. It was completely crazy.

"Of course I'm sure," I said heartily.

"Maybe you should ask Steve first."

There I felt on firmer ground. "He won't mind," I said. "It's not as if you'd be moving into the house with us; you'll have your own place. And you can help out with watering the plants and things. We're trying to landscape the yard, and we'll both be glad to have some help with that."

"Aw, Suzy," he said unhappily. "He might not like it."

"Look," I said, "don't worry about it. You're my father, and you're not going to sit alone in New York going blind, okay?"

"Well, if you're sure," he said doubtfully. (My God, I think now: what must *he* have thought of his prospects with *us*?) Then he said, "What about the light?" (So I can tell you what he was thinking *about*.)

"What light?" I was thinking about which room in the four-square little farmhouse across the yard would make the best bedroom for him.

"You know, the daylight. Does this 'front house' have north light?"

STEPHEN SAID without hesitation, "Of course he should come."

Robin arrived six weeks later. It was only a few years since I'd last seen him, but he looked very thin, somewhat stooped in the shoulders, and unbelievably older than I remembered. He still kept his beard trimmed short, but now he had let it grow right up his cheeks almost to his eyes, like some haggard El Greco saint.

I see my father: the only photo I have from his youth, taken at the "farm" we used to go to with my aunt and uncle (they had a Victory garden there, so this is before 1945), shows him bare to the waist, slender and sinewy, a dashingly mustached young man with a deep widow's peak of upspringing dark hair, carrying a small, laughing child piggyback on his shoulders.

It was a fantastically altered version of this man, skinny and grizzled, that we met at the airport. But after only a moment my vision adapted, and he was the man I remembered from a hundred meals in Village restaurants and visits to his loft-home four long flights up.

Actually, to both me and my sister Liza, Pop in later life looked almost exactly like the comic George Carlin, though taller I think; and had something of the same delivery and speech, not to mention the same sarcastic attitudes, come to think of it. The first time Liza saw Carlin on TV only a few years ago, she called me up in high excitement and incredulity, insisting that I take a look. The facial likeness, along with a similar diction and voice, was enough to raise the hair on the back of my neck. I doubt that Robin ever saw Carlin perform, and he probably would have thought him nothing like himself if he had, but to us the resemblance sometimes bordered on the uncanny.

There was nothing comical about Pop's arrival in New Mexico, though; it was the arrival of a fugitive from his own life.

A few sticks of furniture came after him in a moving truck, including an enormous black easel for canvases, like a bladeless guillotine; a scarred and ancient cobbler's bench (just mid-shin-height to catch you as you walked by) rimmed with a raised rail with holes in it to hold tools (for Pop it held brushes, stuck in upright with their hairs up); and a rickety brown bedside table with one drawer that he had set his telephone on. Whatever else he had owned, apart from a beat-up leather suitcase full of clothes, he had left behind.

The big painting, for instance. I had been eager to see it again.

"Aw, Suzy," he said when I asked about it, "it was too big. There was no way to bring it, so I left it. I cut it up and threw it in the trash. So what?"

His masterpiece. So what?

Oh, Dad.

My youngest sister Patty now tells me that, although I had alerted her beforehand, Pop never got in touch with her about helping him to move. So he must have done the whole thing by himself. I should have gone to New York, of course.

FROM POP'S JOURNALS, 1960:

*It looks as if __Eutrope__ is altogether done. Just a little smoothing and trim-
ming, edges. It gives us back what we meant. Fourfold. We have watched it
fade, from twilight to night. We have watched it emerge with dawn. It asserts
itself in going and coming. Best we have ever done, we think.*

I scarcely ever saw him take a drink after he came to live with us.
Maybe because of this he did not, after all, go blind. In fact his
eyesight began to improve, although in later years he got cataracts
(probably a hereditary weakness; I am now growing my own set).
He wore big bifocals, with oil from his fingertips and crumbs of
crud and dandruff smeared all over the lenses, which he never
washed.

You may as well understand right here, this is not an old man
built on the Dave-of-Wendy's model in those TV ads: some glow-
ingly clean, benignly beaming, successful but modest old gent, nor
yet your basic John Glenn style, either, buffed and bright-eyed and
enthusiastically forward-looking.

This is my dad, who had lived for a long, long time in a real gar-
ret, in real Bohemian poverty—which means he had good taste,
brains, and an artistic bent for which he sacrificed all, thus becoming, to all intents and purposes, what used to be called a bum. An
empty envelope that fell out of his notebooks when I looked
through them after his death had a list headed "cheap meals"
scribbled on it that included "bread and beans."

He had told me once how hobos in the thirties had lived on
bread and beans in their camps beside the railroad tracks: a loaf of
white bread, unsliced, with the center hollowed out and filled with
beans that had been heated in the can over a fire of sticks, made a
nutritious dinner.

We had never been rich on my mom's income, but we'd eaten

well (lamb chops, chicken, homemade dumplings, lots of stews) while Pop worked out ways to eat like a hobo. And said nothing to anyone, of course (he used to insist on paying for lunch when Liz or I went to visit him in the Village).

I put the list in the file next to Einstein's letter.

FROM ROBIN'S JOURNALS, 1947:

Ah, July, the warmth of the year. One has just tucked away a nice little dinner consisting of one fifteen-cent-frankfurter (5 cents in 1945), one seven-cent cup of coffee (5 cents in 1935), one seven-cent "raised donut" made of potato flour (2 for a nickel in 1935), and one cigarette. We have something to be contented about.

This exact time, July last, one was trying to make edible pancakes out of a mush concocted of breakfast food, and succeeded, too. Seems every summer at mid-July the restaurant work dries up; one finds oneself the proverbial grasshopper, and that goes for one's appearance also. By December, will be earning $125 per week again, and throwing it away—again.... One is of a kind which must learn by not one, not two, nor yet three—this is the fourth (since 1937)—periods of privation; but one will learn ...

Me, stacking books to carry from his place back to mine: "Well, what's worth reading in this bunch? How about this Robert B. Parker?"

Rob, my trusty reader and reviewer: "Nah. I never finished it."

"This one, with the cat on the cover?" The cat was why I had included it in the stack I had brought home from the library and put on his table.

"That's not a mystery, it's a romance, Suzy."

"Oh. Well, what's good, then?"

"Ruth Rendell. Get more Ruth Rendell, those are always good."

Ruth Rendell, chronicler of grimness, cynicism, and brutality.

Some of her novels I couldn't even finish, the people were so mean and foolish and doomed. But Pop read them with relish, read everything, read more mysteries and murder stories than he did anything else.

I have mentioned his "alcohol poisoning of the optic nerve" to a couple of doctors since, who all say that they've never seen such a thing—no one has, not since people used to drink wood alcohol, Sterno, and other serious alcoholic poisons during Prohibition days. So maybe something else was going on there, and an over-worked clinician, accustomed to dealing with wine-soaked Bowery bums, jumped to an obvious conclusion. Or maybe Pop never went to the doctor at all but simply gave me his own opinion of the cause and prognosis of his difficulties with vision.

He was never shy about leaping to conclusions, the more bizarre the better. It was one of his favorite forms of entertainment.

FROM ROBIN'S JOURNAL, 1969:

We have yet to see an old man, an old man—80—90—who has a short nose. What's a short nose? Well, a long nose: Durante, Einstein. Got the picture? (though Einstein didn't live to be 80). Observe Bertrand Russell. Can't recall any great men who had short noses—except K. Marx, and he didn't reach 80.

We have never met a long-nosed man or woman who was foolish, intemperate, stupid, or less than superior to us. We have never met a shortnosed, flatchinned man or woman who was not foolish, stupid, or equal to us.

We speak from inner and outer experience.

Nuclear Family Fission

I see my father. I'm in Dad's kitchen with the cracked linoleum underfoot and the old stamped-tin ceiling ten feet overhead, its fleur-de-lys pattern painted over in thick gray-white enamel; the unused stove; and on the sideboard the stained and crusted microwave oven that he heats frozen dinners in. I've come over to invite him to cross the yard tonight and have dinner with us.

Stoop-shouldered, he sits at the kitchen table in a red-and-black plaid shirt-jacket, faded jeans, and his Navy watch cap, with scuffed orange-tan loafers on his feet, which are planted firmly apart. His wiry, graying beard is trimmed rather haphazardly close to cheek and jaw. His eyes are washed-out blue, his brows project gray tangles, and his mouth has a twist to it, an inbuilt crookedness of the lips. But he is a handsome man still, craggy-faced and refined-looking at the same time. That's how my eyes see him, anyway.

Here I am, tall too and getting more stocky than I want to be, with short brown hair and my square, middle-European face, with Pop's Scots-Irish nose stuck into the middle of it. I wear jeans and blouse and Birkenstocks: "Hi, Pop."

Him, petting the cat in his lap with his long, elegant hands: "Hi, Mop."

Me: "Who's a mop? You're the one who won't wash your hair, not me."

Him: "If you call me Pop, I can call you Mop."

He doesn't sound as if he's joking, he sounds grumpy. Which isn't exactly uncommon with him, but perhaps he feels there is special cause; he is sensitive about names, and "Pop" tends to make him scowl almost as much as "Robin."

He's told me that he's always hated his own name, "Robinson," because the short form "sounds like a bird." He was named, he says, after the poet Robinson Jeffers, or was it Edward Arlington Robinson? My memory fails, and not for the first (or last) time. Probably it was a family name anyway, and he's only told me where he wishes it had come from.

We all call him "Robin." No way can he transform himself into some kind of "regular guy" with us by pretending (as he does with others) to be plain old "Bob," or even "Mack."

Me: "Call me whatever you like; I just want you to come over for dinner, how about it?"

Rob: "What, now?"

"No, not now, it's only four o'clock. About sixish."

"Aw, Suzy, I've already got something picked out for dinner tonight."

"Okay, how about tomorrow night instead?"

He grunts assent, his slackening posture expressing his relief at not having to actually do anything yet: the ineffable joy of postponement.

Me (thinking of how I'll switch to noodles tonight, and save the big chuck steak for tomorrow): "But you have to wash your hair first."

Silence.

I see my father; an aging beauty on the long-headed, northern European model, although his false teeth don't fit too well any more (his gums are shrinking) and make his lower jaw look underslung. This is some one I am familiar with but barely know, and now we have to have a talk about personal hygiene.

I sit down across from him at the round table of scarred, stained oak, and I coax: "Come on, Pop; when's the last time you washed your hair?"

Him, grumbling and refusing to meet my eyes (so it's *really* a while ago): "I don't remember."

Me: "I'll bet you don't. I can see from here, there's a skin of gray gunk creeping out of your hairline—you've got cradle-cap, for God's sake, like an infant!"

Him (lying): "It was last week sometime."

Me: "Well, this is this week, so how about washing it again?"

Him (his voice lowers as he gets closer to telling the truth): "If you wash your hair it falls out."

Me (impatient; I've heard this from him before): "Oh, that's crap, Robin."

Him: "It does. You look in the drain afterward, and it's full of hair. You have to clean it up to get the water to run out."

Me (trying reasonable mode, a forlorn hope if ever there was one): "That's hair that was already dead, it would fall out anyway after a while."

Him: "Well, I don't want to hurry it up. And after I wash my hair my dandruff gets worse."

Me (trying for patience; not easy for me, but I'm learning, with him; there's no other choice if I'm not to just strangle him on the spot): "That's not because you wash it. Of course you get dandruff! Your scalp can't breathe, it's fermenting in there because you wear that filthy old watch cap all the time, even in the house."

Him: "No I don't."

Me: "So what's that on your head?"

Him, balefully: "That's because I was reading. If I don't wear the watch cap, my hair's always falling into my eyes when I'm reading."

Me (more patience): "Your hair falls into your eyes because it's too long, and it's too long because it needs to be cut, but I can't make an appointment for you with the barber as long as your scalp is covered with guck. It's embarrassing to everyone, and it's plain cruelty to make anybody wash all that crud out of your hair before cutting it. I end up feeling as if I need to tip him a hundred dollars, and if I did it still wouldn't be enough."

Him (now he's the reasonable one, innocent blue eyes raised to mine): "Why don't *you* cut it? All you have to do is put a bowl over my head and snip around the rim with the scissors."

Me: "Ah, Jesus, I don't believe this! What do you think we are here, a Norman Rockwell painting?"

Him (with fathomless disgust): "Rockwell was a lousy painter. It's amazing to me how a lousy painter like that could be so popular."

Me (unwilling to take an endless detour today through art criticism): "Okay, look: you wash your hair and come over for dinner tomorrow, and I'll take a stab at cutting it."

Him (gruff and sly at the same time; how does he do it?): "Maybe I'd better stay away from all that cutting and stabbing."

Me: "But no bowl. We'll just have to wing it, okay? And you get to live with the result, no complaints."

Rob: "Yeah, yeah. What are we having for dinner?"

FROM ROBIN'S JOURNALS, 1968:

Re "Vanity Hair," J. O'Reilly, New York Mag. 11/4/68—O'R. quotes all these hair-fakirs—and some of their patients—as saying that the chief, the first, the paramount rule is cleanliness (of the hair and scalp): wash the hair (with a gentle castile soap) every day.

I say, shit, bunk, baloney, crap. I spent 4 yrs. on the Bowery—not as a bum, but as a loft resident on Hester St.—and saw more bums (who don't wash, period) with fine, flowing locks of hair—full heads of hair, ranging from black to silver to white, plus beards of all sizes and shapes.

Ourself—we, I—have not washed my head or hair since 1950, that's ten yrs. Bald? NO. It's so goddam thick that we have to trim it every fucking day.

True, we scratch hell out of our scalp every night and day—culling NY's muck out of our fingernails; true, we get a very small handful—maybe 50 hairs—after combing each a.m. (which, according to one fakir, is double what we should get); but we've still got a wildly flourishing head, no sign of a bald spot (at age 57) anywhere. We've got dandruff, too.

So—cleanliness? Bacteria? Germs? Viruses? Clogged circulation?— Bullshit, all of it. My old man had an even fuller head of hair, and I know he didn't bother to wash it—he died with his total wig—64 yrs. His old man had the same full wig when he died, an alkie, aged 80. Neither wore hats.

That's the story: heredity.

Above all, remember this: Never let a barber trim your eyebrows.

Heredity indeed; between him and me, sometimes it felt as if there wasn't much.

What a domestic little scene, you might say; even sweet, if a little on the dry side. Whatever it was, it didn't come for free. We had to create all that between us, because despite being parent and child, we two had not had the luxury of spending my childhood and youthful years together.

One afternoon after school when I was a kid, my mother sat me down in the living room of our apartment on West Eighty-third Street and said, "Suzy, would you mind very much if Robin didn't live with us for a while?"

Mind? I was stunned, horrified, a lot of appalled feelings I didn't even have words to express, which was fine since I was old enough to know a parental *fait accompli* when presented with one; no point bawling over spilled milk.

I don't remember what I replied. I could have said, What do you mean, not live with us? Where would he go? Is he going to live with someone else? (He wasn't.) When will he come back to live with us? (Never.) Why did he have to go? (No answer.) Was he angry with us? (I had never heard him express anger against anyone except the Bad Guys Who Run the World, and none of us are them.) Did this mean he didn't love us any more?

I didn't say any of that. Whatever I did say instead, I didn't cry or make a fuss; I despised fusses, even then. I didn't change the course of events, either, by my questions or my silence or my confusion or whatever came across to my mother.

I don't remember Robin leaving, I just remember him gone. I remember living for what seemed like eons with just my mother and my sister Liza.

Later on, I visited my father by subway in the Village, and in the 1950s by train from Grand Central Station to New Rochelle (where he went to live with his widowed mother until she died), and then in the Village again, on Hudson Street. We talked about

Shakespeare and Cézanne. I didn't ask him all the questions I hadn't asked my mother either.

I was probably scared to hear answers. Also by that time I knew pretty well that adults lie to kids whenever they feel like it and without compunction, for utterly unimaginable reasons, which they invariably describe, when caught at it, as "for your own good." There was no point asking them about anything important.

They were okay about trivia, though, because if it wasn't important they wouldn't bother with lies, except as a clumsy attempt at play in the form of teasing. I remember that I knew such things then because I am reminded of them in dealing with my two grandchildren. I try not to lie to them at all.

My mother told me, as people did then (and probably do now in pending divorce situations in order to give a kid some role besides that of next-to-chief mourner), that I would now have to help her run our household. It would be up to me to take especially good care of my little sister. Robin had often told me that I had to look out for her, so this was old news.

I did not want to look after my little sister. I would have preferred being looked after myself, which I thought was the crux of the family bargain: you put up with being a child, with the daily indignities, the ceaseless incomprehension, subordination, and all the rest of it, without making a horrible nuisance of yourself. What you get in exchange is being looked after, no matter how crudely or spottily or offhandedly. You're not supposed to be taking care of other people; someone takes care of you, because you're a child.

We were living in a comfortable, compact apartment in a big building with an awning on West Eighty-third Street, within actual sight of the green western cliff-edge of Central Park. My parents each had a drafting table in one corner of the living room. Dad's had screens around it for privacy because his work couldn't be interrupted—he had gone from cartooning, animation, and advertising art to illustrating children's stories for Wonder Books; good, paid work for an artist.

My mom drew and colored textile designs to peddle from her portfolio to the rag trade downtown (less good, less well paid, and often irregularly if at all, but still work). She had an eye for the exotic that seemed to please the buyers: paisleys in hot pinks and oranges, wild color combinations—but designs were obviously not serious art, just outlines filled in with colors; they both clearly believed that. Child's play, almost. I was encouraged to color in spare copies with my crayons and colored pencils.

Now Robin's drawing table was gone, his corner was empty, and he wasn't coming back.

He did return, though—it was very confusing—he kept showing up for dinner, once a week or so. Mom must have invited him. They obviously liked each other as much as ever. They looked as wonderful together as they had ever looked to me (he tall and handsome, she petite and beautiful with her blonde hair pinned up for added height, her greenish eyes heavy-lidded with blue eye shadow, velvet mascara on her long, curved lashes).

So what was wrong?

Must be us, something to do with us kids, my baby sister Liza and me. She's sick all the time, and too small for the grownups' problems to be her fault. So that leaves—who? Even though Mom keeps telling me, "Suzy, it's not your fault, this is between your father and me, it's nothing to do with you kids. We both really love you."

But she's so anxious when she talks about this, so tense and intense, that I assume (at least as I remember this) that she's afraid I'll figure out the truth. Whatever I did to make this terrible thing happen must be so ghastly that she can't even bring herself to mention it.

This was a no-win situation, and Mom—no fool—knew it. No

wonder she was anxious. She sent me off to somebody—whatever they called kid-shrinks in the late forties—so the shrink could tell me the same thing, or so I assume. I remember nothing of it. Frankly, I don't remember feeling guilty for very long either. It's hard to concentrate over time at that age, which is one reason we think of kids as resilient.

After a while I was reveling, rather, in the distinction of being the "first divorce" in my class; divorce was not common then. So far as I knew I was the first divorce on my *block*. I was always told I was "precocious," so maybe I was precocious in this, too.

There is a strong memory of people, complete strangers, stopping me on Eighty-third Street as I was going down to Columbus Avenue to buy milk or ice cream—total strangers, mind you—and telling me, or asking me, or practically begging me, to smile.

"Why do you go around looking like a thundercloud? What could a pretty little girl like you have to frown about?"

Nowadays, soaked in volumes of revelations of child abuse, drunkenness, and dope use at home, bullying at school, and childhood madness, nobody would be so naive, or want to borrow so much trouble, as to ask this particular question.

(You'll have to excuse my old-fashioned locution here: I know "nowadays" is a word we don't use any more. We use "anymore," conflating two meanings so as to be able to drop one term; one example, among others, of the ongoing linguistic impoverishment and slovenliness that makes me think that Americans have grown too stupid to hold two similar but distinct phrases, and their separate meanings, in their tiny little brains at the same time. Maybe we've just had to make room in our brain cells for computer-speak and the painfully clumsy euphemisms of ever vaster reams of corporate and government bullshit.

Hear that acid tone? I come by it legitimately, as you will see.)

One of the few good things I can think of about the forties and fifties was that reticence, that automatic assumption of the best, not the worst, about people and situations. I think it was left over from the vast communal effort of the war, and from a benign mis-memory of the Great Depression in which we all pulled together to cope with frightful conditions. Whatever it was, a default civility was assumed that is very attractive now, in nostalgic hindsight.

But considering it carefully—considering the fact that one of Mom's married friends in the building used to come down to visit with a black eye, but nobody talked about it because such matters were simply hidden, out of that perverse form of shame that forced a beaten wife to assume the blame for her own abuse—I can see that our naive optimism, which we now hark back to with such a sense of loss and betrayal, did not come free. Its price, for those caught in the dark side of reality, was very high.

Those were also the days when a "guidance counselor" in junior high school could look me compassionately in the eye and tell me in all seriousness that because my mother was divorced, the chances of my marrying and staying married when I grew up were nil. I probably believed her (for the record, I married in my late twenties and have stayed married for over thirty years, and I hope the damned "counselor's" marriage is the one that fell apart).

I was moderately unhappy. No kid really likes to be the "only" or the "first" anything. It's quite clear when you're small that the only safety is in numbers, and numbers means lots of other kids who appear, at least, to be just like yourself (I already knew I was a fraud in this department, since I read six library books at a time while most kids I knew read none). The thing you learn, when for one reason or another, you are denied the safety of conformity is to despise that safety and all those who have easy access to it, at the same time that you still crave it desperately for yourself.

But I was talking about smiling. My mother herself sometimes regarded me with a pained and guilty expression and chided me for looking like such a "crosspatch." Another lost word, replaced by flatter, duller words, one even descended from television holiday specials meant to keep the kids busy while the adults fuss and quarrel: "grouch," or "grinch."

But why, I said to my child self, why should I walk around grinning like an idiot? Moreover, I was *not* pretty and knew it; my little sister was "the pretty one," as all the world could see and was quick to say aloud.

My mother (who was already taking photos of Baby Liza around to Eileen Ford's agency in hopes of creating a modeling career for the Pretty One) even said so (she was a realist, in her way): "Liza's going to be a beauty, but you have your own kind of beauty, dear. Besides, you're the smart one. You're going to make your way on your brains."

Well, yes and no; my dumb blonde sister got into Columbia University. On the other hand, I *did* make my way on my brains, and when I look at photos of myself as a youngster I do see a kind of grave beauty—a little heavy-jawed, like a marble head of Athena in a museum (it's dispiriting how after forty so much of the outrageous nonsense your mother told you turns out to be, in some way, true). My nose doesn't qualify for beauty on any terms, being my father's for starters, and then having been broken by a boy in third grade in a quarrel over the relative merits of Gene Autry and Roy Rogers.

I frowned because I was angry and humiliated that my family was somehow broken. I had three sets of aunts and uncles, solid couples who never quit till death did them part despite various stresses I only recognized or learned about later. So how come *I* was stuck with the first divorce on the block *and* the first and only divorce in my family?

It didn't dawn on me for a long time that there were reasons, instructive ones, that my grandmother lived alone in her apartment on 107th Street. A huge, oval portrait photo hung on the wall over her dining-room table, displaying a suited, complacent-looking, portly man with impressive black whiskers that divided in the middle to make two points aiming in opposite directions.

That was grandfather Nathan, although at the time nobody ever referred to him except by his European name, Ignatz ("Nathan" came later, when some of my cousins got interested in family history and a child was named for this great-grandfather—no sane adult in modern America is going to name a kid Ignatz).

When I asked about this unseen grandfather, Nana said he was away somewhere. "Florida, maybe."

Liza says that when she went, in her turn, to visit our grandmother, Nana used to point at the portrait and say, "Don't marry a lazy good-for-nothing like Ignatz, darling; you marry a good man. You want to be happy? Marry a nice Jewish man, look after your health, and take care of your teeth."

Since Nana was always stumping around her apartment looking for her own misplaced teeth, she clearly knew what she was talking about in that department at least. On the other hand, surely the worthless Ignatz himself had at least appeared, at one time, to be a nice Jewish man?

I put two and two together only years later, when some genealogical notes about my mother's parents were circulated in the family. Apparently the tradition of strong, ambitious, bright Lilienthal women marrying and then living at least partly without their intellectually restless, fecklessly impractical, and/or philandering husbands went back several generations in Europe, where the marriage-in-name-only was a well-recognized solution to this kind of mismatch.

Just how did my father, a hermit and misanthrope by nature, despite his nature become bound into my mother's family; and what came of that, good and bad and impenetrable? Pop never introduced me to any of his family, so I only knew him at all in the context of mine and my mother's.

FROM ROBIN'S JOURNALS, 1928–35:

Ever since memory first served him, no one forced God on him. His parents were too busy supporting themselves and his brothers and him to do anything on Sundays but think restlessly of more work to be done—they were artists. His old man did those melodramatically tortured and richly Latin illustrations for "The Candy Cigarette" in the American, you recall? And many other stories in the Saturday Evening Post and the rest, slicks and pulps. His mother paints anything, everything, sells one once in a while, and gets nice remarks from the little old Lady in the Times.

Well, they never bothered him, because he was never in their way. Of the boys, the two oldest were, and still are, simply a moron and his duplicate. But what saved him from over or any attention was William. He was, he is, The Boy. Since there must be genius in every family, William was it.

Capabilities unknown, our strange young man was left alone. All through the schools he went to successively because the family was always moving, he seemed to preserve this untouchableness . . .

Most Americans talk about family and "family values" without having a clue as to what we're dealing with here. All of our schematics about this—ideals of the Right and of the Left—fall so breathtakingly short of the variety found in reality that there's hardly anything to do in response but fall down laughing hysterically, turn on the TV, or walk off a rooftop, depending on your mood at the time.

Sometimes I am sorry for Pop, the archetypal loner, hanging

baffled in a web of women and other entangled men, trying to separate from it but always linked by threads he can't quite break—and
doesn't quite want to (no one forced him to keep coming for dinner, or staying in touch with his daughters).

In a simpler time, Liza and I agree now, he'd have been a monk
in a cell illuminating manuscripts, or some desert-dwelling mystic
sitting on a pillar a mile up where he could tease and upbraid an-
gels and devils to his heart's content. There would be a radio up
there, too, and a dumbwaiter-arrangement for hoisting books and
magazines, but no phone; and no need to wash your hair.

Well, we don't always get what we want.

WHEN I CAME HOME from the Peace Corps—two years in
Nigeria, 1961 and 1962—I taught for a while at a private school
on the edge of Harlem, and in the second summer I took a brief
course for teachers at Bethel, Maine, in "sensitivity training." The
instructors said, Try to resolve your hangups with your parents
while they're still around to talk to; it's a lot more satisfactory than
haranguing a headstone.

Made sense to me. When I came home from Maine, I called up
Pop and arranged to see him with the intention of clearing the air
between us. We met in Sheridan Square on a warm September day.

I said, "Pop, let's talk. We never talked about your divorce
from Mom."

We were sitting on a bench, not very close together. He leaned
forward the way he liked to sit, bracing his long back at a slant
with his elbows on his knees. "You want to talk about that?"

"Yes." Then silence: how to begin?

"What do you want to say?" he prompted. So helpful.

Now that we were up against it, I didn't even want to be there. I could not speak, not having the foggiest idea what I wanted to say to him.

"Are you mad at me?" he ventured at last.

"Yes." I waited for the great cleansing wave of relief; felt a twinge of something letting loose inside, an easier breath-draw, that's all.

"Yeah, well," he said. "I wish things had been different. What do you want me to do?"

What the hell kind of a question was that? "I don't know," I said rather testily. How had we gotten to the place where he was the one asking the questions?

More silence. A few cars swished past the little island that is Sheridan Square Park.

I said, "Were you mad at Mom, is that why you left?"

"No," he said. "I wasn't mad at anybody."

"So what happened?"

He shrugged. "Nothing. People can't always get along. What do you want to know for? It was a long time ago."

I knew a stone wall when I ran into one, and besides, who said there had to be a big revelation, a cathartic confrontation? That was not Pop's style, and to tell the truth it wasn't mine, either. *Pace* the nice, warm, bright facilitators at the retreat in Maine, one size does not fit all.

I said we might as well go get a soda or something. That may have been the day that he took me to the bar that Dylan Thomas used to drink at, the White Horse Tavern I think it was: dark, odorous, quiet at that time of day, unconnected in any perceptible way with Pop's colorful anecdotes about the literary hangers-on who still came in there at night to carouse.

On my way home I realized that I was still angry, at myself now as well as at him. I thought I would probably be angry forever, so there was no use thinking further about it.

Later still, when I knew him better, I thought it had been incredibly brave for him, given the man he was, to have asked me that: "Are you mad at me?"

I wish I had been brave enough to give a fuller answer.

Mr. Geniality

Scene: Rob's kitchen, the northeastern room in the front house on Fourth Street. Enter, me, swearing.

"Damn it! Why do they give you those thin paper bags to carry your groceries in, and then the packer jams all the heavy stuff into one of them? Here's your blasted orange juice."

Pop: "Bag broke? They always do that. I heard you swearing out in the yard."

Me: "I wish they'd heard me swearing back at Safeway, the idiots!"

Pop (smugly): "You have a bad temper, and I know where you got it from. You got that temper from me."

Me, incredulously: "You have a bad temper?" I've never seen him do anything other than snarl in a subdued tone at this or that obstacle to his ease and convenience.

"Sure I do. Used to scare me sometimes, exploding like Mount St. Helen's. But I never swore like you do."

"Oh, come on."

Robin, looking over his shoulder at me as he jostles juice bottles into the fridge: "Are you kidding? I learned not to. When I was a kid, if you said 'damn' you got smacked."

"Your parents hit you?"

"Everybody hit their kids in those days. You remember getting spanked, don't you?"

Now that he mentions it, I do. There was a period when I came home from kindergarten every noon and spilled my glass of milk and got spanked for it by my exasperated mother; every day. Years later I figured out that my eyesight was already awful even then, so that I couldn't see the glass of milk because the table top was covered in a thick coat of white enamel.

Me: "Spanking isn't the same as hitting."

Rob: "Want some tea? I just made some. If you said 'fuck,' they'd disown you. It wasn't till after the war that men started swearing in public, and now it's women too."

Me (avoiding Bibi the cat, who sprawls on the kitchen counter looking dead and stuffed by an untalented amateur, as she always looks): "I guess that's a shock, huh." My father, the old-fashioned gent.

Pop (with enthusiasm): "I love it! Some good-looking woman trips on the curb and hollers, 'Shit!' It's wonderful. I love it when they yell, 'Asshole!' That's my favorite swear word, it's the best. It sounds so perfectly like what it is: ASSHOLE!"

Me: "Meaning what? It has a round sound, or a puckery sound, or a brown sound? Or what?"

He wipes a thick blue mug out with a dishtowel for my tea.

"That's not as crazy as you think. Scriabin worked out a whole system of sounds coordinated to colors and numbers."

"Really? When was that?" You never know what strange stuff he'll produce—wild bits of information, if it is information.

"I don't know, late nineteenth century. He was working on a theory of sensation, linking them all together with some kind of equivalences—"

Me (pleased with myself): "Like a unified field theory of music?"

Him (handing me the sticky plastic jar of honey in the shape of a bear): "Yeah, something like that. He was crazy, like all the Russians."

All Russian artists, writers, and composers, he meant, since hardly anyone else signifies.

"Was his music any good?"

Rob: "It was all right."

"How did it sound?"

"It was nothing special. Sometimes they play it on the radio."

"Have you heard any of it lately?"

Rob, sipping his tea: "I don't listen to the radio much any more."

Me, taken aback: he *always* has the radio on (not right now, though, come to notice): "Didn't they fix it last time I took it in? I still have the repair bill. If it's not working again, I can take it back."

"Naw. I just don't listen, that's all."

Uh-oh. I can feel it coming, one of Pop's twists. "How come?"

Pop (as Bibi whines and crawls into his lap, and his hand falls automatically to petting her): "All they do is play the same thing over and over. I'm tired of it."

I no longer hesitate to be sarcastic when he comes out with this kind of thing. I think he does it to provoke a reaction. Why disappoint him? "On our local classical music station, the one with the whole library of recorded music to choose from, they only play one thing over and over? What thing is that?"

Pop: "How should I know? I don't listen."

Me, craftily, as I put in more honey; the tea, poor man's tea, is weak and tasteless, heavily overwatered: "What was it when you were still listening?"

Robin: "The Bolero. Same damned thing, over and over, it could drive you crazy. Ravel wrote it as a joke, did you know that? When he was a student. It was just a stunt, to see if he could get away with repeating the same exact phrase over and over through a whole piece. Now that's all they play, over and over—what for? Because there's a new recording of it out? All they do on the radio is push records."

Me: "Discs."

Rob: "What?"

"It's compact discs now, not records. I walked into a huge store called Discount Records last week and there wasn't a record in the place; nothing but these little shiny discs wrapped up in square packages that tell you absolutely nothing about the music because there's no room for text. I didn't buy anything."

Rob, skeptically: "You don't have a compact disc player yet? I thought you had all the new gadgets."

Me: "No, that's Liza you're thinking of. Her husband buys every new thing that comes along, and then they wonder why they're broke. Well, maybe he wonders; she knows."

Rob: "Then she must have a compact disc player."

Me: "At least one. I wouldn't doubt it for a minute." I look at him, considering; Liz had asked what to get him for Christmas. "Would you like a disc player, Pop?"

Robin, shifting his long legs but being careful not to disturb the cat draped over his lap: "What for? I don't even listen to the radio.

Nothing but ads pushing the new records, and they think we're so stupid we don't notice that it's just new technology reworking the same old music so they can sell it to you all over again."

What can I say to this? I've just seen an article in *The New York Times* about the transfer of LP recordings onto disc and how it's cheaper than making discs from scratch, so current performers are finding it hard to get their work out in the new format. Pop may be crazy, but he's not stupid, and he reads all our magazines and has kept up a subscription to the *Village Voice* (although he complains that the coverage of the gallery and museum scene is completely commercialized and useless).

"Come on, Bibi, let me up," he says irritably, pouring her out of his lap. "I can't just sit here all day, I have to walk the dog."

She jumps onto his vacated chair and curls up. He glares down at her, brushing cat hair off his pants. "Look at that. Every time I get up, she grabs my chair."

Me: "I thought I saw you take the dog out already this morning, before I went shopping." I surmise that what Pop really wants is the privacy to smoke without me seeing him; the doctor has told him to stop.

"I'll go get a burrito for my lunch at that little joint across from the post office."

Me (recoiling): "Jeez, Pop, that place is more like a phone booth than a store. They can't *make* anything there; it must all come in frozen."

"Sure, they use the microwave to warm stuff up. They have really good burritos, and George likes a bite. Gives him something to look forward to, you know?"

"Well, as long as you're going, how about walking him further up the street? More exercise is better for him than snacks of junk food."

Him: "Nah. I don't like to stay out too long. People keep talking to me. They don't even know me, and they say 'Hello.'"

"No kidding." I perk up, thinking, Hey, he might start making some friends for himself in the neighborhood. "Do you stop and talk?"

Rob, disdainfully: "What for? I don't know them, and I don't want to know them. Yesterday this nosey old guy walked up to me and asked me how old I thought he was. I didn't answer, so he said, 'Ninety-one.' Boasting about it, as if I should care. Then he asked me, 'How old are you?' I didn't tell him. Why should I? It's none of his business."

Me, getting up too: "Well I guess you showed him, all right. Thanks for the tea."

FROM ROBIN'S JOURNAL, 1958:

Women—at the Lion—at times throw themselves hopefully at me. I am polite. I can not deal with women, hardly with other men. I know what these women want and respect it, but it seems I __am__ a hermit. An exile from life.

He got a letter, once (that I know of), from one of his former fellow-workers at the Head. She was a waitress, and she was coming out West on a vacation with another young woman who worked there. I said I'd enjoy meeting them.

Oh, he said, he wasn't going to answer, let alone invite them to stop by. "If you let people visit, all they do is borrow money from you."

This startled me. Pop had always spoken warmly of the Head, of the conviviality of the place, of the boozy, smoky, cheery nights when the Clancy Brothers came in after a gig for drinks with their admirers; of when Pete Hamill of the *Village Voice* came by to drink, argue, and sing with cronies; and of the old chef, a souse of a Frenchman, much admired, who had once offered to teach Rob the skills of Continental cooking.

Robin had of course refused, because, he said, it was "too much work." A straight answer, at least, and it's not as if he didn't know what he was refusing, after all those years in restaurant kitchens. It *is* too much work, if you're not called to it: he told me enough stories of drunken chefs, crazy chefs, larcenous chefs, for me to understand the toll this *métier* takes on its peripatetic workers. And it's also possible that he shied away from adding their professional eccentricity to his already formidable personal oddness. An artist needs some sense of proportion, after all.

So he never wrote back to the waitress at the Head who had taken the trouble to track him down. He admitted that he had not even left the people at the Head his new mailing address (how the girls had found him at all he couldn't say).

This should not have come as a surprise. Let me digress a moment to tell you how I met my half-brother, Ian.

Rob had never told me anything about his first marriage (in fact I was in my late teens before I knew there had *been* a first marriage), and Ian knows nothing about it either. He says he thinks it didn't last more than a year. All of Ian's mother's relatives who might have known something about it are dead now, and wouldn't talk about it when they were alive.

Robin did say once that his first wife had "run around" on him, and he had left her, and she had later died in a fiery car crash while driving at high speed one night with her latest beau, whom I understood from Pop's remarks to have been a violinist; so romantic.

My father did not tell me that I had an older half-brother from that marriage; my mother told me that. Ian was in the Air Force at the time, and about to marry and have kids of his own. But Robin, when I asked him excitedly about this rumored older brother, clammed up and refused to divulge anything.

I called Pop up one day to arrange lunch with him and I heard him talking aside to someone. I asked who it was, and he admitted that Ian was there with him. I demanded to talk to this long-lost brother of mine.

I was eighteen or so at the time; Ian was maybe twenty-four and, he told me later, had only just finished tracking down his father (of whom he could never get one word from his mother's family) via the IRS. Having just discovered that he had a couple of half-sisters living right there in the city, he was very excited, not surprisingly; and it was no hard job to make an appointment with him to come up to our apartment on the West Side to meet us. We were pretty excited ourselves; I had sometimes fantasized about having an older brother, thinking of course only of the positive possibilities, picked up from my fiction reading.

He looked very much like his father, and he was at that time a poster boy for the Air Force, slim and blond and athletic-looking. He said he had been raised by his mother's family, based in Baltimore, but had spent most of his young life in military schools. He was very handsome in his spit-and-polish uniform, but beyond the fact of his long-lostness not unusual, which was no great surprise given that he had been living in barracks, essentially, since age six or so under paramilitary discipline. Whatever corners he had originally come with seemed to have been knocked off, leaving an affable, attractive young man.

I asked Robin later why he had never said anything about us to Ian or Ian to us. He said, "He's not my kid. He's illegitimate."

Given the fact that Ian was pretty much the spitting image of Robin, I found this statement ludicrous and said so. That was when Robin explained about the first wife, who was "wild."

It only later occurred to me that perhaps it was easier for Robin to justify having left his first wife and, presumably, contributed nothing thereafter to Ian's upbringing (whether by choice or by being banned by the ex-wife's family), if he believed that the boy was not his child. But I never checked this or any other theory out with Pop, who obviously didn't want to talk about any of it if he could help it.

As the years wore on, and later as Ian came by the house on Fourth Street from time to time and his resemblance to Robin intensified with maturity, Robin allowed his certainty on the question of illegitimacy to fade into the background and vanish. He never again in my hearing claimed that Ian was not his son.

When, some years after Robin's death, I checked the story of the "wild" first wife with Ian, what I learned was that Ian's mother had come from a wealthy and prominent family in the South, and that she and Robin had married very young and apparently secretly, because her family had moved heaven and earth to have the marriage annulled.

Well, consider it from their point of view, if you can stand to: she was some sort of heiress and he was a penniless young art student, youngest son of a commercial artist, without prospects or possessions. The outlaw couple's brief union was swiftly canceled, as if it had never occurred. If Ian was sent away to military school as a very young child (by his mother's mother, who had guardianship of him), it was to get him out of sight and out of mind, because he wasn't supposed to exist at all.

The mother went on to become a drunk who died many years later, running away with her eighth (prospective) husband in that crashed car; and it was she who was the violinist, not her beau, as I had wrongly supposed. I was embarrassed to realize that I had without a moment's hesitation or question performed the com-

mon cultural vandalism of erasing talent from a woman by ascrib-
ing it instead to a man who is linked with her, in this case by fiery
death.

I can glimpse a possible tragedy of young love in their story, or
anyway the dim lineaments of one. It does not suggest the encouragement in Robin of a lasting trust in the warmth and support of
family relationships or in the transcendent glory of romantic love.
If he was an antisocial curmudgeon in his later years, he had some
reason to be.

So far as I know, he never had a visitor in all the whole eighteen
years that he lived next door to us in New Mexico, except for an
Indian from the pueblo north of us who apparently had used to
stop by and bum money off the old man who had lived in the
front house before Robin. This Indian, Robin told me with some
annoyance, came by one afternoon asking for "Bill" and a buck
or two.

My father sent him on his way empty-handed.

FROM ROBIN'S JOURNALS, 1946–51:

*Often a person is an ascetic not because he dislikes sociability, but because
sociability melts down his reserve, his defenses, his ear for corruptness, and he
becomes a fool, a child again, under the delusion that he is free, secure, at play.*

Las Palomas

When you say you live in the North Valley, people assume that you mean you have a rambling, modern "designer home" built (or remodeled out of an ancient adobe wreck) on Rio Grande Boulevard or Guadalupe Trail; these are "horse properties," fenced acreage with tennis courts and old cottonwoods throwing dense, gnarly shade over the ground.

We lived in the North Valley, officially, but not in those stately precincts. We lived on North Fourth Street. Fourth is the historic Camino Real that used to connect the outpost of Santa Fe with Mexico City, when the Spanish invaders ruled an empire reaching deeply into North America.

Our house, 8918-B, had been owned by a retired woman who had been renting the place to Gypsies. No, not hippies with a Gypsy "lifestyle," real Gypsies: a wizened grandmother with gold front teeth and a long velvet skirt; a skinny wife, dressed likewise, who worked at a treadle sewing machine, the sole piece of furniture in the small front room; a swarthy, huge-bellied man lying on the bare springs of the only bedframe in the place, watching a small black-and-white TV set; and three little kids running around bare-assed with a tiny white puppy stuffed, squirming, down the T-shirt of one of them.

They were evicted by the owner of the house once she had us as buyers. On their way out, the Gypsies took a halfhearted whack at smashing the plumbing under the bathroom sink, a gesture of retaliation that I could hardly find it in my heart to resent. By then they, or someone, had kindly disposed of the dozen junked cars and the battered trailer that had occupied the long, bare front yard when I first saw the place.

My real estate agent was a woman who had just obtained her license. Previously, she had been a stewardess on a cross-country bus; this shows you how far removed in time all this was from the present in anybody's reality. I had not known there even was such a thing as a cross-country Greyhound bus, let alone a stewardess on it.

Jill had gradually shifted from showing me new, architect-designed adobe "homes" with incredibly high prices to showing me ancient, tumble-down ruins, which were what I could afford but was not willing to live in. The money I had inherited from my mother would not stretch to cover the upscale prices of the former or to rehabilitate to liveable conditions any of the latter.

I had about decided that an adobe house in the Valley was a hopeless dream (it was at the time the dream of every in-comer susceptible to the antique—by U.S. standards, that is—romance of the place). But before I could actually give up, Jill said, "There's a house out on North Fourth that I'd like to show you. It's not much to look at, and it's a rental right now, but it's on a bus line into the city and it's not expensive."

She blinked her carrot-colored eyelashes anxiously at me and added in an apologetic tone, "You don't have to get out of the car if you don't want to."

No doubt she was thinking about the dirt yard, the dead cars, the three tall, stringy elms clustered in the front, and the tiny rectangle of a house with its north wall practically right up against a junk shop, next door. But I did get out, even though I saw how small the place was and how neglected, and I thought, ugh; awful. It wore a dingy layer of whitewash over cracked and peeling stucco. The front room's "picture window" faced directly on the yardful of jalopies and the rumbling traffic beyond.

Then I stepped inside, where it was cool and dark but light enough for me to see the brick floor of the front room and the wood floor of the raised dining room a few strides beyond it, the pine-paneled walls, and the ceilings, which were low but supported by thick, round wooden beams still showing the marks of the axe that had shaped them.

The place was fourteen hundred square feet all told, priced at ten thousand dollars. I said, "I'll take it."

We discovered many little things "needing work" as the subsequent renovation process progressed, like the fact that the fireplace had no flue, only a space between the wall and the kitchen paneling for smoke to filter up through, in the process hardening the ends of the white fir beams above to the consistency of iron. After Nicky Garcia, my contractor, finished fixing the place up for us with a gusto and ingenuity that stretched my dollars to the utmost, there wasn't much money left to use for yet another house purchase.

But thank you, Mom; there was *enough*—for a down payment on what became Pop's place when old Bill moved out and it came up for sale.

We called it the front house. It had four square rooms, tall wood-framed windows all out of true, and both a front and a back porch, with the screening busted out. The outside stucco was painted a faded green and the tall pitched roof had to be re-covered in sheets of corrugated metal.

That was where Robin came to live, by himself. Well, except for first one scrawny stray cat (Bobo) and then another (Bibi); and some pigeons upstairs.

THE JUNK SHOP next door to our house had a big bare yard en-closed in a chain-link fence and full of wagon wheels, rusted farm implements and other stuff; this was "Pauline's Antiques." Steve and I had bought a couple of fine Indian pots from Pauline. Her better-than-junk stock was housed in a large barnlike building next to the little house she lived in, inside the eight-foot fence.

Pauline had come from Arkansas twenty years before and set up in business with her husband, who shortly left, or died, or both. She was on her own and apparently content that way, sharp and full of opinions, a good neighbor. She kept a lookout on our place when we were gone, as we did on hers when she went on buying trips into the countryside, driving her old Ford pickup.

We had crime out there, most of it petty thefts. The neighbor-hood thief was a boy of about twelve named Eddie who lived with his mom in a trailer behind a local restaurant, when he wasn't so-journing in Springer, the juvenile corrections facility. I heard from one neighbor about spotting Eddie up on his roof one night, with a pillowcase full of swag (surely he was making this up?). When Pop looked out his kitchen window one afternoon and saw Eddie and a pal of his walking around looking at our car (a 1968 Dodge Dart), inside the doorless adobe garage that we had built to block the noise and smell of Fourth Street traffic, we knew what that meant.

That evening when Steve got home from the office we all three set to work digging holes and sinking two posts in concrete bases, so we could lock a heavy chain between them across the entry to the garage. No car was leaving that place without the key to the big fat padlock I had bought at Chase Hardware that afternoon, along with the chain, the concrete, and the posts. All I had needed to convince me of the need for immediate action was the sight of the prints, in the dirt floor of my garage, of Eddie's neat little pointed boots.

Somebody pulled onto the verge of Fourth Street out by our mailbox while we were working, paused there—two slim, silhouetted figures in an old white Pontiac—hit the horn hard a couple of times in strident protest, and roared on up the street.

To give Eddie his due, it was said (at the lunch counter where I went to get superb Spanish food cooked by a white southern woman on the premises of a Japanese gift shop) that his mom was wheelchair-bound by chronic illness. She lived, they said, hand-to-mouth with a brood of kids in a trailer, so the kids had been encouraged to be a little sticky-fingered to support the clan.

Maybe so, maybe not. Even when you think you know, you don't.

Next to Pop's place, to the south, was a barbershop, and then came Ortega Road, cutting across Fourth Street east and west. On the south side of Ortega was a scrofulous-looking house set far back on its weedy yard. There a dog was left out to bark continuously all night, on that curious country assumption that if you lock a dog out in the cold, it automatically becomes a "watchdog" rather than a lonely, frantically bellowing maniac.

Further down Fourth was the co-op called Osha, an organic market where I did a good deal of my shopping and cashiered for a couple of hours each week. Across from the co-op stood a coffin factory—a long, windowless building adjoining a neat little adobe house at right angles to it, the whole covered with rusty-looking, galvanized tin roofing and as silent, appropriately, as a tomb. Next to that, a ratty, narrow trailer park that angled back from the street was enclosed in crooked chain link, the robber-stopper of choice. This was before the era of razor wire; chain link was enough. All the chain-link fences along Fourth were dented and bent from being run into by drunk drivers.

Picture all the buildings as old, with softened contours because they were mostly made of mud brick, one story high, with flat roofs or rusty tin roofs with a low pitch. They were all set back from the street on long, narrow strips of land that ran back to the irrigation ditches, where the willows, red salt cedars, cottonwoods, and Russian olives grew in lines parallel to the course of the invisible Rio Grande. Front yards were covered with patches of green weeds (and, rarely, flowers) or brown, dried-out weeds and dust, depending on the season.

Picture four narrow lanes of blacktop running between these fenced front yards, a nearly shoulderless road, north and south. Fourth, like most streets in the Valley, was overhung here and there by scrawny Chinese elm trees, of which every single leaf on every single twig was half-eaten by elm-beetles and curled brownly in on itself in a disgusting, zombielike mimicry of true foliage.

Pop said he liked the place.

July 10, 1974

Dear Liza,

Suzy gave me your mailgram and said, "Write." So, I'm writing.

I've been here 4 months and 10 days, and I like it, I like it. After NYC, this should come as no surprise. The really hot days—90 to 105 degrees—of June are gone, and we've been getting rainstorms. So it's cool, in more ways than one. Suzy & Steve have been wonderful. I have all the privacy I could want. Work around the place, weeding, planting, bringing young trees from the Rio Grande & transplanting them (with Steve); keeping watch over the place if they're away, feeding the cats and pigeons, birds, & especially, the hummingbirds, of which we've got three. I've made only a couple of sketches and my eyes are about in shape for painting. Haven't touched a drop of booze—beer, wine, whiskey—since Nov. 7, 1973. Haven't been tempted, either.

There's a starling here that sits on an electric cable outside my kitchen window, mornings, & chirps and hollers at 6:30 ayem—just because *he* feels great at dawn, for Chrissakes! So, I get up early. I used to cuss at him, but he's so goddamn funny I can't help liking him for it all. But the hummers are something else. I can stand 6 inches from the feeder & look them over as they guzzle. They are unbelievable. They look *me* over, too. Curious, nosy, cute as Hell.

Enough of rustic joys and splendors, already.

Write me a note when you can. Regards and same old love to you and Duncan.

As ever,

Robin

FROM MY SPORADICALLY KEPT DIARY,
MARCH 3, 1975:

The day before yesterday, Robin triumphantly reported that two of his birds are now literally eating out of his hand.

A flock of pigeons had long ago found their way in through gaps under the eaves of Robin's house, where the pitched roof had been casually tacked to the outside walls. These birds roosted in the attic, which was a shallow space with a floor of skinny rafters that wouldn't hold much weight. You could only store a few lightweight things up there, so the birds were not disturbed much by us. There was a ladder to the attic when we bought the place, and a hole in the ceiling by which to enter.

We put in a flight of steps that you pulled down with a cord, but even then there was very little traffic into that unheated, fragile space. Only Robin used the stairs, to go up and feed the birds. He talked about them, worried about them, and watched them gather home each night. As a young man he had known people who kept pigeons on rooftops in New York.

"They kept them for food," he said. "Squab; it was a delicacy in those days."

He would drive down to the feed store, about two miles south on Fourth, to buy food for them. I said they were wild birds and could forage for themselves, but Pop said there was nothing around for them to eat but weeds, and that wasn't enough. And they flourished on his feeding; the little flock was growing.

In time I suggested that he clean up after them a bit, since there was a lot of mess accumulating up there. He said they got scared when he poked more than just his head and arms through the trap door, but he would try. Knowing the man as little as I did then, I thought: He loves the birds, so why would he allow them to live in squalor? I had conveniently put out of my mind the squalor he had lived in himself, in New York.

A year or so later Robin got sick. He panted; he couldn't help Steve dig holes for planting for more than a few minutes at a time. It's just from smoking, he said, when we expressed alarm. I told him to quit smoking, for Pete's sake. He said he would.

Then one day he staggered into my kitchen and flopped down on a chair, gasping for breath.

I said, "Pop! What's the matter?"

"I can't catch my breath," he wheezed.

He looked awful. I thought of all the people I saw around town trailing those little oxygen tanks on wheels, with a tube coming out to feed a mask over their noses. Emphysema, I thought, from the goddamn smoking!

I helped him into my car and we drove to my doctor's office. We sat outside in the Dodge for a few minutes because he couldn't muster enough strength to climb out. He started to cry with no sound, just tears sliding down into his beard.

"Don't cry, Pop; what's the matter?" I said, embarrassed and full of pity and thinking about those little tanks on wheels.

"They'll put me in the hospital."

"If that's what you need, that's what they're supposed to do."

"Who's going to feed Bibi?"

Bibi; the cat.

"I'll take care of her for you, don't worry. Can you get up now? Come on, Pop, you're scaring me. Your lips are turning blue."

"All right, all right, leave me alone a minute."

"Listen," I said, "it's okay. Go ahead and cry if you're scared, that's okay. It makes perfect sense. Everybody's scared of doctors and hospitals."

He said angrily, "I'm not crying about that!"

"Oh," I said. "What is it, then?"

"It's little Beakless Betty. She'll die if I'm not there."

I stared at him. His eyes were closed, the tears running and running.

"What?" I said. "What? Look, tell me about it and I'll take care of it."

"You can't, nobody can do it but me. She's one of my pigeons. She has no beak."

"No beak?" I said, horrified. "How did she lose her beak?"

"I don't know, how should I know? She was there with the rest of them when I moved in, living in the attic, and I saw right away that she had no beak. Maybe it froze off. Anyway, she was very shy, she was nearly starved when I started feeding them up there. I had to coax her to come close, because with no beak she couldn't pick up the food from the floor when I threw it, and the other birds would grab it all anyway and shove her out of the way. So now I throw it out to the end of the attic for the other birds, and they go scrambling after it. But she comes to me and eats out of my palm."

"How, if she has no beak?"

"I don't know," he said, "she just shoves the hole in her face down on my hand and gets some somehow."

So this was at least part of what he'd meant, about birds eating out of his hand: how incredibly gross, but this was not the time to say so. I said, "She must be a pretty smart bird, then, Pop. She'll be okay. I'll feed the pigeons for you, and I'll look out for her specially. Come on, we have to go in now, they're waiting for us. You look terrible."

"Take it easy, will you?" he snarled weakly, blotting his face with his sleeve. "I can't walk fast, I have to rest. I can't catch my breath."

Sure enough, the doctor packed him off to the hospital, declaring his condition a mystery. Everybody came around and did tests on him. They sent for a specialist from Atlanta. Our doctor was thrilled by the enigmatic nature of the whole thing. Robin himself seemed to enjoy the attention and being waited on hand and foot by the nursing staff, who liked him for his wisecracks and his good looks and for flirting with them.

Meantime I went up into the attic every night on the ladder and threw out feed for the pigeons. I didn't see any beakless bird, but to tell the truth I am somewhat squeamish, and I wasn't looking very hard. They all were afraid of me and stayed well back in the shadows until I stepped down out of the trapdoor again.

After a huge medical bill had been run up, somebody figured out what was wrong: Robin had psittacosis, also known as parrot fever, from living with the damned pigeons overhead. He never did clean the attic out, and their accumulated guano got kicked up into the air in all the excitement every time he fed them. He had been breathing pulverized bird-shit every single day for a year.

We hired a couple of guys, through an ad in the local paper, to come get the birds out of the attic while Robin was still in the hospital (this was in the days before the doctor started throwing you out after an hour with tubes still flying from the needles in your veins). They went up there after sunset, flung bedsheets over the birds when they were sleeping, gathered them in, and put the stunned pigeons into sacks. Then they drove over the mountains and released the birds on the far side, except for three or four solid-color ones that one of the men kept to add to his own flock.

A few birds found their way back long afterward—I spotted them hanging around Robin's roof at sunset—but by then we had blocked the little windows they had used to get in and out of the attic space and stuffed newspapers under the eaves. We had to trap the stragglers, using a humane trap from Animal Control, which we set up on the back porch. It took days, but finally they too were gone.

There had been upwards of three hundred pigeons in that attic. Robin had started with a dozen. I found a couple of empty sacks that the feed had come in; he had been buying it for them down Fourth Street at the feed store.

It was for chickens; the labels on the sacks read: "Laying Feed."

The guys who cleaned the attic out for us didn't bother picking up any carcasses of dead birds, so naturally when Pop came home and climbed up there, he found old Beakless Betty, curled up dead in a corner under the eaves. He told me so, but there were no reproaches.

He had expected the worst, and sure enough, it came.

FROM ROBIN'S JOURNAL, 1954:

New York Times: "Mystery of the Whooping Crane Solved. Nearly extinct birds' breeding hideout found in Canada." Poor Whooping Crane, that's the end of him. We always did wonder where he hid out.

Green Truck

R obin (opening my freezer compartment—his own didn't work, so I stored the frozen meals he bought for himself): "I gotta get a dinner out for tonight. 'Beef Tips.' That's a pretty good one. The fish ones are terrible, I don't get them any more. They used to make good fish ones, but they stopped making them. They always stop making the good stuff, ever notice that? They get you used to it and then they stop and make you buy inferior junk instead. We going shopping tomorrow?"

Me: "Yup. Hey, you want a cup of tea? I'm just making some. Sit down a minute, have some tea."

Robin: "Okay, tea would be good. But not that stuff Steve likes, that smells like shoe polish."

Me: "You mean lapsang souchong? That's what he likes. It isn't like shoe polish. It's smoky."

Robin: "Whatever it is, I don't like it."

Me: "Fine, you don't have to have it. How about some Earl Grey?"

Robin: "Earl Grey? That's the one that smells like flowers. Not that I could smell it anyway. When the humidity goes down so low my nose dries out. I wake up with these crusts in my nose, they drive me crazy."

Me: "So blow your nose. Are you out of tissues again? Put 'em on your list for tomorrow, then."

Robin: "I can use toilet paper, but it doesn't do any good. You have to get your finger in there and dig around, and sometimes you tear that stuff off and it hurts and it bleeds—"

Me: "For Christ's sake, would you mind not talking about this?"

Robin: "Heh, heh."

Me: "Heh, heh, yourself. Forget your nose, you've got a *real* health question here. This 'beef-tips dinner' says it's under four hundred calories. No wonder you're so skinny, if this is what you're eating! It's dangerous for older people to let themselves get so thin. If you get sick and can't eat for a couple of days, you've got no extra weight to drop."

Robin: "Aw, Suzy; I never get sick."

This was irritatingly true; apart from his entirely self-caused bout of parrot fever, he didn't. "Can't you find any frozen dinners that aren't low calorie?"

Robin: "They're all like that."

Me: "What about the Spanish ones, with tortillas and beans and all that?"

Robin: "Aah, they're no good. They're too much trouble to make."

Me: "Trouble? What kind of trouble can there be to making a frozen meal?"

Robin: "You have to cook the tortillas separately and all kinds of crap like that; it's a pain in the neck. I tried the fajitas once. I'll never do that again."

Me: "Why, because you had to put a couple of tortillas on the stove to warm?"

Robin: "It's a nuisance, Suzy."

I am flummoxed by his definition of "a nuisance." Grit in your running shoes, absolutely; a misplaced file, a power outage, the dog chewing up the seatbelts in your car at four hundred dollars a pop. But putting two tortillas in the toaster oven?

It took some time to get a sense of the particular density, the damp, woolly weight, of Pop's inertia.

For example: the truck.

Out here you need wheels to get around—the city even then covered ten square miles or so and bus service was spotty at best—and I was thinking about his independence (and my own writing time being less vulnerable to intrusion, if he could get himself where he needed to go without me).

I thought he might like to drive across the Corrales bridge and north to where he could see the mountain even better, and paint. I took him up past Bernalillo once and parked on the side of the road, facing east-southeast. The mountain looked powerful from up there, broad-shouldered and backward leaning, with the whole Rio Grande valley between us and the wide tilt of the mesa rising to the foot of the deeply eroded slopes.

He looked, but he didn't say anything.

Pop had cut little color reproductions of Cézanne's paintings out of art magazines and taped them to his walls. He put up no other decoration, apart from suspending on wires a couple of small, marionette-like puppets he had bought somewhere, refugees from Sicilian puppet theatre by the look of them, and a foot-high model of a Renaissance angel blackened with scorch-marks (he had bought it in a junk store on Canal Street and was convinced that it was a model made by El Greco for the elongated figures in his paintings). I was sure our mountain was earmarked for him, if he could just get out to find a good view of it.

I told him, "This is a western city, Pop, it's laid out for cars, not pedestrians or public transport. You're going to have to learn to drive."

"I can drive, Suzy," he said in that testy tone. That was when I found out he'd been born in California, not in the east. I was surprised. As long as I'd known him, he'd lived in or near New York.

"Great," I said; "but when's the last time you actually drove a car?"

He admitted that it had been decades ago. People in New York City didn't have cars, if they could help it and had any sense.

We found him a little green Mazda pickup truck with automatic transmission and a rotary engine, used and shipped up from Texas. I tried to teach him to drive again myself, but the first time I caught myself shrieking at him to "step on the brakes, for Christ's sake," with him yelling back at me, "I am, I am," I realized this was a bad idea. I found a driving school that advertised instructors who specialized in teaching older drivers and turned the job over to them. Rob got his license, somehow. I didn't ask.

Pretty soon he drove the truck into an irrigation ditch along Second Street and we had to have it hauled out again by a wrecker. The truck wasn't damaged and Pop wasn't hurt, except for a bloody nose. Wide and deep, the ditch runs all along north Second Street behind the field in back of our property, even though there are no farms there left to irrigate. I couldn't blame Robin for driving into that big damned thing, making a too-wide turn. But it made me nervous.

He needed to be independent, though, he really did. I let it alone and hoped for the best, and the best is what it got: there were no more accidents.

He used to drive himself down to the bank on Fourth Street once a month to cash his Social Security check, which was not enough even then. When I realized how little he was buying at the supermarket on our joint errands there, I checked with him and elicited the grudging information that he couldn't both eat and pay me even a token rent, not on that income. I stopped collecting rent. Instead, we asked him to look after our house for us when we were away, and to do more landscaping work with Steve on the property, mostly watering new plants.

Our yard started out in wasteland mode, all dust and weeds except for a couple of stands of disease-ridden Chinese elms (they are really Siberian elms, but everybody around here calls them Chinese elms). A local benefactor once gave the city a forest of these trees, to plant for shade because they grew fast. Then it turned out that the damned things worm their roots into underground pipes for water, and are unkillable. The stumps sprout even without any water, without any light, without anything. They are zombie-trees.

I got the ones in front cut down to make way for something better. We had no cash to spare at that time for store-bought trees to plant in their place, so we used to go down, all three of us—I would dragoon Robin into coming with us, and this was early enough in his new life with us for him to cooperate—to the banks of the Really Big Ditch, the *acequia madre*, that ran a couple of miles west of us, alongside the Rio Grande. We would take a morning to dig up a few of the young Russian olive trees that grew wild there. They look like willows but have thorns and little green fruit, and they are tough.

We hauled them home in Pop's truck-bed and planted them in the front yard. Pop took some real satisfaction in the whole process, for he'd help later with the necessary watering to keep the young trees alive while they reestablished themselves (the water table has dropped many feet since then, and those trees, full grown now, have all died).

From Rob's Journal, 1952:

One increasingly fascinating aspect of trees is their serene ignorance of the laws of perspective. Mountains, hills, forests all bow to the optical illusion of perspective. But the individual tree is a complex structure, the sole pictorial aim of which seems a quite successful demonstration of form and volume, pure, without benefit of perspective or isometric mumbo-jumbo.

As one looks at a tree, one sees that its branches go out in all directions, creating rhythms and great closed spaces which seem solid as concrete. Vanishing points vanish. A tree and perspective have nothing in common.

I only rode in the truck with Robin a few times, when my Dodge Dart was out of commission. Robin never would drive into town proper, fearing that he would get lost; and I saw how tense he was at the wheel and didn't encourage extra excursions.

He didn't go out sketching the mountain, either; or rather he went out once or twice, and that was that.

"I don't know where to pull off and park," he said. "I can see it fine from here anyway."

There was a sketch propped on his easel, very faint and tentative, of one of the piñon trees in my back yard. I know he occasionally sent off a drawing or a painting to his brother Irving in California, but I think they were all old works, including a small oil study of a head, labeled "Don Quixote," that I had my eye on. But I was not consulted, and one day it was gone.

He soon settled into using the truck only to go to the bank. He got himself a wheeled cart to lug his groceries back from the co-op on foot, since the place was less than half a block away. Things he couldn't buy at the co-op he got at the nearest supermarket; I took him down there with me once a week to shop.

I drove him to the public library one morning, thinking he would like it and would go there himself in the truck, or even on the bus that ran, infrequently, all the way into town, a straight shot down Fourth Street. Robin had lugged books out West with him, and had always spoken with respect and admiration of the great central library in New York, at Forty-second Street.

He spent an hour in the Albuquerque main library and said he wouldn't go back. "It's full of bums sleeping," he said. "Worse than the Bowery."

Well, yes (the library is in the middle of the city's vagrant-ridden downtown); but I hadn't really thought he would mind. There had always been bums in the Forty-second Street library, too, taking shelter there. The guards came through periodically and woke them up. You could stay in the library as long as you were reading, but not if you were snoozing. The situation in the Albuquerque library somehow gave more offense, and that's how I came to be in charge of bringing Robin books to read.

He would not go anywhere but to the bank, unless I drove him. I think his idea of independence didn't include that kind of mobility. It had subtler parameters.

About those nose-crusts: we had installed a big rectangular gas heater in his place. I put a pan on it, with water he was to keep topped up so that when he heated the house in winter there would be some moisture evaporating into the air.

Sometimes he bothered; mostly not.

FROM ROBIN'S JOURNAL, 1952–59:

We have often thought of getting a station-wagon model car—some cheap make like a Willys—and traveling over this country, painting. The object, of course, would be to find motifs wherever possible. When we think of certain beauty that exists in every section of the interior and on both coasts, it hurts not to be able to see it.

Bredds and Muffins

I see myself, standing at the counter in the kitchen of my house, chopping scallions and looking out of the window at the piñon tree we had planted in the back yard, and beyond that the alfalfa field, and then the great, long, laid-back face of the Sandias.

Pop stalks in, wearing jeans and a checked cotton shirt and the scuffed brown loafers he shuffles around in all the time, with white socks. He's growing his beard longer, wiry and white, with a few wild tufts curling this way and that.

"We going shopping?" he demands.

"Yes," I say, filling a Mexican green glass tumbler from the kitchen tap. "I told you—right after lunch."

"It's after lunch now," he says, following me to the table in the dining space adjoining the kitchen.

"After *my* lunch," I say. "I am not geared to eating lunch at eleven a.m. And I'm driving, right?"

You can see that a certain amount of friction has begun to arise here. I was not supposed to have to run Pop on his domestic errands. Steve says he's having some trouble feeling as positive about Robin as he once did, because unless we insist, Pop doesn't do anything. Literally. "How can he just sit there all day and do *nothing at all*?"

I say in Pop's defense that Robin is retired after many years' hard work in a hard business; he's taking some well-earned down-time. But I think Steve is repelled by a vision of "retirement" that scares him—is *that* what it's going to be like? Might as well be dead. And I can't say I don't feel the same way, at least sometimes.

It wasn't supposed to be this way.

I sit down to my tuna sandwich and glass of water. I have not slept well; the dog at the corner of Fourth and Ortega barked all night again. It has barking partners all over the neighborhood with whom it keeps up a running commentary from dusk to dawn. I hate that dog. I hate everybody.

Robin sits down too, eyeing my food with deep disapproval as I eat. Finally he snaps, "So when are we going? If you go too late, everything's gone."

"Everything's gone from Safeway?" Tuna falls out of my sandwich onto my jeans. I retrieve it.

"The blueberry muffins are gone."

I refuse to hurry. "Then get a different kind of muffin, Pop, it won't kill you to do that once. Relax. Look, you see this sandwich? We'll go when I finish eating it, like this. There, happy now?"

"It's about time," he mutters.

"What does that mean?"

"Never mind, forget it. Well, are we going?"

Through my annoyance, I have to admire him: what a blaze in the faded eyes, what a mutinous set to that long, grizzled jaw! But I know too, by now, if you let him order you around once, it never stops.

"No, we are not going," I say with deliberation. I sit back. "Not if you keep acting so crabby."

"Well of course I'm crabby!" he snarls. "I've got a lot to be crabby about!"

"Really? Such as what?"

"Forget it. Let's go, if we're going."

"Remember last Thursday? We went shopping, just like today. Only we went really early, right after breakfast, remember?"

He doesn't give me the satisfaction of an answer, just sits glaring at the table. It's a round oak kitchen table on a pedestal, like the one in his kitchen but a little bigger. I got both tables from Pauline, next door.

I press on. "Do you happen to recall what you said to me when we got home?"

"I didn't say anything to you," he growls. "What was there to say?"

"You said, 'We went too early. The delivery trucks hadn't come yet. They didn't have any blueberry muffins.'"

He looks me in the eye. "So what?"

I sigh. "So lighten up, Pop. The world's not coming to an end on account of blueberry muffins, one way or the other. Come on, let's go."

"I have to get my hat," he says sullenly, getting up. "It's going to be hot again. Always the same thing; the weatherman says, 'another sunny day.' Sunshine, sunshine, that's all they ever talk about."

We go out to my car, a new one because the Dodge has finally proven more costly to keep running than it's worth. Now I have a white Corolla that has, thank God, air conditioning, which I turn on. "Pop, this is New Mexico, in the *southwest*, what they call the *Sunbelt*, where people retire because of the *warm, sunny climate.*"

"Yeah, but they never say it's going to be *hot*, ever notice that?" he says, jamming on the dark straw hat we got for him in town last month; he's worried about skin cancer, quite rightly, with that skin. " 'Warm temperatures today.' Warm! Ninety-six degrees! It's a goddamn oven out there already, and it's not even noon!"

I tell him he's right, it's going to be a scorcher, and I lean out past him because he's blocking the view out of the passenger side window. I have to turn left onto Fourth without getting us killed.

Robin grinds on bitterly, "They do it to fool people into thinking the climate is nice and moderate so more dopes will buy houses and move down here."

That's a jolt. "Are you saying you're sorry you moved out here?"

"I didn't say that," he mutters. He resolutely does not look at me. "I'm talking about the weather reports. I'm just saying it's a scam, that's all."

There, an opening: I pull out and turn left, and we do not die. "What do you mean, a scam? You think the local chamber of commerce is making payoffs to the weatherman to soften his reports?"

"You never know," he says darkly.

I have to laugh. "You want to watch that old-man's paranoia, Pop, it can really screw up your head."

"You're naive, that's all," he says contemptuously. "And they never tell you the low, ever notice that? They give you the high, but they keep quiet about the low. The only one who tells you the high *and* the low is Howard Morgan."

I hit the horn as a jerk in a pickup pulls out of the Shady Lanes trailer park right in front of me. "So watch Howard Morgan."

"I do; only sometimes he's not on, and he's going to retire soon anyway."

"Oh my God, call off the future, the weatherman is retiring! He's announced that he's going to retire?"

"No, not yet; but he will," he says in that emphatic, distinct way he does when he's ticked off. "He's getting older, isn't he?"

I shake my head and slip into the right lane just past Ranchitos Road. "We're all getting older. I, for instance, am getting older, faster, than anybody else for miles around."

Fortunately, there are blueberry muffins.

FROM ROBIN'S JOURNAL, 1960:

So, up betimes, and read ye Gospel, according to Nicolas Hilliard (1547–1614), viz.—"This matter only of the light let me perfect, that noe wisse man longer remaine in error of praysing much shadows in pictures after the life, especially small pictures which ar to be wiued in hand: great pictures placed high ore farr of requier hard shadows or become the better than nearer on story worke better than pictures of the life, for beauty and good favor is like cleare truth, which is not shamed with the light, nor neede to be obscured, so a picture a littel shadowed maye be borne withall for the rounding of it, but so greatly smutted or darkened as some usse disgrace it, and it is like truth ill towld."

Amen. So, had break-fast, 2 bredds peanut and apple-buttered, ½ banana, and three cuppes of ye instante coffee—with vapored milk and thatte sugar whiche ys used on pasties (the whiche last wee had nonne of).

I am surely not the first person to be driven to distraction by my father.

My mother said she always had to pry Robin out of the house to go see people socially, any people, although he invariably had a great time when he got there. I remember them going out a lot at night, leaving me alone in the apartment except for my baby sister. I used to fantasize about dying while they were out, just stopping breathing there in my bed, and how sorry they'd be when they got home and found me.

Mom once told me that Robin left because he wanted to be more than a commercial hack, and he couldn't support a family as a "real" painter—nobody could in those days (except maybe Norman Rockwell). She said she got the divorce because she was tired of providing all the motive power for their married life, all the initiative, all the ambition.

The last straw was when Wonder Books, a publisher he worked for on commission, offered to make him one of their lead illustrators. He refused. He said, according to Mom, that he didn't want to compromise his standards or spend his time doing pictures for books like *The Shy Little Horse* and *Old Man Rabbit's Dinner Party* (both on my bookshelf now; the illustrations are sweet, delicate, faintly cartoonish).

So he quit working for Wonder Books, and Mom asked me, "Would you mind if Robin didn't live with us any more?"

FROM ROBIN'S JOURNALS, 1945:

If you explain painting, any painting, to a woman as a <u>thing</u>, a carrier which affects people, is impressive, contributes to her prestige as a possession; if you can explain painting, any painting, to a man as an idea, or a carrier of ideas, which can stimulate ideas in him, then you can make art understood.

I had work of my own now, in an outbuilding on the Fourth Street property, the goatshed (I'm sure that was what it was originally) that I had converted into a tiny, cool studio. Fiction got written there, often in the dead of night, when I would wake up suddenly full of ideas that wouldn't let me alone. I pulled on robe and slippers, and padded out there to work in blessed, uninterrupted quiet until my eyelids began to droop.

I asked Robin to read my second novel in manuscript. A futuristic, feminist fantasy of a tribe of women living like Amazons in a barbaric future, it had no men in it, not because I had planned it that way but because every time I tried to write a male character into it, the scene I was working on would drop dead on the page. As a reader myself who had grown up on books that almost always hinged on the actions of male characters, I had been extremely reluctant to try writing about only female characters, and I was very nervous about the results once I had done it. I was anxious for reactions from male as well as female readers, and I finally worked up the nerve to ask Robin's help.

These early readings of my books in manuscript are not just a formality. I count on presubmission readers to give me the feedback I need to fine-tune a book so that it will do its work for readers coming to it cold. Steve did this kind of editing wonderfully, at least before the demands of his law firm became so all-enveloping as to make spare time impossible to find.

Pop read my book per my request. "It was okay. Kind of flat, though—not much happening, without any men."

And that was all. It was like dropping a story into a black hole. I was let down, even hurt, of course. Fortunately I had lots of other input to steer by. Another male reader had told me that there was a lack of tension in the book because of the absence of men. I think I was disappointed that Pop had had nothing more original to say than the same thing.

He read two more of my books in draft after that; he was a smart man, a well-read man, whose opinion I hoped would sharpen my own eye for the faults and the strengths of my work. But I never got more than a sentence out of him about any of them, and after a while I gave up and took him off my list of presubmission readers. He was probably relieved.

Which is not to say that he never gave me good words; I mean words meant to be good, and meant for me, not jokes. It's amazing how you never outgrow your desire for such words from such sources.

There was the time he said he was surprised at the way I had turned out (though I can't remember what sparked this comment). "You were this frowning little girl, very critical and sharp; sulky, even. And now you're this big, laughing woman."

I blushed and said I was glad to hear it, although upon consideration I am not so sure. For all I know, he meant that I had fallen away from some grim, cramped faith of his own that precluded laughter. Even then I think I sensed also a thread of accusation— how could I have come up so cheerful in a world that he knew to be so treacherous and mean?

But I chose to take his remark as a compliment, an expression of gratified surprise (after all, if I turned out okay that let him off the hook of having contributed to any neuroses of mine by being gone when I was little). That way it made up for some of those flat, useless comments on my work.

Reading the journals later, I saw that I had gotten off lightly.

FROM ROBIN'S JOURNALS, 1942:

The American Girl, as presented to her forerunners by Hollywood and the magazines, will be almost noseless, she will have buttock-sized breasts and breast-sized buttocks, and she will be able to sit on either in perfect comfort and probably at the same time.

I see my father, on his back porch with the sagging screening repaired with patches. He tells me proudly about the hummingbird.

It got trapped in the porch screening, having flown in through an unmended tear. He stalked it, trying to catch it to let it out again, until in its terror it flew straight at the screening and got stuck there with its needle of a bill wedged into the mesh. He carefully closed his big, fine hand around its vibrating body, carried it outside, and let it go.

He's read that hummingbirds are so highly strung that just touching them can cause them to die of terror. This bird, he tells me, lay very still in his hand, its heart pattering wildly against his palm, until he opened his fingers and flipped the tiny creature aloft.

We think about that together, savoring one of those moments that feel blessed because life has happened instead of death.

Then he says, "Irving saved my life once."

Irving is his next-older brother, the English professor in California whom Pop sends paintings to. I keep my voice casual, resisting an impulse to pounce on this rare invitation into Pop's past. "He did? How?"

"It was in a fire, in the house when we lived in Montara, in California. It happened at night, and we were all asleep. I remember Irving yanking on my foot—I hated when people did that, my old man used to do it to wake us up for school—so I kicked him to make him stop, but he wouldn't let go. He was yelling, 'Get up, get up, the house is on fire!' He shoved me out of the bedroom window, onto the porch. He saved my life."

Me: "You never told me that before."

Robin shrugged. I said I wished I knew more about his family.

"Why?" he said. "Family 'history' is crap, nothing but lies and baloney. Only southerners give a damn about families anyway, ever notice that? Them and their genealogies."

"Weren't any of your ancestors interesting at all?"

Him, with disgust: "Slave-owners, newspapermen, a couple of

bankers in Kansas. I never could stand that Kansas branch of the family; bunch of purse-mouthed reactionaries."

(I never met any of these people, so I can't vouch for his estimation of them; but in hindsight this may have been an accurate, not to say a generous, judgment. The state board of education of Kansas not long ago decreed, in its boneheaded wisdom, that evolution was no longer to be taught in its schools.)

Me: "Are you still in touch with any of those relatives?"

Him: "Nah, what for?"

Me: "Well, I hope you don't mind if your other daughter comes to visit for a weekend. Liza's got some free time and fares are low right now."

Robin: "Oh yeah, she told me on the phone. What's she coming all this way for?"

Me, refraining from pointing out that she hasn't seen him in years and that he is her father too: "Just trying to put some mileage on her pedometer."

Robin: "Maybe she'll leave that husband of hers and move here. Maybe she's coming here to case the joint."

Me: "It's not likely, Pop."

Robin, with satisfaction: "He isn't going to live much longer, you know. His lips are blue. That means a heart condition. Ever notice how blue his lips are?"

Me: "Nope, I never have."

Robin: "Well, they are. And he doesn't have long earlobes, either."

Me: "Huh?"

Robin: "Men with long ears don't get cancer."

Me: "Oh."

Robin: "So if the heart condition doesn't get him, cancer might, and then Liza could move here. How would you feel about that?"

Me: "I'd feel fine. The older we get, the better Lizzie and I get along, especially now that we have you to keep in touch about, y'ol' fart."

Robin: "The two of you talk about me? What do you say?"

Me: "Nothing, I was kidding. How old was Lizzie when you left?"

Him: "You're changing the subject."

Me: "Yup. How old was she?"

Him: "Three or four, I guess. You were born with black hair, like an Eskimo, and she was born with white hair. Isn't that funny?"

Me: "I remember she was kind of sickly as a child."

Him: "Liza? No, no, she was a little Tartar. I never saw anybody with so much energy."

Me, wondering what this could mean, coming from Mr. Inertia: "I remember that she had a nurse in her room at night when she was little."

Him: "That was because she had that sleep thing, where you stop breathing. She grew out of it. The pneumonia was later. That was what changed her. Before that, she ran everywhere on the tips of her toes, so fast you couldn't keep up with her. But then she got sick. She was never the same afterward. That pneumonia nearly did her in."

Me: "I barely remember, really. It's all a blur."

Him: "What do you want to remember for anyway?"

Me: "I don't know, must be a brain tumor or something. Humor me." Strike, I thought, while the iron is hot. "How did you meet Mom?"

Robin: "I told you that already."

Me: "Tell me again."

Him: "There's nothing to tell. We were in the WPA together. We got married. I have to go in and watch Donahue. We going shopping tomorrow?"

FROM ROBIN'S JOURNALS, 1945:

Surely, it takes great skill, inventive coquettery, imaginative evasiveness, dogged persistence at meaningless duties for a woman to inspire, prod, stimulate by denial, and finally ignore and comfortably outlive her fortune-amassing, cardio-carcino-ulcerous insurance ridden drone? (Who, if it were asked of him, would say that all he really wanted out of life was a little less love and a great deal of sex.) Surely, America's coldly beautiful woman is her genius.

Mom

I should have asked other questions, of course. I should have asked what I really wanted to know: What were you doing when you first saw my mother? How did she look, what was she wearing? What did you say, what did she say? When did you decide to marry, and what made you decide, and how and where did you ask her, and what did she answer? What did you think your future would be like together? What were your dreams?

How did you feel when she told you she was pregnant the first time, what plans did you make then, what did you hope for, what were you scared of, where were you both living at the time?

What had to change after I was born, what did your relatives say, how did I look when you first saw me? Did you want to name me after my grandmothers, or was that Mom's doing, and how did you feel when she changed my name legally to "Suzy" because she didn't like the way New Yorkers flattened the *a* in Joanne?

Did you like that perfume she wore all her life, did you buy her Arpège even though you couldn't afford it? What was she like with her friends and your friends, and who were they, and what did you all do when you got together; and what was she like with her own family in those days, with her sister and brothers and with her aunts, those old, fireplug-shaped sisters that Nana fought with all her life?

The thing is, I don't see my mother; not unless I have a photograph to remind me. I like the one taken of her in Mexico, on someone's flowery patio, in a tan cotton dress with a luscious-looking, deep green shawl wrapped around her shoulders.

Robin knew her, I didn't; not the young Maxine. She was nearly thirty when I was born. By the time I was old enough to notice anything much but my own tastes and moods, my mother was worried, serious, and chronically tired. Her laughter was often shrill with anxiety, her thoughts busy, I believe, with frantic plans to get another, sounder father for us girls and support for herself. In any case all I saw was the side of her that she turned toward Lizzie and me, not what she was to her own generation.

And of course when I wondered about my parents, I naturally tended to wonder about *him*, not her; I wondered about the mysterious one, the one who was not right there day in and day out, impinging on my life, leaving me shopping lists to attend to and sometimes dinner to cook, if she was going to be late getting home from work.

Mom was also inclined to load me down with her career anxieties. The older she got, the more she dreaded being fired by Burlington so they wouldn't have to pay her a pension (she was an executive by then, heading their design studio). Terrified of being replaced by some rising young male assistant, she dyed her hair blonde to hide the gray, armed herself in skillfully applied makeup to look younger, and lied herself blue in the face about her age. There were no laws against sex discrimination or age discrimination then. She was vulnerable to the whims of management, and she needed to talk it all out.

I used to lie in bed in the mornings until the very last minute before leaping up and flying off to school so there wouldn't be time to talk over breakfast, but when she could she confided her fears to me, who confided in no one.

Well, who would want to know that stuff—my friends whose parents stayed married and who had a father's salary to live on? Besides, repeating any of it would have felt like a betrayal of my charming, laughing, beautiful mother, who made sure she appeared to other adults to have few real cares in the world. She was a sociable creature by inclination, and few people enjoy the company of the fearful or the morose.

My load of uninvited adult confidences was heavy and ever growing, and in time it pushed between my mother and me so unbearably that I pulled away. I couldn't stop myself; it felt like sheer self-preservation to me.

I was pulling away when she died one Saturday morning in the hospital. I had been concealing the fact that Steve and I had already decided to go live in New Mexico, unable to break it to her while she was trying to recuperate from a broken hip. I didn't want to face the emotional storm that was sure to come crashing down on my head when she found out.

So there were a lot of questions I never asked her either, because I had already had too many grim and frightening answers to questions I hadn't asked. And I didn't ask Robin now, because getting answers from him was like pulling teeth from a concrete jaw.

And anyway, maybe it was not my business. Pop made you very aware of that kind of boundary, even when he didn't say anything direct about it.

In Robin's journal I found a clipping of my mother's obituary:

Mrs. Maxine Szanton McKee Powers, the stylist for Burlington-Craft Doubleknit Division of the Burlington Knit Fabrics Company, a part of Burlington Industries, Inc., died yesterday of a heart attack at the Columbia Presbyterian Medical Center. She lived at 845 West End Avenue.

Mrs. Powers had worked previously as a designer for Lowenstein & Co., and Fair-Tex Mills. She studied art at the Sorbonne, the Parsons School of Design and the Fashion Institute of Technology.

She is survived by three daughters, Mrs. Stephen Charnas, Miss Liza McKee and Patricia Powers; a brother, Dr. Victor L. Szanton, and a sister, Mrs. Barney Tobey." [*Robin has underlined the words "died yesterday" and added, "(1 pm, Sat., 5-24)."*]

We talked to her last Wednesday. She sounded ok. Suz called us Sat. eve. Went to services yesterday.

Lizzie came to visit us on Fourth Street, and we two sisters sat in the living room with Robin and talked one winter evening. We had a bottle of Glenlivet that I had bought for Steve for Christmas, that he seldom remembered to drink. We turned the lights out and just watched the fire, in that little front room that was paved with brick, with the rounded kiva fireplace in the corner like a stylized pregnant belly projecting its rounded center into the room.

Liza, with her long blonde hair and svelte figure, held up her glass of scotch and made a face.

"Ugh, you drink this stuff? What is it? It's awful!"

Me, hating it too: "Steve likes it."

Robin: "It's the best there is, the only liquor I ever really liked."

Liza: "You probably shouldn't even be drinking it, because of your eyes."

Me: "Oh, pooh, it's a celebration; how often do you come here on a visit? Anyway, a little bit can't hurt."

Robin, sitting on the couch glass in hand, in clean blue jeans, clean shirt, with his longish gray hair gleaming dully like pewter: "You girls don't drink, do you?"

Me: "Not this stuff. A little wine, in which I have very low, cheap tastes, thank God."

Liza: "I used to drink scotch when I was living with Duncan, but only because *he* drank it. I get crocked too easily, just like Mom used to. You're not much fun to be with when you get falling-over crocked. I think it runs in the family."

Robin: "She was no drinker, your mother; that's true."

Me: "Remember how pretty she was? Uncle Jule took that wonderful, dreamy photo-portrait of her; it used to hang in the hallway at Nana's, remember?"

Robin, dismissive: "She was more beautiful than that."

Liza: "I remember how she had those gold flecks in her eyes—"

Robin: "Freckles."

Liza: "I got the blue eyes, but no flecks. I always wanted those little bits of gold, too."

Me: "I used to think of them as tobacco crumbs. No, really— they were exactly the color of cured tobacco with sunlight on it, very rich."

Robin, pouring more into his glass: "I never saw eyes like hers on anyone else."

Me: "Myopic eyes, which is where I got mine from. And she

had that thyroid condition, too, that's why her eyes looked so big; you know, a little bulgy."

Robin: "She never could see worth a damn without her glasses, but she was so vain about wearing them, she'd rather bump into things. With eyes so beautiful, who could blame her?"

Me, picking up on his lowered guard: "Pop, why did you leave?"

Robin, not looking at either of us: "I didn't want to go."

Liza: "Then why did you?"

Robin: "She told me to."

Somebody's glass clinks against their teeth.

Me: "What?"

Robin, with thick, covered emotion: "She threw me out."

Liza: "Here, your glass is empty. How could she throw you out?"

Robin, staring at the fresh inch of liquor in his shot-glass: "She asked me to go, that's all. So I did."

Me: "But why? I don't remember any fights or anything—"

Liza: "And you used to come for dinner sometimes afterward, even after you moved back from New Rochelle. I could never figure that out—why you lived someplace else, when you two seemed to like each other so much still."

I'm thinking how Liz and I used sometimes to tell each other that they would get back together, after one of these evenings.

But Robin is speaking, his voice fainter than before, weighed down and bleeding at the edges: "I loved her. I never stopped loving her."

We stare at each other, appalled, because we see the brightness of tears on his cheeks.

"I still love her."

We move in awkwardly on either side of him on the couch and pat his shoulders a little, muttering soothing idiocies—"It's okay, Pop, it's all right, don't be unhappy."

We've hardly ever touched him since childhood, and we're not good at it, but after a while he sighs and blots his eyes on his sleeve, and we move away again and talk about other things.

We had him on the ropes, and we let him go.

There are some things you just can't do; and you're not very sorry about it later, either.

FROM ROBIN'S JOURNALS, 1953:
Like the last step in the cellar stairs upon which we think our foot is rest-ing—we step down and plunge headlong with a swift realization of error we will not forget for a long time: love.

Recently Lizzie told me that during the years between my relo-cation to New Mexico and Robin's departure to join us out West, she used to visit him in the Village much more often than when I had still lived in the City. Her boyfriend, a dark young man with a brooding mien—a movie star's son—thought highly of our fa-ther, appreciating in him the self-made intellectual that Pop actu-ally was. The two youngsters used to meet him in Central Park at the Bethesda Fountain Restaurant, under the tall statue of the angel. They'd order a pitcher of *sangria* and look at the lake with the rowboats on it and shoot the breeze.

One day Duncan was busy, so Liz came alone. Robin, as usual on these occasions, got a little sloshed. He said to Liz at one point that she shouldn't come to meet him without Duncan, because with her there alone, so beautiful, Robin felt tempted to come on to her.

After that she came to meet him with Duncan or not at all.

She speaks of it now with exaggerated incredulity, humor, and a touch of tart resentment. It makes me uneasy to hear about it, because it suggests a side of him that I never saw: the hidden man, the sexual man.

So is it dishonorable and shocking that our dad felt attracted to my sister—who at that time looked a lot like our mom, but our mom when she was a young beauty—or is it admirable and honorable for him to have warned Liz about his feelings? Neither? Both? How am I to judge this unwelcome and startling news?

What's judgment got to do with it?

False Teeth

A phone conversation: me and my sister Liza, the one whose husband buys all the new gadgets and has (does he?) the dreaded blue lips and short ear lobes. She calls Robin up to talk with him now that he's been living with us, and she and I phone each other more often, too. We talk about—what else?—our father.

Me: "Hello?"

Liza: "Your father is crazy. He says you won't allow him to have a new thermometer."

Me: "Yaarrghhh!"

Liza: "No, really: he says he wants one, but he's afraid to ask."

Me: "He's not afraid to ask; he *did* ask, and I've been looking for one for him, but it's hard to find one with numbers big enough for him to see from his window."

Liza: "Oh. Uh-huh. Has it got something to do with him not wanting to have to actually get up out of his chair and step out onto the porch to read the thermometer?"

Me: "What do you think?"

Liza: "I think I've never known anyone as lazy as our father, and besides that, he lies."

Me: "Sure he does, just to get a rise out of you! Anyway, he only wants a thermometer so he can read off the low temperatures and foil the weather conspiracy."

Liza: "It's almost as bad as the coffee conspiracy. You know about that one?"

"You mean about how they grind up the coffee and store it carefully for years in faulty cans so that it's never shipped to the supermarket until it's completely stale and flavorless? Yeah, I know about it."

Liza: "Does he really believe this crap? I mean, why would anybody do that, can you think of one good reason?"

"Only that as you get older your taste buds dry up."

Liza, musing: "Oh, that's right, I read that too: they die. Ick; a mouth full of taste-bud corpses."

"Don't get gross, you're starting to sound like him."

Liza, anguished: "My God, are we going to, ever? Kindly put a bullet through my brain if that ever happens! Like if I ever start grousing that they play the same music over and over on the radio—"

Me: "Has he told you about the Hollywood Conspiracy?"

Liza: "Told me about it? The last time he got onto that one he said, 'You should know all about it, you live there.' Like terrorists in black ski masks meet in my living room every Thursday. He can't really believe this stuff."

Me: "Believe it? He lives for it. You know the dry cleaning one?

Dry cleaning wears out your clothes. The dry cleaners are in ca-hoots with the clothing manufacturers to wear out everything faster so they can sell more clothes to poor idiots like you and me, who wash and clean our stuff instead of wearing it till it falls off of its own accord, like certain other people. Or he would, if I didn't in-sist on taking out a load of his laundry with ours once a week. Even so, he gets a bit ripe sometimes. It's embarrassing to have to insist that he take a bath before coming over for dinner."

Liza: "He used to smell like tobacco. It was sweet, almost fruity. I liked it."

Me: "I did too; but he smoked a pipe in those days, it masked everything else. He got worried about cancer of the tongue or something, so he gave his pipes to Steve."

"Yuck! You mean Steve smokes pipes that Robin had in his *mouth?*"

I tell her the pipes are fine, expensive ones (many of them birth-day and Christmas presents from Liz and me during the old days, back in New York), and Steve gave them a good cleaning, though frankly it strikes me as a little gross too.

"I wish," I sigh, "I could get Robin to brush those teeth of his, at least, before he gets in the car with me."

Liza howls, "Those teeth! Where the hell did he get them? What *century* did he get them? They look so awful I was sure they were real, until when he was eating dinner they started hopping around in his mouth. Can't you get him some new ones?"

Me: "Nope. He's very proud of those teeth, says the dentist who made them for him was 'a real artist.' He used to tell me he had his real teeth pulled when he was forty so he wouldn't have to pay dentists any more, but my dentist here says the old liar must have lost all his real teeth from gum disease. He won't be parted from those false ones even at night. He says if you sleep without your false teeth, your cheeks fall in and you start to look old."

Liza: "Ah; that explains all those old people hanging around in nursing homes with their cheeks fallen in, I guess. Ignorant assholes."

Me: "No kidding. He hates old people. I thought I'd take him to one of the local senior centers for a couple of afternoons a week so he might strike up a friendship or two of his own, you know? Something besides me and that damned ugly cat for him to relate to for a change. Nothing doing, he says; why would he want to 'hang around with a bunch of old people?'"

Liza: "Take him anyway, maybe he'll be so pissed off he'll get up and walk home. At least he'd get some exercise."

FROM ROBIN'S JOURNALS, 1940S:

Psychologists might be interested to know that there seems to be some relationship between rotten teeth and abstract or non-figurative painting and drawing: I have not seen photographs of Picasso, Braque, or Mondrian in the pornographic act of smile, but of the seven-odd abstract painters I know—Diller, Holtzmann, Greene, Spivak, Browne, De Rivera, Von Wicht, Rinehart, Gorky, and Hoffman—five have lost most of their teeth and the others don't show theirs. (My own, of course, led me to the thought by way of their interesting little vacuums.)

As the youngest of four brothers and the only one not living with a wife at the time, in 1952 Robin was selected (I can't imagine him volunteering) to move up to New Rochelle and live there as a sort of caretaker for his widowed mother, and he did so until she died seven years later.

I remember meeting his mother once: a large, shapeless, white-haired woman with a mournful, hooting voice and watery blue eyes. She was living with Robin upstairs in a little wooden house in a dreary part of that rundown town (or so I remember what I saw of it at the time). I was in my teens. It was a long train ride out there, all alone, and it was unsettling when I arrived. There was a strong atmosphere in that house: a hovering cloud of grim compromise, of putting-your-head-down-to-get-through, of unchosen but immovable circumstance.

Robin said later, with a mixture of pity and harsh disgust, that Marcia McKee had had some talent of her own and had painted, but, discouraged by her husband's cutting remarks on the subject, had given up. I saw some of her watercolors in New Rochelle: pallid things, still lifes, dim in memory like the woman herself.

It was clear that Rob despised her for her weakness, but despised his father even more for his hardness.

"There was no love in that house," he said in damning summary, and he said it more than once.

There was a rumor that Robin's mother died of malnutrition. Liza says it was no rumor, Pop told her himself: "I forgot to feed the cat, so maybe I forget to feed her, too. Heh-heh."

How heartless that sounds. Maybe it was just one of the man's outrageous teases; either way, I can't get worked up about it. I didn't know the woman. My only grandmother, as far as I was concerned, was Nana, Mom's mother. She used to joke that when she met Robin's family—his mother, father, and three brothers— it was "just like going in the forest, they were like big tall trees all around."

Nana was about five foot one. Pop was six foot three, and not the tallest in his family.

When she could no longer take care of herself, my uncle Vic

moved Nana (against her furious protests, I am told—I was away in the Peace Corps at the time) out of her New York apartment and up to Ansonia, Connecticut, where he and his family lived. I heard later that she used to sneak out of his house and wander down the street, stopping strangers to tell them that her son was holding her prisoner and starving her.

Uncle Vic was a doctor. Nana had a weight problem (she had the central European fireplug shape and referred to herself as "stout") and a heart condition that made her weight dangerous, so he had her on a diet.

"My son and his wife are starving me," she would say, pleading for rescue from these monsters. "They want me to die."

Sometimes grown children seem to torment their old parents with tyranny and spite, but you don't always understand what you're looking at, or what you're told.

I HAVE A PHOTO of Robin's parents outside a house in the East somewhere, with snow on the ground and the roof; the picture was taken in the thirties, to judge by the clothes (though that's not so easy to tell about people muffled up in overcoats and scarves). His mother's face, much younger than when I saw it, is on the boiled-potato model seen in some women of British stock—an undistinguished shape with undistinguished features afloat in it. His face is long-jawed and craggy, rough granite without a glint of humor. I look at that face and I know what the word "dour" means, a cross between "dire" and "sour."

I can see what drew Pop to my mother and her family. It wasn't just Mom: she was an elegant, petite blonde with big green eyes and an infectious smile, built on a fairly voluptuous Continental pattern rather than the bony American one. But it wasn't from her that he soaked up his surprising Yiddish and German vocabulary, because my mother's mother was something of an anti-Semite and had done her best to train the Jewishness out of her American-born sons and daughters. She couldn't root her background out of herself, though.

So I suspect that Pop got his peculiar overlay of Jewishness from Nana herself, her and her shouting, laughing, quarreling sisters and that whole, hot-burning, Viennese first generation; and from Jewish guys who worked with him in the old Paul Terry studios, drawing animation cells before the war.

He must have been freezing to death in the northern forest of his own family.

ME (looking in on Pop after lunch): "Hi, Pop. I want to make a stop at the co-op before we go to Safeway; let's get going."

Robin (looking up from reading the *New Yorker*): "What, NOW?"

Me: "Yes, *now*, of course now. I'm standing here now, not to-morrow. You ready? Let's go."

Him, shifting as if to rise, growling: "You never give me any warning."

"Warning of what? We go shopping every Thursday afternoon."

"Yeah, but I'm busy, Suzy."

"Busy." I look at him. He's just settled back mulishly into his chair, brooding over the glossy pages of advertising in his lap, and he doesn't want to move. With a martyred sigh, I cave. "Look, what do you need? If it's not too much, I'll pick stuff up for you."

Now, this is risky. If he gets the idea that he can get me to go do his shopping for him just by saying that he's "busy," he's liable to try to take advantage to a degree unimaginable in any normal person. But I just don't have the energy today to coax and kid him into hauling himself to his feet and walking out to the car.

Him: "I'm out of oat bran flakes. That's all."

Me, adding this to my list: "You're still following the oat-bran wars?" There's been a lot of back-and-forth in the news about oat bran as an effective anticancer agent (or not).

Him (relaxing now that he knows he won't have to get up after all): "Oh, I don't care about that. The big C either gets you or it doesn't. I eat bran because it bulks you up; you know what I mean. You want nice firm, shapely turds, not runny blips—"

Me: "Excuse me, can we not talk about your bowels this morning?"

Robin, with offended dignity: "It's important to me. I don't want to get caught short while I'm out walking the dog."

Me, flipping open his cupboard doors to see if there's anything in there that needs replenishing: "I understand that. But I've been hearing from you about this particular subject since long before we got the dog. You need more instant?"

Robin, putting the magazine aside to concentrate on a favorite subject: "Nah; coffee gives you gallbladder cancer, don't you watch the news? There are other times you don't want to get caught short, lots of them. Wait till you get old. How old are you, anyway?"

I tell him: I'm well into my forties.

Robin, suspiciously: "You don't look it. You're that old already? Watch out for osteoporosis. You should take calcium."

"I do."

Him, careering along as if I haven't spoken: "Otherwise you could get all, you know, *puckleback*, like your uncle Jule's wife."

"A widow's hump, you mean? I take calcium, I told you. Look, I have to go—I brought you the book review section from the Sunday *Times*. I haven't read it yet, so bring it back over when you're done with it, okay?"

He takes it and glances at the cover page and mutters peevishly, "Dickens, again?"

Me, on my way out the door before I bean him: "Yeah, 'Dickens, again.'"

He glares down at the image—a *fausse-antique* engraving—of the massive, bearded face of Charles Dickens on the front page. "Why are you so good to me? I don't have any money."

"See you later, Pop," I say, and I go.

FROM ROBIN'S JOURNALS, 1960:

Shakespeare was 49 when he retired, after having produced the greatest literary art on record over 25 years, dying 3 years later at 52.

We retired from the commercial art and restaurant world at 49, after having produced nothing; and embarked on the career which we had never actually forsaken, but which burst at last from us. Now, we know nobody. Nobody knows us. We don't even know ourself. Nicht. The future? We see nothing in it to prevent any reader of these absurd volumes from thinking of them as a sort of diary of a madman. If mad we must be, better it is to go mad with a brush in one's hand than a knife.

But we don't believe it. More likely, it will be a case of gradual, dull, grinding, petering out and expiration. Like a rat with delusions of being a man, and an artist at that . . .

Liza calls to ask what to get him for Christmas (again; this is a seasonal quest). I tell her about how he warned me not to become like Aunt Carol, with her "puckleback."

"'Puckleback!'" I mimic. "What is it, Yiddish? Viennese? Where the hell did he learn expressions like that? He's a Scottish Presby-damn-terian, for Christ's sake—"

"No he's not, he's nothing and proud of it," Liza points out.

"You know what I mean; he knows more Yiddish and German than either of us two. He's like Mom and Nana rolled up into one. I swear, he's Jewisher than we are!"

Liz, very dry: "Well, that doesn't take much. But I know what you mean; sometimes on the phone he says things, like, oh you know—so-and-so is such a *putz*, or Suzy is *meshuga*, and it sounds so natural, you'd think he was Jerry the butcher on Columbus Avenue."

Me, refraining from pointing out that Jerry was the Italian grocer (the Jewish butcher on the other side of Columbus was Harry): "Maybe he thinks he *is* Jewish. That's what he tells these door-to-door evangelists when they show up here in their suits and ties. 'I'm not interested; I'm Jewish,' he says, which is not that common out here, remember; and they take off stumbling all over each other in confusion, and he stands on his porch laughing like a hyena, the old fraud."

I remind her how, in the photos Ian took when Steve and I had our outdoor wedding, Robin, in his blazer and pressed pants and loafers and yarmulka and white beard, looks like a gaunt Old Testament patriarch.

In my hearing, he turned to Stephen and muttered, "Take good care of her." Given our odd, stilted relationship I found this rather moving; I, literally, hadn't been sure he cared. I was just as surprised when he agreed to hold the pole supporting one corner of the *chupa*, which was not easy in the brisk breeze that was blowing on that chilly October morning at the Ward Pound Ridge Reservation, near Pound Ridge, New York.

Liza laughs about Pop and the evangelists in my yard. "For an old curmudgeon, he sure knows how to keep himself entertained."

I say he entertains himself mostly by watching TV and monitoring his damned bowels, and she should send him books for Christmas. "Mysteries. He likes mysteries, that's all he reads now."

She is quiet. Then she says, "That's all? He used to be such an intellectual. I never knew what to say to him."

"Oh, come on, Liz!"

"No, I mean it. I never graduated from college, remember? And he always seemed like somebody who knew everything."

Liz went to a private high school for kids headed for performing careers. That kind of education doesn't encourage higher levels of traditional schooling; the goal is to get your acting (or singing or dancing) career going as early as possible. This is particularly important for girls, since the job opportunities for female actors thin out alarmingly as they age; it's not as true for the boys, but holds for all to some extent.

I finished college and a fast-track Master of Arts in teaching at NYU; Liz started at Columbia but quit after a year, and it may be that this was in part our mother's intention. Mom could barely manage to pay for one college education, let alone two, on a single, woman-scale salary.

Liz's shyness about the old man was rooted in this difference, among others I suppose. It's a painful thought. Pop never went to college at all. (His attendance at the Art Students' League in New York was sporadic; when I ordered his transcript, they sent one for only 1931–32, saying that was the only year that he was in serious attendance.) He's an autodidact, but with someone who seems to know so much about so much anyway, that's pretty daunting in itself.

I answer lightly: "God knows, the damnedest things come up

sometimes when you talk to him, even now. Yesterday I saw something in *Art News* about Willem de Kooning—"

"Ugh, yeah," says my undereducated sister, "all those hideous pictures of fat women in horror-movie makeup."

"That's him. So I mentioned this article to Robin and said I'd heard that de Kooning was a brawler with a reputation for barroom fights. Robin said, 'Oh, for Pete's sake, just because one time he heard some guy saying that all artists are fairies, and he was fed up with hearing that crap so he turned around and busted the guy in the nose. Broke his glasses. The guy was a dentist.' I asked him how he knew and he said he was there."

"In the bar?"

"That's what he says."

"Jeez."

We are quiet, thinking about that. I say, "He used to know everybody in that scene, when he lived in the Village. I hate to think of all that memory and experience disappearing for good when he dies."

Liz says, "You're a writer. Get him to talk about those days, and write about it."

I explain how in the face of direct questions Pop blanks out. He says, "I don't know any more. Whaddya want from me? It was a long time ago." But if I mention a name, like J. Robert Oppenheimer, he says, "Oh, yeah, we heard him talk once at the Museum of Natural History, your mother and I." So I ask, "When was that? What did he have to say?" And he scrunches up his face as if I'm being completely unreasonable and grumbles, "Aw, Suzy, who remembers?"

Liz says, "What about all those notebooks? Those black, leather-bound sketchbooks. I looked in one once; it was full of his writing."

I've peeked too. "Have you ever tried to read his handwriting?

It's the writing of a paranoid, smaller than microbes and proof against anything but the Palomar telescope. Anyway, he told me to leave it alone, I can read the notebooks when he's dead if I want to."

Silence. Then she says, "What do you think he writes in there? Does he write about us?"

"Who knows? He doesn't write about anything in them any more, as far as I know. Not since he came out here. He reads a lot, but mostly just browsing the magazines and papers: the *Guardian*, *Art News*, the *Voice*. And the *New Yorker*, which he only looks at so he can complain that the cartoons are no good any more. Listen, for Christmas? Send mysteries."

FROM ROBIN'S JOURNAL, 1960:

We have written down, poured out in ink an immoderate sized stream of somewhat sheer drivel since about 1930, when we took the habit. However, it has been good therapy, cured us of any itches to write. But for downright ineluctable modality of the risible—it's not too horrific, despite the Omega Comedic thread that weaves in and out, as above. Hell, we've got to entertain ourself <u>some</u> way.

The notebooks stop with 1969. Living in the front house on Fourth Street, Robin wasn't writing, and he wasn't painting. Lizzie says she asked him if he was painting, when she called, and he always said no.

When he first came out West I took him to Langell's, the local art supply store. We stocked up on tubes of paint, canvas and sizing, turpentine and oil, everything he said he needed, including a painting box he could carry brushes and colors in when he drove the green truck out to find a good spot to work; but that never happened.

. . .

ROB, sitting at his kitchen table with Bibi on his lap: "So Dufy's finally visiting America, and he gets on the train heading across country. His young guide who's riding with him to translate and show
him around keeps promising him this wonderful light, light that
European painters would die for, in the famous American Southwest.

"All the way across the country he's talking about this light, to lure
the great painter on. So finally one morning the train pulls into the
Albuquerque station and the guy wakes Dufy up and rushes him to
the doorway—'Hurry, hurry, Maître, come see the wonderful light!'

"And Dufy steps out onto the platform and looks around, and
he says three words and gets back on the train and sleeps all the
way to Los Angeles, where he turns around and heads right home.
He said, 'Trop de lumière.'"

Me: "Great story! Is it true, do you think?"

"Sure it's true, Suzy."

It probably isn't; I read recently that Degas was the only French
painter of note at that time who came to America, and he never
went west of New Orleans.

"What about you?" I say. The same little sketch, on a stiff-
backed pad, has been sitting on the vast black easel for months: a
tree trunk and a couple of branches. "Too much light, Pop?"

"Nah." He sits thinking, calculating how much to say. We're at
his kitchen table; I'm going through his mail (which he lets pile up
there till I get to it), dumping the endless supply of junk into a
paper bag between my feet.

Finally he says, "You told me there was north light in this house."

"Yup. There it is, in the next room." In fact, light is streaming in
through the tall north window, I can see it from where I sit.

"I thought it would have lots of big windows in the north wall."

I sigh. It's amazing how much I sigh when I'm talking to Pop. I try not to let the sighs sound as annoyed as I feel, as annoyed as you feel when you open your hand to give your best and the recipient says there are flies on your best, it's no good.

"Pop, this building is a farmhouse. It wasn't built to be an artist's studio."

"There's just the one window," he goes on, carefully not looking over his shoulder at the room we're talking about, "and it's in the wrong place."

"Well, it's what we've got, Pop. We can't put in a skylight because of the attic up there. I did think about it, but the way the house is constructed, there's no way."

"And," he forges doggedly on, now that at last he's begun, "the walls are pink. Who painted them that color, anyway?"

Well, they *are* pink: hot pink, in the Mexican style of strong interior colors. I didn't notice. I don't paint, I write. The color of my walls doesn't matter—though the walls of the little cabin where I work are in fact white; I painted them myself, after I finished the rough interior with mud plaster.

"With a color that strong," he explains, "you can't see the colors you're trying to work with. It throws everything off. It makes reflections."

Guiltily, I tell him that when I sell my next book, we'll paint the walls.

But we never do; it isn't necessary, because he doesn't even draw, let alone paint, the whole time he's with us. I never smell the good, strong tang of turpentine in that house. I never find him sketching on the porch or stretching a canvas. He spends his time in the kitchen, reading or watching TV. I know because that's where I find him whenever I walk in there.

When I ask him to help me get ready, a few months later, to

paint the walls white in the northwest room, he says, "Nah, don't bother, it doesn't matter, we'd just have to shift everything around."

I should have done it anyway.

Or maybe not, because then he'd have had no excuse.

FROM ROBIN'S JOURNALS, 1938:

I shall never buy the artist's beret, I shall not grow a beard, I will dress in ready-to-wear clothes, smoke my pipe privately, and try to remember to get my hair cut fortnightly instead of annually. I WILL NOT WEAR A HAT.

George and Bibi

I bring Robin his mail. We share the big gray mailbox that lists to starboard on top of a cedar post out by the street. Day and night, four lanes of traffic whiz by, trying with more or less success to avoid the shambling drunks walking home from the bar a half mile down Fourth at Ranchitos Road. Our mailbox leans because the drunks pause and lean on it, sometimes.

Pop gets occasional letters and his Social Security check. Not today; just the *Village Voice* and some ads.

The TV is on—he keeps it on the kitchen counter next to the sink, so he can watch without moving from his chair at the oak table. Usually his cat, the slab-sided gray cat with the skinny tail, occupies his lap.

Today she's out somewhere. He's watching on his own, with the sound turned off.

Me: "What are you watching?"

Him: "Geraldo. He's got wheelchair-bound lesbian adoptive mothers with abusive partners on today. Same old thing."

Me (checking to make sure all the ads and junk mail are his, not any of mine mixed in): "So turn it off. Who's forcing you to watch?"

"At least it's better than Donahue. He only does Hollywood. He worships Hollywood, ever notice that? He wants to be in movies himself, that's why he has nothing but people from Hollywood on his show."

Me (innocently): "Isn't that where they film the show?" We have had this conversation before, but I just thought of this reply; it can't hurt to try.

Him, snarling a bit: "That doesn't make any difference! Hollywood has a stranglehold on the whole country. Everybody wants to be a movie star; that's why George Bush holds so many news conferences. He's hoping they'll hire him for one of the sitcoms."

"We did, Dad, didn't you notice?" I say, thinking of the sitcom called "Babbitt in the White House": the reign of President George Mealy-Mouth Bush.

"You can always tell a movie actor," he says. "They're all *polished*, they have a kind of glow about them: health, that's what it is. They spend all their time working on their health, so they can blind the rest of us with their glow. Bush has it, you must have noticed that. So you know he's a movie actor, or wants to be."

I make a face. "That's the glow of money, Pop. All rich people have it."

He grunts. "He wants to be an actor, like Reagan."

Me: "Baloney. He's a Republican. He wants to be king, not some measly actor in the movies."

Him, glaring disdainfully at me from under the brim of his broken-crowned straw hat (it's summer again, he's laid the watch cap aside): "What's measly about it? You know of any other country that elected a two-bit, brainless, cataleptic movie actor for its leader not once but twice, and when they couldn't get him for a third time they took his straight man instead?"

I sit down, grinning, and stretch my legs out in front of me.

"You think the country runs on plots," I chide him. "George Bush sneaks into office on a conspiracy run by Frances Ford Coppola and Steve Bochko. Do you really think the world is so simple?"

"You think it isn't?" he snaps back, his false teeth clicking with vehemence. "So Kennedy gets nailed but Reagan survives; and Martin Luther King dies on the porch of some motel but whatsisname, the governor of Mississippi, George Wallace—"

Me: "Alabama, isn't it?"

Pop, bitterly: "*He* survives, and his wife gets to be governor."

"Come on, Robin, no she didn't."

"Well," he says, "almost; same thing. What about Italy? The CIA has been running Italy since World War Two."

Me (taken aback by the grandeur of the claim): "What? Where'd you hear that? Was that on the news?"

Him, triumphant: "Of course not, they wouldn't put that on the news—Hollywood wouldn't let them! It was in the *Manchester Guardian*. You don't even read the papers you subscribe to."

Me: "Jesus, you're in a mood today. What's going on, Pop?"

I'm slow, but I do eventually pick up on the signs: something is bothering him, and it's not really Hollywood.

"Sure I'm in a mood," he growls. "I've got good reason to be in a mood."

Alarm. He's into his seventies, it could be anything: symptoms noticed but hidden, fears unexpressed—I recognize the pattern all too well, from my own inclination to anticipate the worst and stay away from the doctor to avoid confirmation of it. I ask him if he's feeling okay.

"I'm fine," he barks. "What are you talking about?"

"So what's the problem?"

He glares at me. "I'm having a fight with Bibi."

Bibi; the cat.

"A fight with Bibi?" I say. "How can you have a fight with your cat?"

"She won't eat her food," he says resentfully, "and then it sits there and gets hard as a rock and she comes in from outside and yells at me for fresh."

I am baffled; I've always had a cat of my own, and this just isn't my idea of a problem. "So don't give in to her; let her eat what's there."

Him: "She won't eat it, Suzy; I'm telling you. And then she drives me crazy, rubbing my legs and whining."

I stare at him, feeling a little like Alice talking to one of Lewis Carroll's characters. "Robin, you're the man; she's the cat. There must be a way you can take control of this situation."

"Like what?" A stony glare.

"Like quit catering to her every whim, for starters. When she gets hungry enough, she'll eat."

Him, sitting back, disgusted with my incomprehension. "Yeah, but meantime she's such a pest I can't do anything. Anyway, she can't eat that stuff when it gets hard, she hasn't got enough teeth left. The food has to be fresh, or she can't eat it."

"Robin, you're a smart man. I know you can figure out what to do about this."

He mutters, "I should never have fed her yogurt. All that acid dissolved her teeth."

I stand up. I've had enough; I'm always having enough, with Pop. "You fed her yogurt because she yelled for the yogurt you were eating, and you always give in to her."

He looks down at his hands, his long, elegant old hands with the nicotine stains on the fingers, and mourns, "She's seven years old and she can't eat hard food."

The cat is a stray, nobody knows how old she is. I groan. "Stop, go back to watching Geraldo, will you? You're breaking my heart."

I have to be careful, though. The last time he was crabby like this, I thought he was just being his usual grouchy self. But talking to Liza on the phone, I got the real scoop: he had caught his foot on his own threshhold and fallen, and had to drag himself to the kitchen sink to reach up and grab hold of the counter and lever himself upright again. He wouldn't tell me about it, though; didn't want to bother me, he told her. Didn't want to complain.

About the cat's gourmandizing, yes, but about crawling around on the floor for half an hour trying to get up? No, he wouldn't think of it.

You could lose your mind.

FROM ROBIN'S JOURNALS, 1940:

Democracy is an expensive myth maintained by opportunism; monarchy is an expensive myth maintained by incest; and Fascism is an expensive myth maintained by the firing squad.

Pop took our dog for walks enthusiastically and without complaint. He adored George from the word go, falling (apparently) for my scheme of adopting a dog solely for the purpose of luring him out for the healthful exercise he would otherwise not take.

And though Pop sometimes came home slapping dust from his pants because George had pulled him down on the ground again, somehow he never got hurt. He would fall on the dirt shoulder of the road, toppling like a felled tree (as I realized later, when I actually saw him fall)—but his long Celtic bones were as resilient as sword blades; he never broke a thing.

George, being part malamute, was headstrong, like—I've read since—all that breed. He had a bad habit of lunging after a truck going by if a dog in the truck-bed barked at him. And because George was big, an eighty-pound black-and-tan alpha with an amused look on his broad, low-domed head and little laughing brown eyes sunk deep in velvet fuzz, every other dog that whizzed past safe in a moving vehicle naturally let out a volley of barks just to let George know what a lollygagging dipshit of a poodle he was, a zeta if he was anything.

Of course we tried to cure George of his bad habit. We tried everything—courses (he went through obedience school twice and was both times voted Mr. Personality but never did actually graduate); a hired trainer; even, I am ashamed to admit, a collar with an electric shock device on it operated by remote control. This last resort of desperation occurred after he had nearly dragged me into the path of an oncoming semi in response to the usual provocation.

Without even thinking about it, I did what some dog-training manual or other had advised: grabbed George by the scruff of his neck and somehow flipped him onto his back (as another pickup full of mutts roared past, all of them yelping with joy at his predicament).

I straddled George, held him down, and yelled into his face, "NO, DAMN IT, NO, NO, NO! Do you hear me, god DAMN you?"

I was petrified and trembling, of course, having nearly been yanked into the path of onrushing traffic, and my fear expressed itself in fury. George lay there quietly but let out a faint, grumbly growl in the back of his throat.

"WHAT DID YOU SAY?" I screamed at him, shaking him by the ruff with both hands. "Don't you DARE growl at me, you brainless twerp!" And more along those lines, till my throat hurt and I let him up; there were no hard feelings from George that I could detect—he trotted home with me as brightly and confidently as ever. I was the one who felt like an idiot.

That was before I got my new contact lenses. I had given up my hard lenses because the blowing dust got under them and scratched my corneas. Meanwhile, I wore glasses with lenses so thick that they miniaturized everything.

When I got new, soft contacts and really saw George, I was stunned: he was the size of a small brown bear, with a head as big as my own. He must have thought me completely unreasonable, objecting to his lunging announcement to those cowardly traveling dogs that he could whip their hairy behinds any time. Like the true gentleman he was, he had refrained from biting my face off and had just lain there instead, complaining under his breath and enduring my irrational abuse, until I had returned to my senses.

SO LIZ SAYS on the phone: "He really shouldn't be walking that dog."

Me: "What? He's not whining about walking George, is he? I don't believe it. You should see how he fusses over him."

Liz: "He doesn't want to complain; he knows how much Steve loves that dog."

Steve and me both. I don't answer, waiting for the bad news.

Liz: "But Robin says his balance isn't so good."

Me, with passion: "His balance is fine. He's just too damned lazy to pick up his feet when he walks, so he catches his shoes on anything sticking up the least little bit above ground level."

Liz: "Well, whatever it is, the dog makes it worse. He's pulling Robin down a lot. You have to do something."

Me: "Damn it. We only took on the dog as an excuse to force that lazy old fart to get some exercise."

"I know, you told me. But you've got to come up with something else. So you knew this was happening?"

"Well, once or twice, and no harm done, apparently. You mean it's all the time now? When did you find out?"

Liz: "Oh, it's months ago now. He didn't want to make problems for you."

Me: "Ha. Not telling me things is such a good way not to make problems for me, don't you think? What things, anyway? What else is a problem, besides George, I mean?"

"Oh, he's always saying this is wrong and that's wrong, silly little stuff, like how the exhaust fumes from Fourth Street get into his house and are slowly poisoning him, but then he says, 'Don't tell Suzy, you know how she gets.'"

Me: "Oh, yes, I get livid and beat the crap out of him, right? It's ridiculous!"

Liz: "It's no joke, Suzy. He says that stuff to me and I know it's bullshit. I tell him so, and then he laughs, because he knows it too. But what if he said that to somebody else? He could get you into a lot of trouble if people thought you were abusing him or something."

Me: "People like who? This is our father, remember? Who won't talk to people who say hello to him on the street because it's none of their business whether he's having a 'nice day' or not? I can't worry about it, Liz."

But I do worry. I worry about the falling-down part.

We keep working on George. The electric collar—you can't buy one of these, thank God, you must hire a trainer who uses it and work with him—had no more effect than anything else. George had his alpha duties and he insisted on doing them, like the honest dog he was.

So, reluctantly, I told Pop to forget it, I would walk George (in fact I already walked him nights, usually with Steve, all three of us relishing the hard dirt side roads under chilly moonlight between ramshackle Valley houses and fields).

Robin set his heels and balked. He liked walking George, he could handle George, he *insisted* on walking George; and he would not be moved. This may have been partly sly punishment of me for saddling him with George in the first place.

What you have to understand is that I had not wanted a dog; I'd had one, Tinky the mutt, when I was a girl in New York—including morning runs to Central Park to get in a walk before school, chewed sheets and shoelaces, and clothing to replace. I was well aware of what a serious and time-consuming responsibility a dog is when properly kept, and I figured I had taken on a pretty whopping extra helping of responsibility as it was (Guess Who).

But Steve and I had noticed this big furry fellow slumped in a disconsolate heap on the evening of Election Day in 1984 outside the Federal Express office, where Steve had to mail off some documents at the last minute. The dog was still there when we came out, the office was about to close up, and the people behind the counter swore they had no idea who this animal belonged to.

He had no collar, let alone I.D. tags, and he wasn't in a part of town where he would stumble upon friendly householders to cadge a drink or a bite to eat from. This was an industrial strip right beside Interstate 40, and it was rapidly closing down early so workers could go vote. More likely he would wander into traffic and get himself killed (in fact, a persistent sensitivity in his front paws suggested that he might have arrived in the area in the first place by jumping out of a pickup truck on a slow stretch).

Steve wanted to take him home for the night and then lug him up to the Humane Society next morning (that was where we got our cats). I put up a valiant defense, knowing that Steve and I were both way too softhearted about animals to involve ourselves only tangentially in George's fate. Since I was arguing against my own deeper inclinations, this didn't get me very far. Finally I said, "Look, I'll call him; if he gets in the car with us, we'll take him home for the night."

Figuring that he'd be too shy of unknown people to climb into a vehicle with us, I held open the back door of the Corolla and hollered, "C'mon, George!"

He jumped up, tail wagging, and leaped into the back seat to settle down next to Steve and lick Steve's nose all the way home. We took him to the Humane Society the next day as planned. They had grave doubts about placing such a sizable adult animal. To make taking George more palatable, we said that if nobody claimed him, they should get in touch with us.

They got in touch with us.

We talked about it. Looking desperately for a way around the fact that we really weren't set up for a dog, we nonetheless stumbled upon a brilliant idea. Since we had finished landscaping the place with ditch-side trees and had (madly) hand-built our adobe garage so wide that its roof had to be beamed with used telephone poles, there was no longer enough serious work for Pop to do around the place to get him up off his narrow butt once in a while. George might function as a health strategy, on a stealth basis.

In due course we collected George (neutered per Humane Society requirements but unaffected by it so far as we could see) and brought him home. We had to build him a pen outside, a large dog run with eight-foot chain-link fencing enclosing George and a huge old cottonwood, for shade.

It was necessary: this dog who had no hesitation about entering cars had never been inside a house before. Coaxed indoors, George vacillated wildly between being terrified of doorways, steps, and wood or brick floors, and lifting his leg to mark the place as his own.

There was the incident of the vet's files ... but that was their own fault, since whenever I walked George up there for an exam or a shot, he would rear up to look over the counter and they would coo and burble and give him a cookie. Or six. His mild, interested, completely confident face was irresistible. So of course he had thought he was on his own property, where people knew how to treat him right; and there were all these nice files in the bottom shelf along the wall, just waiting for his signature.... They forgave him; people always did.

When I went up Fourth with mail, I would hear from the guys at the post office about how when Robin walked up there and bought a burrito at the burrito stand across the street he always got a Coke, too, and put the lid with some Coke in it on the little ledge where the burrito man laid out the food to be picked up. Then George stood on his hind legs and lapped Coke from the lid like a gent in a thick fur coat (and handcuffs).

Or Pop would come in and tell me how George insisted on stopping every day to dig a little in one spot in front of Pauline's fence, where he had found a cookie half-buried one day. "He thinks there's a cookie-mine down there," Robin said. "He's an optimist, he never gives up hope."

Or how a kid walking by stopped to ask what that box-thing was on George's collar (it was the electric charge-box, which we hadn't taken off even after the trainer and his lessons were gone, in hopes that George would somehow be reminded that it was *supposed* to sting him if he dashed after a truck). Robin had answered, straight faced, "Oh, that? That's his radio. He listens to rock-and-roll, can't you hear it?"

Daytimes George would lie on the yellow couch while I worked, my guardian (in case the Seventh-Day Adventists should detect my hidden presence and mount an attack on the studio). Then at the end of the evening Steve and I would sit on the couch with him, hugging his big barrel of a body and singing to him, "Goodnight, Georgie," to the tune of "Goodnight, Sweetheart," before shutting him in for the night.

Oh, all right, it sounds crazy; it was crazy. It was to make him feel better about not sleeping in the house with us. Yeah, okay; to make *us* feel better.

One week when we were out of town Robin took over this task of singing George to sleep, but he said he'd never do it again: George had sung with him, lifting his face and hooting, "Loo-loo-loo!" and had licked his beard. I think it was what Robin took as implied criticism of his own singing that incensed him rather than the dog-slobber, but as it's Robin I'm talking about, I can't say for certain.

Still, when George fell into the basement it was Pop who rescued him (not Pop's basement or mine—we didn't have them—George's basement). We got George a large doghouse and set it up off the ground on bricks so the bottom wouldn't rot out, and we put a bale of hay outside the doorway as a sort of front porch. George would lie in the doorway watching the yard with his head and front paws on the bale.

When nobody visited, and it was still a while before I would show up to feed him and play fetch with him, George would dig. This began as recreational digging but became a serious, even an artistic endeavor. I had to line the entire inside of the pen with big rocks to keep him from tunneling out. Resourceful George began tunneling in, digging ditches that wound among the roots of the big cottonwood and under the doghouse.

One night Pop, whose place was closer to the pen than mine, heard a commotion of scramblings and distressed cries; pulling on his robe and shuffling outside with his flashlight, he found that George's excavations had collapsed: the doghouse had fallen into the pit, with George inside.

"Almost broke my back, hauling him out of there," Robin told me the next day, proudly and with some defiance: he had put his back on the line for his buddy and was daring me to rebuke him for not getting help instead. A bond like that is not easily overridden. It's a wonder he didn't teach the damned dog to smoke so he could share a pack with George now and then.

At my insistence, Pop began to carry a long, lightweight stick with which to tap George on the shoulder if he got out of line and his position threatened Pop's balance. And if there continued to be falling incidents, Pop chose not to call them to my attention. So long as they both seemed to enjoy their outings so much, I could live with trading Robin's greater safety for the certainty of the only exercise I knew of that the man would willingly undertake.

I understood by then that animals were the only people Pop really had any use for at all.

FROM ROBIN'S JOURNALS, NEW ROCHELLE, 1952:

A small gray cat name of Bubba, whom we have reared now for almost a year, begins to push us, move us over a little, and to assume her rightful place in the household—as the boss. You don't draw or paint a creature like this—though it has been attempted, from Pisanello to Renoir—for a cat's beauty is not static. Not this one, anyway. Unusual in that her nose, pro-file, is bent in a true Roman bend over a British lion chin which juts out like Edward the Seventh's beard. She greets us each am with much ecstatic demonstration, so that we instantly forget our own weariness . . . a distinct pleasure . . .

Chinatown

The phone rang one night when Robin was having dinner with us. I took the call. An unfamiliar voice, a man's, low and thick, asked for Robinson McKee.

I said, "Who's calling, please?"

"Irving McKee."

Excited, I rushed to hand Pop the phone. "It's your brother!"

Robin took it, scowling. "Hello? Yeah. Oh. Oh." Long pause. "I don't want it. No. I won't take it. No, I'll say the same tomorrow. Yeah. Goodbye."

He finished his meal without a word and left.

I trailed after him across the starlit yard. "Pop? What's going on?"

"A phone call," he said. "That's all."

"Irving doesn't call you often, does he?" I followed him into his house, chagrined that I hadn't been quick enough to grab the opportunity, however belated, to have a conversation at long last with my unknown uncle. "What's up?"

Robin didn't answer at once, but I didn't give ground. I was alert now, almost alarmed. It had to be something serious. None of Robin's family had ever tried to contact him on Fourth Street, so far as I knew, which had not struck me as unusual. He had never introduced me to any of his brothers when we were all living back East, despite my requests to meet them.

I had run into one brother once, one of the twins, at the Hudson Street loft. Robin hustled the man out as soon as I arrived—a lean, grim-looking individual with a pointed nose reddened and running from a cold, who must have spoken two words to me all told. ("Hello." "Goodbye.") If that much. Robin had had nothing to say about him except that he worked at a factory somewhere upstate as an accountant.

The family background, I had since learned from Ian (who took an interest in such things), was actually what some might consider distinguished. It included a soldier who had fought in the American Revolution, some newspaper editors, a judge or two, various businessmen, drunks and ne'er-do-wells, and a political cartoonist of the nineteenth century who used the pen name Petroleum V. Nasby; I have found his pictorial current-events commentary occasionally reproduced in high school history books. Rob's father had been a commercial artist and cartoonist himself, so the arts focus had some fairly sturdy antecedents.

There was also reputed to be some obscure connection to the family of Arthur Conan Doyle through Robin's grandmother; and a mayor of Sacramento who had died falling down the steps of City Hall at mid-day in a drunken stupor. I don't know whether any of that was true. Robin was hardly reliable on the subject of his family, only on the subject of his *feelings* about his family.

He said of his immediate clutch of relatives: "I couldn't get away from them fast enough—bunch of blue-nosed Philistines. Every year I get an ad for something called 'The Book of McKee'—as if I wanted to read about that bunch of dullards! Forget 'em. I try to."

Then there was a story he could occasionally be led to repeat, about how his father had gone into the Mexican desert with a geological engineer and the engineer's "woman," and how the engineer had abused the woman and Robin's father had more or less rescued her and taken her away and married her. This was Marcia, the mother I'd met in New Rochelle, for whom (along with my mother's mother) I had originally been named. Pop's eldest brothers, the twins, had traced the geologist later when they heard he'd gotten rich and presented themselves as *his* sons. They had been thrown out, with menaces, for their pains.

Rob seemed to believe this tale himself. According to him, the twins were the get of the engineer and only half-brothers to himself and Irving. He said that one twin was a mean cuss, and the other was a sweetheart who could mend any broken machine in the world and make it run. All the older brothers ever did was fight, according to Pop; the McKee household house was always full of tall, angry young men squabbling and hitting out at each other.

"It wasn't a close family," he'd told me. "The old man was a real sourpuss, mad all the time. It was because of his ulcer. He got it from working with that drawing board, one of those heavy old drawing boards of inch-thick wood, that he held on his knees so the edge pressed against his belly. He was in pain all the time so he was cranky, and our mother had no authority in the family because he wouldn't let her have any. It was just fights and arguments all the time."

Except for Irving, Robin had been only too glad to leave the whole lot of them behind when he moved to New Mexico.

Pop was proud of Irving, a Shaw scholar with a respected biography of that author and many monographs to his name, who went to England now and then to do research or to teach. I knew a couple of things about Irving that Rob had let slip in conversation: that he hated recorded music and would never even listen to the radio, only attend live concerts. That he had no children. That he had married a great beauty.

I used to think that Robin was ashamed of me, and of Liza, and that was why he didn't want us to meet our uncles. Later, I thought he just didn't want to deal with it, whatever "it" might turn out to be.

"Why did Irving call?" I said. "Jeez, Pop, you could have asked me if I wanted to talk to him before you hung up!"

"He's dying. He has colon cancer."

"Oh," I said, and stopped there, with my mouth open: what could I say? Irving was the only person in his family Robin had ever expressed the least regard for. I didn't know how to offer comfort, or if he wanted comfort offered. He had kept me an outsider to whatever relationship he had with this brother of his, so how could I say meaningful words about it now, at its end?

"He wants to leave me a hundred and twenty-five thousand dollars in his Will," he said.

"My God!" I said. "You're kidding! How'd he pile up all that on a professor's salary?"

He shrugged. "He wrote books, and he's always had a good head for investments."

"But still," I said, "isn't there his wife?"

"Frances? She's taken care of, he says. This is besides that. I told him I don't want it."

"What?" I said, gaping at him. "Why not?"

"I don't want it, that's all. What do I need that kind of money for?"

I stared at him. "My God, Pop—how about for paying doctors if you get sick?"

"I'm never sick," he said.

"No, okay, not right now," I admitted, "but what about later on?"

"I'm not going to get sick, Suzy."

I sat down across from him at his kitchen table. "Pop, don't be an idiot, please. Call him back and tell him you'll take it and gladly."

"No."

I flailed around for convincing arguments. I pleaded, I cajoled, I explained, I projected probable futures in which that money could grow to an amount that could buy him security in his old age even if some driver should come barreling down Fourth Street one night and wipe out both Steve and me in one magnificent crash.

Robin wouldn't budge.

"*Why* won't you take it?"

"I don't want it. I'm not going to call him back and change my answer."

I swore. "I'd call him myself, if I'd ever met the man!"

Robin said, "You still couldn't make me take the money."

Too angry and upset to sit there talking to a stone wall about this, I got up to leave. "Just do me one favor, will you? Think it over. Think about it, all right? Think about changing your mind. Will you do that?"

"Yeh," he lied; and I walked out.

FROM ROBIN'S JOURNALS, 1959:

1930–1959: 29 yrs. We labored, slowing down gradually, in the market: 29 yrs. Our Dark Age; now we are free—for a year, free!— And we have two score canvases, 200 papers that nobody wants . . . And no money . . . A high rent, a leaky-roofed-studio, puddled floor . . . but for Irving, we should be a stiff . . . But for a chinese lightness of mind . . . dead.

I didn't tell Steve, not then. I couldn't. Both his kids were in college or grad school, so we were still struggling to make ends meet. The man so we were still slowly buying Pop's house from on a real estate contract sometimes came banging on our front door, scowling like a villain in a melodrama, when the monthly payment was late because our cash flow wasn't flowing so well.

I didn't even tell Liza about the rejected legacy, not till years later.

Yes, I was upset, even furious about it; but I also kept having this funny feeling that it wasn't our business, in the sense that we could never see through to what it was really about; like when the guy tells Jack Nicholson's character in that movie, "Forget it, Jake; it's Chinatown."

Irving had been helping Pop out financially for years, I knew that much; buying a few of his paintings, too (so far as I know, he was the only person who did). Maybe that seemed to Robin like more than enough. Maybe it was a question of dignity.

And what kind of person calls up the proposed beneficiary to tell them *beforehand* that they're going to leave him a fortune? Why? It could have been some kind of twisted power trip on Irving's part.

I figured that, stubborn as he was about it, Pop must have had good reasons, and I let it go at that. Irving died a month or so later.

When I visited his widow some years afterward, she told me that the money had gone instead to the hospice where he had been taken care of till the end. I told her, over chicken salad that she served me for lunch in a small, plain front room of her suburban house in Sacramento, that I was sorry never to have known my uncle.

She said gently, "Oh, it's probably just as well. He was a manic-depressive sort of person, and he drank to control his moods. I don't think you would have liked him much."

FROM ROBIN'S JOURNALS, 1952–59:

Of three brothers, which we have, one feels a strong bond to only one—which would astonish him, if he knew it—the more so since we expect no advantage. Simply, it exists. A times we have drunkenly, unreasonably railed at him, as now. But he hath held a Yaleish reasonableness. Him we would hold, though three thousand miles separate us. Why? Who the hell knows? For he knows least what we attempt by way of paint . . . Perhaps it is his even keel, his good wife, his eventful life—they're barren of children—who knows? A search for the ideal existence? A good wife, an eventful life, <u>and</u> having children—Oh, Suzy, oh, Liza—who knows, the ache. . . . Such metaphysical dawdlings!

One actually poured half a glass of wine—good red burgundy—back in its gallon jug.

Flash-forward to Thanksgiving dinner years later with my mother-in-law, Juliet.

Steve and I met in some ways with a peculiar symmetry. His father died just before he met me, and my mother died just after our marriage, leaving each of us with one widowed parent to look after. Julie had recently moved down from her condominium in Santa Fe to a "retirement community" in Albuquerque, called (let's say) Gracious Gardens. In her apartment there she continued the tradition of serving Thanksgiving dinners, which suited me because I had no patience for cooking and no taste for entertaining.

Robin always came with us, with protestations and grumbles. He liked the food (Juliet was an accomplished cook) and put up with the required bathing and dressing for the sake of an excellent, rather formally served meal once a year.

We're sitting around Julie's table in the dining alcove adjoining the kitchenette, all very elegant, but small with so many people in it.

Julie (a tiny woman with a round, smiling face and close-cut white hair, wearing a tailored suit, a strand of pearls, and shoes especially made for her because of feet ruined by fashionable high heels): "How is the squash? Too sweet?"

I said it was delicious, which it was. I said I was impressed by how she could whip up this fine, big meal in an efficiency kitchen.

Julie: "What?"

She had been increasingly deaf since her thirties.

Me: "I really admire you, turning out a meal like this!"

Julie: "I just can't remember whether I put the orange juice in the squash or not, isn't that terrible?"

Steve: "The squash is fine, mother."

Julie: "Hah?"

Steve: "The squash is fine."

Julie: "I didn't hear you, dear."

Steve: "The squash is delicious."

Julie: "Oh, good. You know where I got that recipe? It was from a newspaper story about Wallis Simpson, it was her favorite squash recipe. Robin, do you like the squash?"

Robin (in his gray slacks and blazer, white shirt open at the neck; he's trimmed his beard, too, and looks fairly dashing for an old crock): "Huh? Yeah, it's good."

Julie offers him the dish: "Have some more."

Robin, sitting back and neatly blotting his mouth on his napkin: "Not me, I'm saving room for pie."

Julie: "Well, I just hope the pie is good tonight."

Me, to Steve: "How does she hear him, when she can't hear what anybody else says to her?"

Steve: "It's a plot to drive you crazy."

Julie, to Robin, winningly: "I always make too much food. You could take some squash home with you. Didn't you take home some pie last year, Robin?"

Robin, with gusto: "You bet. It was wonderful. Even Bibi ate some."

Julie, looking around appealingly: "What did he say?"

Me: "He said his cat ate some."

Julie: "Goodness, I didn't make it for the cat to eat! I won't give you pie to take home so your cat can eat it!"

Me: "Don't worry, I'll fight the cat to the death for the last crumb of that apple pie; she won't get a lick of it!" Julie's pie was unbearably good.

Julie: "Hah?"

Me: "I promise, it won't be wasted on the cat."

Robin, impatiently: "So when are we going to get this pie? Talking about it is making me hungry. Isn't it time yet?"

Me: "Jeez, Pop, hold your horses! Julie hasn't finished her dinner."

She is, in fact, a dainty but thorough eater, and often ends a meal apologizing for holding everybody up.

Robin: "She's just like Nana at Thanksgiving, jumping up and down to get things from the kitchen so she never gets to eat her own food."

Me: "I remember that. But I don't remember you being there."

Robin, offended: "I always went to those dinners, up until the time I left. She didn't make turkey, though, she made a couple of big fat chickens, and boy, were they good."

Me, warming to the subject, so to speak: "Mmmm, yes. I also remember Uncle Victor chasing all us kids around with a huge hypodermic needle, to give us our polio shots. It sure made Thanksgiving fun."

Robin: "It was a good thing you had an uncle who was a doctor. That was the only way we could afford those shots, in those days."

Me: "Were we poor? I don't remember feeling poor."

Robin: "Sure we were poor. Everybody was poor, it was the end of the Depression. The animation business didn't pay anything much, and your mother was just getting started freelancing."

Julie (who has not been able to make out a word): "So what do you think of the latest estimates of the cost of the savings and loan failures?"

Me (used by now to her making abrupt breaks into ongoing conversation so as to make room for some participation on her part): "I think that at some point people are going to have to admit that Ronald damned Reagan and company have wrecked the country."

Robin: "Ah, they'll never admit it."

Julie: "What did you say, dear?"

Me: "I said I haven't seen the latest figures because the whole thing makes me so mad I'm afraid it'll give me a heart attack."

Julie: "I didn't hear you, darling."

Steve: "We think it's terrible."

Julie, indignantly: "Well, of course it's terrible, and they keep revising the figures upward. What's going to happen? Everybody here at the Gardens is very worried."

Robin, again with gusto: "They should be. It's only going to get worse."

Julie: "Hah?"

Me: "He said, we're all worried."

Robin, glowering with ferocious satisfaction at his plate: "It's going to be another depression, just like last time."

Julie, anxiously: "Some people here have moved out because they can't afford the maintenance payments any more. You know, the management promised not to raise them more than five percent in one year. Last year they raised them twelve percent."

Me, knowing she won't hear me: "Great; if it gets too bad, you can move in with Pop."

Robin: "WHAT?"

Me: "Gotcha."

Julie: "What did you say, dear?"

"It'll work out all right in the end. Isn't it time for dessert?" I get up to cut the pie.

NEXT MORNING Pop came over for a cup of tea, as he'd begun doing almost daily.

Ladling in the sugar, he observed, "Julie sure has a nice setup at that place."

Me: "Yup." A short answer, in a short tone.

I have been worrying about him. This morning he brought the dog back, turned in my doorway to go to his own place, and toppled back flat on his butt on the ground. His balance is terrible, much worse than I thought. I'm just starting to panic a little, wondering what in hell we're going to do if a time comes when I can't take care of him here at home.

Julie needs care, too, but her situation is secure. Steve saw to it that she got the insurance money due her from her husband's death. She also had money from a New York building she owned a share in that was sold at just about the time she needed a down payment for her place at Gracious Gardens.

Robin: "I wouldn't mind living in an apartment like that, with a dining room where they serve you meals when you don't feel like cooking."

I rounded on him at that; I couldn't help it.

"Then you should have taken that money that Irving wanted to leave to you, because I sure as hell can't afford to install you in a place like that."

Silence. He looked into his cup.

"Pop, tell me, will you—why didn't you take that money?"

Robin, muttering: "Frances would have been angry."

Me: "What? Wait a minute, I thought you told me Irving had

already provided for her. The hundred-twenty-five thousand was extra, you said."

Robin: "She would have been angry."

I put the kettle down with a bang on the stove. "Jesus Christ, Pop, I've met Frances, and she's not like that! You're crazy, you know that? You threw away a chance for security because you were worried about annoying Frances, who's living very comfortably in Sacramento on all the rest of the money Irving left, and who hasn't spoken to you in years?"

Robin: "Well, she was his wife. The money should be hers."

"She gave it to the hospice."

"He said it was a good place."

"Why didn't you take it?"

He glared at me. "What would I have done with all that money? I don't know anything about handling that kind of money."

Light dawns, and it's angry light. I yell. "Damn it, you were just too lazy to deal with having something to invest and look after! Too much work for you? Or were you too chicken to risk a frown from Frances, and that's why you said no?"

Robin, gravelly and sullen: "It doesn't matter now anyway."

Me: "Not as long as you're healthy, it doesn't."

Robin, defiantly: "I've got Medicare. And they don't let you have pets in that place Julie's in. I asked her."

Me: "I could fucking kill you sometimes, you know that? All this time I thought you had some kind of good reason for refusing that money."

Robin: "I did have a reason. I didn't want it."

FROM ROBIN'S JOURNALS, 1939:
If the Lord is my shepherd I shall not want much, being a sheep.

The Death of
Fred Astaire

Me (on the phone with Liza): "So this morning he tells me that Fred Astaire died. I said, 'Oh, too bad, but he had a long life, he did all right; how old was he?' And Robin says, he was eighty-five or whatever it was, and then he adds, 'That's pretty old, for someone so active.' I swear, that's what he said. I think I've figured it out. He has a sort of conservation of energy theory of life: if you don't use any, you never run out."

Liza: "Suzy, he has a theory about everything. And he really does think he's never going to die, you know."

Me: "What do you mean?"

Liza: "Well, we were talking about the greenhouse effect last time I called. He saw some program about it on TV. And I said, 'Well, that's one thing you won't have to worry about; you won't be around when it really starts to hit in 2025.' And he said, 'Why shouldn't I be around?'"

Me: "Did you remind him that he's an old man?"

Liza: "He knows, he knows. He just thinks if he sits very still and barely moves a muscle, Death won't notice him and he'll never have to die."

Me: "Death won't have to notice him. If he doesn't get up off his *tuchus*, his already lousy circulation will get lousier and at some point his damn feet will have to be amputated. I am going to end up pushing him around in a wheelchair because he was too damned lazy to get up and take a few steps once a day. In which case I will kill him myself. Did you know he's started smoking again?"

Liza: "Oh, yeah, he told me. But I'm not supposed to tell you because you'll just get mad."

Me: "You're not supposed to tell me? Do you know what it *smells* like in his place? And there are cigarette burns all over his table top."

Liza: "But look, at his age, how many pleasures does he have? And what difference can it make in the long run, since there sort of isn't much of a long run?"

Me: "Oh, not a lot I guess. But really, keeping secrets from me is ridiculous. Especially a 'secret' like that, for crying out loud! Anyway, he could have told me."

"Well, yes; but he's scared of you."

Me: "Scared? What are you talking about, he's *scared* of me?"

Liza: "He knows you could kick him out any time you want to. Nobody said you had to take him in the first place."

Me: "F'Chrissakes, if I hadn't dragged him out here, he'd be a homeless bum on the streets in New York right now."

Liza: "No, he'd be dead by now. That's what I mean."

Me: "That's what you mean, what?"

Liza: "He left us, we didn't leave him. You don't owe him a thing, and he knows it. Why do you think he didn't call up and tell us he was having trouble with his eyes in the first place? You had to drag it out of him, because he knows neither of us owes him anything. He's just goddamned lucky, and believe me, he's well aware of it."

Me: "Oh, piffle. He couldn't see to write your phone number down; and we'd just bought the front house and it was sitting here vacant. What the hell was I supposed to do? Any human being would have done the same. You'd have done the same, if you'd been able to."

Liza: "Yeah, well, maybe." My sister is a realist; and she'd never been as close to Rob as I had, if "close" is the applicable word. "How are his eyes now?"

Me: "Fine, except that we're waiting for his cataracts to ripen."

Liza: "Yuck, what a disgusting expression."

Me: "It fits. Disgusting is his middle name."

Liza: "Well, at least he's trying. He's proud of only smoking a couple of cigarettes a day now."

Me: "Great, wonderful. I'm fed up with being put in the position of the cop who has to nag Robin about stuff he should have the sense to take care of himself. I haven't said anything about the smoking, and I'm not going to say anything about it. It's between him and his doctor."

Liza: "Listen, you do whatever seems right, I won't criticize you. As far as I'm concerned, you are a saint."

Me: "I can't be a saint, I'm Jewish. So when can I ship him out to you again for a visit?"

He has visited her, once, since coming to live with us.

Liza: "Never. I'd be back on Valium in five minutes."

Me: "Ahah. Being a saint means never having to say, 'Bye, Dad, have a nice time at Lizzie's.'"

"You know," she says darkly, "what happened last time."

What happened was that I called up on the third day and asked if maybe she'd like him to stay over for the upcoming weekend.

"NO," she said on the phone. So he came home as scheduled, that Friday.

"Come on," I say, mostly to get her goat. "It couldn't have been that bad."

Liza: "Suzy, he sat in a chair in the middle of my kitchen and ordered me around as if I was his slave. That's what happened. 'What's for lunch?' he'd say, and I'd tell him hamburgers, and he'd say, 'How about a BLT?' And he expected me to make it for him, too. And that night that Al got home right on the dot for this fancy dinner we took him to, and Robin shoots up out of his chair and snaps, 'Are we going to eat now?' I thought Al was going to deck him."

"Aw, you're exaggerating," I say.

Liza: "And I couldn't get him to take a shower, not once in three days. He had a million excuses. Newton kept jumping up on him and shoving his face into Robin's armpits, you know how cats are: they love a good, strong stink. It was so embarrassing!"

Me: "I read that old people like to be able to get a whiff of their own scent now and then. It reassures them or something, makes them more comfortable."

Liza: "Well, he must be very comfortable, then. I used to think you were exaggerating with some of the things you said about him, but that visit cured me."

Me: "You should have told him, get cleaned up; otherwise, no lunch. For that matter, you should have told him to make his own damned lunch!"

Liza: "I did ask him to do things for himself, Suzy, I'm not a complete pushover. But he just sat there grinning with Newton dozing on his lap, and he wouldn't get up because that would disturb the cat. He said he wasn't going to do anything: he was on vacation."

Me: "Vacation."

Liza: "That's what he said."

Me: "He's been retired for years. Vacation from what?"

Liza: "Don't ask me. All I can tell you is, he said he wasn't going to lift a finger because he was away on vacation. Did I tell you, Al never drove so fast to the airport in his life, he was so ready to put Robin on that plane. So nobody says a word in the car, until all of a sudden Robin says, 'Did you know that chimney sweeps all used to get cancer of the scrotum?' Al said, 'No,' and not another word, but on the way back he said, 'Where does he get this kind of stuff?' I told him it was probably true, because if it's weird and disgusting, Robin knows it. Al couldn't believe it, he had to go and look it up, and he said, 'My God, it's true.' I mean, this is this man's idea of *conversation*."

Me: "I am going to kill him. You wouldn't mind if I just killed him, would you?"

Liza: "Anything you do about Robin is fine with me, as long as you don't send him *here*. Our father is the laziest living human being on the planet. Do you remember the first cat he got, when he came out there?"

Me: "You mean that ratty old stray that wandered in and found himself in paradise?"

"That's the one. Remember what Robin named him?"

I have to think for a second, it's a while ago now. "Bobo."

Liza: "Right. Now he has another one, and what does he call her? Bibi. Do you see a pattern there?"

Me: "I see a certain lack of imagination, yes."

Liza: "No, it's laziness, don't you see? If he'd been in charge of naming the two of us, we'd have been Lola and Lulu or something."

Me: "Thank God for Mom, then. You're right, Lili."

FROM ROBIN'S JOURNALS, 1943–45.

We smoke because it is a simple thing, requiring no thought and little effort, conveys an easy distinction, and is something over which we exercise complete direction; few criticize, most do it, it is considered desirable, and gives a little thrill to the throat and lungs, possibly related to the sexual response.

I'd walk in and find him at his sink, the whole kitchen stinking of fish oil, and Bibi sitting on the oak table, watching.

"She's waiting for her tuna," he'd say. "I had that steak you gave me last night, but she wouldn't touch any of it. She hates beef. If you're going to the store today, get some ice cream, will you? Strawberry. But not sherbet, Suzy. She wouldn't touch that sherbet you got me last time. I had to eat it all myself."

I'd think about walking over there one day and finding him dead in his chair facing the TV, or having to ship him off someplace and paying for his keep out of our savings. Either way, I'd think, what the hell was I going to do with Bibi?

And I'd think about how a friend of mine who's into these things told me, reading my palm, that I'm going to have a long life. So the chances are that a day will come when some younger folk will be in charge of an aging me, seeing to it that I'm looked after, as Julie is looked after at Gracious Gardens (if I'm lucky). So maybe somebody younger will be looking to me to explain about the old days (which get older faster than has ever happened before in recorded history) and offer the wisdom of experience to try in the new ones.

So I need to know how to do that, Pop. Show me a little, give me some hints. I'll probably need to know how to do age, and I'll surely need to know how to do death. You can give me that, at least. Here's your chance to do something a father can do.

Take it. Don't just sit there radiating discontent and grousing about how your cat bullies you. Talk to me; teach me.

But I didn't know how to ask, and he didn't know how to offer, so that conversation never happened. I think it seldom does.

BOBO HAD BEEN a sinewy stray who used to stand yowling and fussing at my Siamese cross, Little Eyes, in the back yard, or out front by the rusty outdoor watering spigot. Flakey (the cat that had come out with us from New York) had been killed in traffic by then. He crossed Fourth one too many times and was flattened coming back at dusk, probably because I had missed him and was calling him to come home. Steve found the corpse in the morning, under the mailbox post.

So then I got Little Eyes, with his Siamese voice and coloring and the build of a Mack truck to go with the tiger stripes around his legs. He had dignity and presence, and I seriously considered dedicating a book to him (he is the hero of the first piece of short fiction I ever got published, about a space pilot and her talking cat). After eight years of whatever kind of love it is that we have with our cats, I discovered that he was infected with feline leukemia. A bad bite in his back that he'd gotten from Bobo would not heal, and a blood test confirmed the vet's guess as to what the problem was and where it had come from.

Little Eyes spent his last few weeks sleeping on a towel folded on the lower platform of a two-level TV stand, which I had positioned over the floor vent from the furnace because he seemed to be cold all the time. I'd been irrigating the fang punctures through the loose skin over his hip with a sort of squeegee bulb, twice a day, with medicated saline, pumping it through while he purred the way cats do when they are scared and angry but too weak to defend themselves or run away.

When I saw that he was not getting better—that in effect I was torturing him to no purpose—I stopped the treatments. He still kept trying to go outside, when he wasn't drooping slackly on his improvised bed over the heat vent. So one morning I made arrangements. Then I picked Little Eyes up and carried him out through the French doors across the tiny brick patio, and set him down on the ground.

He blinked and squinted and wove around a little on his shaky pins, and then he staggered out into the back yard and slept in the sun all day. I'd go to check up on him and find that he had moved to another spot a few yards away from the previous one, unable to rest comfortably anywhere; I'd been right to phone the vet.

After five, the vet stopped in on his way home. We found Little Eyes sleeping in the long grass by the fence.

He tried, unsteadily, to avoid us; Steve and I caught him easily, and we crouched down next to him, hemming him in.

I held him down as gently as I could (he resented being interfered with while he felt so lousy, but he had barely any strength), stroked him, and talked to him—telling him what a great guy he was, and how he was going to stop feeling so terrible really soon now—while the vet slid the needle into the vein in the front leg. Little Eyes hissed and flashed his fangs, and then he settled weakly down under our hands again, growling faintly. The vet asked if we were ready, and we nodded, and he undid the tie-off on the cat's upper foreleg.

Little Eyes slumped flat under my palm as if all his insides had been sucked out at once into the ground. His pupils instantly flooded the whole surface of each eye with inky darkness. It was amazing; it happened so fast, that transition from life to total absence of any perceptible trace of it, that I have never since hesitated over the necessity of putting a suffering animal of mine to sleep. I just hope somebody will have the guts to do that for me, if a time comes when I need it as badly as Little Eyes did.

I kept bursting into tears without warning for weeks after, partly because I missed his loud, demanding voice, partly because my stubborn clinging had prolonged his pain several weeks for no other purpose than to postpone my sorrow once he was gone. I felt as if I had betrayed a trust, and there was no remedy now.

Meantime Bobo, the feline buccaneer who had cost me my talkative friend, had himself vanished, not to be seen again by any of us. Doubtless he had keeled over somewhere in the big alfalfa field, dead of his own illness.

I took Robin down to the Humane Society to adopt a new cat. He picked out a young female with faint tortoise-shell markings, one of a litter that had been found starving, motherless, in the ruins of a half-demolished house up near the mountains.

She wasn't with us very long; she was sweet, but there was something wrong with her. She entertained Robin immensely with her odd behavior: she would jump very high to get onto the table, like a Pop-Tart propelled out of the toaster slot. When she went outside, she walked into things.

I concluded that there was something wrong with her eyesight, but Robin wouldn't hear of it; not until she got out one morning and he found her crying by one of the elm stumps, lost and afraid. She was only a few yards from his back porch.

The vet said, "You never see this, hardly ever: she's got no retinas. We think it's from a nutritional deficiency when they're kittens. That's why you never feed a kitten puppy chow: it hasn't got the right nutrients for a cat, and the eyes won't develop properly."

So Pop had this blind cat, which he called Goldie because her eyes were a brilliant gold color; her eyes that saw nothing. He was charmed by the idea of a blind cat that was so smart, and so special, that she could still figure out how to survive on her own for a good while before being rescued, and how to jump up onto a table that she couldn't see.

But he was also worried that she might get killed by local dogs or traffic because of her handicap, and he complained anxiously about the trouble he was having keeping a lithe young cat locked up indoors, safe, when he himself wasn't a very spry mover.

The vet called me to say we should bring her back to his office, he had a place for her: a veterinary college up in Colorado had had a blind cat as a sort of cross between a demo model and a mascot for years, and it had died. They were interested in acquiring Goldie in its place, as an example of natural feline blindness that the students could take a look at as part of their training.

I told Robin, "Your cat has got a job offer in Colorado."

So he thought about it, got excited by the idea, and came with me to say goodbye to Goldie and send her off to work in veterinarian school.

His next cat was that scrawny, rat-tailed, yogurt-swilling whiner, Bibi.

Many years later I reminded this vet of the story of Goldie

while he was tending to another of my animals. He looked away and cleared his throat. "Well," he said, "that didn't work out after all. The vet school was interested, but after you brought her in, they called and said they had decided not to replace their cat."

"Oh," I said. "So what happened to her?"

Well, what do you think happened?

I said he should have called me before putting her down. He said she couldn't have had any kind of life, not once she'd been outside already.

I never told Robin. I couldn't. I hated it when the world conformed so grimly to his low opinion of it.

FROM ROBIN'S JOURNALS, 1968:

There goes Ketsela, the Lion's Head cat: she'd been depositing turds and piss around the place, wouldn't use her box downstairs (the floor of that cellar is always <u>wet</u>). So, the boss decreed she had to go. Carlos, 2nd cook, wanted to take her. We bundled her into a box, tied with strings (Tues. night), and sent them off. 20 minutes later, he comes back—K. halfway out of the box. . . . Nice try . . .

Well, today—no K. Tom, the weekly porter, said he'd seen a regular cat-carrier down in the cellar all week. Today it was gone. So was K. How and how long will it take her to get back? Over the Brooklyn Bridge? On the subway?

Goodbye, baby, we loved you.

BOOK TWO

Falling Off the Cliff
as He Fled from the
Tiger, the Man Saw a
Flower Growing on the
Cliff Face and Thought,
"How Lovely!"

Cedar Street

I knock on the French doors into the in-law apartment Rob's living in now and stick my head in; he's sitting in his deck chair, a pale wooden folding frame with two dark blue cloth slings, one a seat, one a backrest. It's easy to move, but he never moves it from its place close by the side of his bed. He sits there looking at the TV that flickers silently under the small west window, the images dimmed by the afternoon light from outside, the sound turned off.

He's got his Navy watch cap on, and the heat is turned up too high as usual. The big room that he lives in here on Cedar Street is sweltering. Bibi is curled on the bed, sleeping on the gray L.L. Bean blanket with the colorful stripe near the top, a moth-eaten scrap of gray fur.

I walk over and turn the thermostat down. I no longer apologize for doing this, or discuss it. He always turns it up to eighty-five degrees, which would be fine, except that the heating bills—which come to me, like all his bills now—are killing me. The first time we got into this, he said he was cold, and I told him—he was sitting there in his jeans, slippers, and an undershirt—to go put a shirt on, and some socks. He said disdainfully, "You mean you save money by turning the heat down and putting on more clothes?"

He no longer turns his head to watch me adjust the thermostat, let alone comments.

"Hey, did I tell you?" I say. "I'm a gramma! Maggie's had her baby."

Robin, eyes on the TV: "Well, it's about time."

Me: "What?"

Robin: "You've been telling me about it for months. So are they going to name it after Steve's mother?"

Me: "Well, no. The sonogram was wrong."

Robin: "Wrong? There was no baby?"

Me: "There was no girl baby, no. They were all set for little Juliet, but they got Nathaniel instead."

Robin: "They must be pissed off."

Me, sitting on the low cupboard built-in by the door, where he keeps his clean sheets: "I think they'll manage. Maggie's sister has two boys, so Charlie and Maggie were hoping for a girl. They don't mind, though. Maggie wants more kids, she'll have other chances."

No answer.

Me: "Why have you got the sound turned off?"

Robin: "What's the point of listening? It's always the same thing."

"Yeah? So tell me what's going on here, since you know the whole story without having to hear a line of dialog."

Robin, pointing: "That one, Melanie, is in love with her sister's husband; he's a dope smuggler, he's in jail——"

"Okay, okay." Who knows, maybe he's making it up, or maybe he's got it right; he watches the soaps all the time now. I see my father, the self-taught intellectual who seemed to know everything— from the secrets of how the world really runs to the technical secrets of the great painters of the past—as he sits there and watches the soaps with the sound turned off.

Me: "Pop? How did you feel when I was born? Were you happy to have a daughter?"

"I don't remember; it was a long time ago."

"You told me I was born right after midnight."

Now he looks at me, and I can see the memory click in behind his faded eyes (it's 1990; Pop, soon to be eighty, has been with us for almost fifteen years). "That's right, I was waiting outside; they didn't let you go into the delivery room in those days, not like now. The nurse came out a minute after midnight, maybe two minutes, and said I had a daughter with a lot of black hair, just like a little Eskimo."

He stops. The spark has dimmed again; I'm not even sure it was real to begin with. He's told me this before, it could be just rote recitation now.

"What else?"

"I don't know. Your mother would remember."

My mother, of whom I have very few memories because Robin has taken up all the space labeled "parents," through sheer longevity and proximity.

"Here's something I remember," I say. "In the bathroom in the mornings when you were shaving, in our first apartment, at 102nd Street: I'd come in and play on the floor with this little ceramic cat I had, black and white, very small, with a bright red ball under its paw. You used to crack your toe knuckles on the tiles while you were standing there."

Robin: "Crack my toes? Why did I do that?"

Me: "To make me laugh. You used to do that kind of thing. Mugging, making faces—"

"That's how we did close-ups of our cartoon characters, by mugging in the mirror and drawing what we saw."

"I remember one morning I had strawberries on my Cheerios—"

"Cheerios," he murmurs. "That's all you'd ever eat for breakfast for years. Drove your mother crazy."

"You said, 'Quick, look out the window, there's a bird on the windowsill!' or something like that, so I looked, and you stole one of my strawberries and ate it."

An injured stare. "I only did it a couple of times. It was a game. I wasn't really trying to steal from you."

Me: "I thought you didn't remember things."

Robin: "I remember that."

Me: "Maybe you do, maybe not. Maybe you remember it because I've told you about it before, and you tucked it away in your memory as if you'd remembered it yourself, so now we think we share a memory. It could be just a story we kick back and forth, you know, but about something that neither one of us really remembers at all."

Pop, with satisfaction, looking back at the screen: "You lost me."

Me: "Bullshit. You're the guy who read *Finnegans Wake*, and a ton of other rarefied stuff most people have hardly even heard of. You're so loaded with brains they leak out of your ears."

Pop: "Is that what that stuff is?"

Me (falling for it *again*): "What stuff?"

Pop: "Well, sometimes while I sleep this dark brown gunk oozes out of my ears and I find it on the pillow in the morning—"

Me: "Oh, for God's sake, I don't want to hear about your goddamn bodily secretions today, okay?"

Pop: "Anyway, I'm an old fart now, I don't have to be smart any more. Maybe I've got Alzheimer's."

Me: "Maybe I've got fleas."

Pop: "Or Parkinson's. I could have Parkinson's. My hands shake a lot."

This is true; I have noticed that he can hardly sign his name legibly any more.

I say firmly, "You don't have Parkinson's."

Pop: "They used to think you got it from exposure to mustard gas in World War One, but I think it's from drinking. Like Pauline, next door at the old house on Fourth Street; she had Parkinson's."

Me, startled: "She did? She never told me that."

Pop: "She had that tremor in her head all the time, didn't you see that? Sure she had it."

Me: "She's still alive, you know."

Pop: "Then she still has it."

Me: "But Pauline doesn't drink. It was that sister of hers, the one who came to live with her for a while. She was the one who drank."

Pop: "Then Pauline *used* to drink; she drank some time in the past, or she wouldn't have Parkinson's."

Me: "She doesn't have Parkinson's, I told you."

Robin, impatient with my denseness: "Sure she does. Look at the way her head shakes."

One's friends are desperate for encouragement because no one else gives a goddamn about the work they consider worth doing. What love one cannot give to women, one gives circuitously to the things one's friends have done with love. One's children grow out of one's sight, and it is a shock to see them again; the beauty of infancy gone; a new, harder-to-know beauty stretching their frames.

Sometimes I think he just jerks me around for the fun of it, like cracking his toes on the bathroom floor, but for his own entertainment this time. Must be better than TV with the sound off, anyway.

The scene, you will notice, has changed; in 1986 we left the Valley, with its rural-suburban mix, for the city itself. My allergies forced us to move to a section of town set on the plateau above the river bottom and less afflicted with the noxious weeds that take over the Valley each spring. We chose a house in a tiny, once outlying but now totally encapsulated suburb just down the hill from the central campus of the state university, an area of tiny lawns and old trees and small, pretty houses clustered around a neat green park.

Our house was not one of the fancifully varied places on the next street up but a newer construction on the westernmost edge of this vest-pocket neighborhood. It was a frame-stucco cottage, with a very modern-looking skylight that reared up over an atrium that had been created by joining the house to a smaller, newer unit on the same lot. This adjoining structure, a two-room apartment partially dug into the hillside that was our southern boundary line, had looked like good in-law quarters for Pop.

"Moving?" he'd said with alarm. "You mean I'm going to have to live with you, in the same house?"

"No," I said, not in the least insulted; I'd have been just as horrified at the idea of sharing living space that closely with him. We had bought the new house on Cedar Street because it was the only one I could find in town with decent and *separate* lodgings for Pop and that little gray mummy, Bibi. "Come and see it, I think you'll like it."

In search of "in-law quarters," I'd looked at basement bedrooms with mazes of pipes hanging an inch from your scalp and cinderblock walls colder than a Hebridean sea cliff; at mansions with guest houses larger than our whole house on Fourth and priced accordingly; at attic rooms with sloped ceilings and slanted floors and ancient wood-framed windows that would never again.

And then we found this house, with the adjoining apartment for Pop and the garage done over as a studio by the previous owner (this last earmarked as a work space for me). There had been some haggling about the "extra" kitchen in Pop's place. The local neighborhood association was rabid on the subject of any amenities that would create a rentable apartment, as a defense against the area being taken over by student housing, because of the university just up the hill.

You could hardly blame them. The real student ghetto lies a half-mile south, and it is not a pretty sight. Those streets are heavily afflicted by the neglect and the ceaseless petty crime and vandalism that tend to creep into neighborhoods that are dominated by high-density, high-turnover rental properties.

So Steve worked out language that would satisfy the neighbors. We swore that the apartment (which had been created illegally and on the sly by previous owners, so naturally the neighbors were furiously suspicious from the outset) could never be rented out but only used by my actual, blood-related, non-school-attending father. Pop and I looked at Cedar Street together. Pop pronounced it good, pending Bibi's approval.

Fortunately Bibi settled right in, once we installed the cat door in Pop's entrance into the small, enclosed back yard.

But it turned out that this pleasant neighborhood was not territory made for George Dog.

On our third morning in the new house Robin came home limping, with grass stains on his pants: George had pulled him over again, and Robin had just missed crashing down on one of the metal sprinkler heads in someone's front lawn. George was a country dog at heart, made for wide-open spaces. Here he found so many places to mark, so many new dogs to be put in their place by appropriate roaring and lunging! So many smells, so little time! It wasn't his fault; it was his nature, bold and exploratory and proprietary, that was putting my father in serious danger.

I looked again at the sidewalk outside our new house—no soft dirt shoulders here, like the ones along which the drunks tramped home on Fourth Street. Here it was concrete, sprinkler heads, high, sharp curbs, and driveways cut slantwise across the sidewalks every few feet.

George had to go back to the Humane Society, where they were understandably dismayed to see him again (he was much bigger and a couple of years older). But I made sure they kept at the desk the biography and vita of George, written by me with all the wit and warmth I could command, for the information of prospective new owners.

In a mere three days George was adopted by a couple in an outlying town, so he moved away to a place very much like our old home in the North Valley and, so far as I know (or wish to know), lived there happily ever after.

. . .

POP'S APARTMENT was a spacious, white-walled room, with a kitchenette and bathroom tucked into the east end of it and a tiny adjoining bedroom. In the main room, which was either dark (there were few windows, and they weren't large) or cozy, depending on your mood, was a working fireplace with a thick adobe *banco*, or bench, built opposite. Pop's books went into the shelves on either side of the fireplace (although after we moved to Cedar Street, I never saw him reading anything but a newspaper, a magazine, or one of the paperback mysteries I brought him from the library).

There was no place in there for a bed, really. The loft over the closet had been constructed as the main sleeping space, romantically raised up under the high brightness of the clerestory skylight. This arrangement was plainly out of the question for an old man who now had trouble walking, let alone climbing a ten-foot ladder.

Pop put his easel and his painting table in the tiny bedroom to gather dust. His narrow bed from Fourth Street just fit against the wall of the main room by the French doors, which opened into the oddly shaped atrium that joined his place to ours.

It was not an elegant arrangement, but it worked.

The same faint sketch of a tree occupied the easel in the side room, keeping company with his hot-water heater, boxes of odds and ends, and blankets. The huge old tweed coat that he had brought from New York—and never used here—hung on a sagging wire hanger in the open closet space in there.

We got a new dog to walk Pop, a sleepy, aged Afghan cross, and after she died, a nervously intelligent red Doberman. There was a small corner grocery store a quarter mile down the hill where Robin went to shop for odds and ends, taking red Kate with him and trundling the same old two-wheeled cart he'd used on Fourth Street to go to the co-op (though now he complained about having to lug it back with groceries in it).

He responded to being in the city by wearing his better clothes and keeping his beard trimmed. I had to nag him less about those things, much more about not heating his place up like a steambath.

New quarters, new complaints: neighborhood kids took a short-cut from the higher street to the lower, which meant running over the roof of Pop's apartment and down the narrow path between my high back fence and the even higher one of my neighbors up-slope from us. Pop stalked out and yelled at them once, so now they do it just to annoy him, as a game. We're having a gate with a lock fixed across the narrow dirt path between my yard wall and my neighbor's; ridiculous, but necessary for peace in the house.

And someone is calling Rob's new phone number and hanging up, sometimes three or four times in an evening. We think it's a kid doing sitter duty at a neighbor's and amusing herself with random calls on their phone. I ask Pop to keep track of the times and frequency of the calls—"Here's a notebook, here's a pen, you can keep them handy on the table by the phone"—so we can alert the phone company and they can get to work identifying the offender and putting a stop to it.

"Aw, Suzy, what for? It won't do any good," he says; and he stops talking about it.

The truck, which he doesn't drive any more—the city traffic is too daunting—stands parked at night outside his window in the driveway. Steve revs it up in the morning and drives it to his office because the firm has moved too and there's no easy way to get there by bus. Pop complains that the truck makes horrible fumes in the morning when Steve warms it up (its rotary engine takes quite a lot of warming up) and the smell seeps in at his window. But we can't park the truck on the street in front of the house, because you can't see anything on our street from the other side of the hill. The truck would be sideswiped or worse by some jerk zipping over the crown of Cedar Street and roaring downhill past our place.

Pop's nose torments him anyway: he used to constantly smell exhaust on Fourth, too, despite the masses of weeds and trees between his house and the roadway. He often looks accusingly at me and says, "You've been eating garlic," when I've been doing nothing of the kind and nobody else smells anything on my breath.

For a few seasons of our Cedar Street occupancy he comes with us to the chamber music concerts held in a lecture hall just up the hill at the university. He dresses in his gray slacks and blazer for this, and he looks very distinguished. He never falls asleep during the music (Steve does, sometimes; but Steve works all day and most evenings as well).

Once, I persuade Robin to go to the seasonal welcoming party for the musicians (as a board member of the music festival for a couple of years, I am invited). They were the Guarneri Quartet, who for a while in the eighties made Albuquerque the last stop of their winter tour and stayed on afterward, taking an extra week or so as a vacation.

Pop came back from the party saying that he had enjoyed himself, a little. He had spoken to the cellist, David Soyer, asking a question about the man's instrument. Soyer had told him that this cello had been with him when he was in a traffic accident, in a taxi in Manhattan; and the cello had been "hospitalized" to be mended. Robin asked if the cure had worked. "No," the cellist said. "It's never been worth a damn since."

My father, who won't answer questions from strangers on the

street, has no problem approaching one of the premier musicians of our time for a chat.

I remembered this story when I heard, many years later, that these musicians had made it a practice not to bring their finest instruments—including the Guarnerius fiddles of various sizes from which they took their name—to New Mexico, because they were afraid of the effects of the aridity here.

Then Robin began declining to attend the concerts. Liz told me, "I asked him why he never goes any more. He said, 'Whatever they're playing, I've heard it.'"

But when I kept on inviting him, eventually he said, "I can't get up those steps so well."

The auditorium seating did have a very steep pitch. I hadn't had the heart to press him. He was having more trouble than ever walking—bent forward from the hips, shuffling along, he was suddenly beginning to look like an old, old man. He had also developed a rash on his ankles, and we were having no luck persuading it to heal.

His doctor recommended an exercise class—water exercise—to try to boost the strength and circulation in his legs and his aerobic capacity. I made sure Pop had money for cabs and enrolled him in the exercise class at the nearby rehabilitation center at St. Joseph's Hospital.

I drove him there the first time and walked through the place with him, watching him cast a jaundiced eye on the rehab work going on in the treatment rooms. And I told him there was no argument about it, he was to go to classes for the elderly at the pool.

He glared at the floor. "Yeah," he said, with that heavy, angry irony that I knew meant he would comply, but under bitter, persecuted protest.

And he did, several times a week, for a year or so.

As it turned out, he liked the instructor, Jackie, a thin, strong, no-

nonsense woman with an almost tangible warmth toward her elderly charges. Every time I insisted to Pop that he eat more because he was getting too thin, he'd say, "That's what Jackie says at the pool, too."

He sometimes spoke about the men he met in the locker room there, and how they bored him with their talk about their operations and their ungrateful and unpleasant children and dead wives and vanished jobs. It sounded as if he was complaining about dreary strangers he didn't like to be with, but I think he came to appreciate some masculine company of his own generation: men who knew what a woman was supposed to be, and how potent swear words once had been, and about occasional hard drinking as a plain part of normal male life.

And he liked talking with the cabdrivers who took him down there and back and whom he overtipped outrageously. I would run into them for years afterward, when I ordered a cab for a ride to the airport on one professional trip or another. The driver would remark that he used to collect an old gent at this address and take him to the pool at St. Joe's, and how was old Mack these days?

And I'd tell them, and they'd say, Oh, too bad, he was a nice old man, very smart and entertaining.

This story has its inevitable end, of course, and we're coming to it; but I promise you a surprise first, a good one. At least one.

ROBIN HAD always looked young for his age (a trait he has passed on to both Liza and me). Now the years were catching up with him at ferocious speed. He slept with a washrag under his cheek because his mouth leaked while he was sleeping. Sometimes while he was talking to me he would mop irritably at his lips with a tissue. I remembered my grandmother doing that, too, when she was nearing eighty.

For Robin's eightieth birthday, Ian and Liza both came to New Mexico. Ian and his wife, Cathy, brought Pop a VCR. Robin took one look at it and barked, "What the hell is that?"

He never did use it, although Ian took great care in setting it up for him. We thought Rob would enjoy watching movies at home, but he complained that the rented movies were stupid and dull and the sound was bad (actually I've found the sound to be a problem myself), and forget it. Mostly I think he couldn't cope with the machine, or didn't want to bother trying.

For dinner that night we all went to a restaurant downtown in a handsome old hotel, the second Hilton ever built; the lobby has great dark beams in the ceiling, big faded murals of Indian dances, and polished quarry-tile floors. The restaurant, in its current incarnation (it's had many), had waiters who sang show tunes during dinner. We'd never gone anywhere like that before, and it sounded good for a laugh if nothing else.

So off we go: it's not Pop's actual birthday yet (that's Wednesday), but it's the Saturday night that everybody can be there; and that's fine with Pop. Wednesday is his pool day, and he doesn't want to go have dinner after a pool session—too exhausting, too much to do in one day.

He's wearing a new pullover that I gave him under his blazer and his good flannel pants and he looks nice, distinguished even; but he is in a mood. He grouses about going, he grouses about how dark it is in the restaurant, he grouses about the menu ("more boring southwestern shit and fake French," he says), he grouses about his chair (it's too low), and the food takes longer than it should to arrive (too much performance in the kitchen, perhaps).

When the waiters start in on a number from *The Phantom of the Opera*, Robin snarls, "What now, are they going to *sing*?"

Every time somebody starts a song, Pop snarls, *"Jesus!"* in tones of deep disgust. He sits glaring down at the table while we talk about China—I had gone there for a professional meeting the summer before—because Pop won't join in any conversation.

Finally I lean over and tell him, "Pop, this is your birthday party. Ian and Cathy have come from Phoenix to be here, Liza came from Los Angeles. Either you stop crabbing and whining and being nasty to the staff and embarrassing all of us, or we're getting up and going home right now, and I'll open a couple of cans of beans for our dinner, okay?"

He subsides, with black looks and his chin sunk on his chest so that he glares out from under his ferocious, tangled eyebrows. He manages not to die of fury when the wait staff sing "Happy Birthday" for him.

The evening is never mentioned again between Robin and me.

On his real birthday, a few days later, somebody goes through the locker room at the pool and steals the men's wallets, including Pop's, while everyone is in the water.

"Some birthday!" he snarls.

For a while there, after his cataracts came out, he'd been so elated at the recovery of bright color that he was actually cheerful. He was admirably stoical when I came in three times a day to put stinging antibiotic drops in his eyes, and there was a degree of physical ease that developed between us around this little ritual; briefly. He told me that Monet had had cataracts removed back at the turn of the century, when the operation was still unthinkably crude. Afterward the great impressionist had wanted to destroy a whole series of his own late paintings because the true, natural colors were distorted into yellows and reds that had been all the color that the cataracts had let through.

But then Rob had gotten used to seeing clearly again, and his habitual glumness had returned. The birthday party seemed to focus and intensify this mood. The books people gave him sat unopened on the shelf. He slumped in his deck chair all day, glaring at the TV.

FROM ROBIN'S JOURNALS, 1948–52:

Whenever one feels overconfident, full of sowsilk, boastful, bloated, one goes and stands before one's full-length mirror. One tries different poses— fingers hooked in belt, hand in rear pocket, etc.; one walks toward the glass and away from it.

Soon, one is oneself again: for one sees that all one's gestures, poses, postures and actions are not so unconsciously calculated to conceal or to minimize anatomical and physiological faults.

It is the recognition of the unchangeableness of those faults that returns one to sanity, to maturity: There are one's knock-crock knees, skinny arms, crooked hips—one up, one down—narrow chest, overdeveloped thighs and calves, off center (to the left!) Adam's apple, flat chin (compared to the 10 cent coin Miss Liberty), one's infantile nose, bulging eyes and blackened bags—oh, well—one does not recommend the treatment.

"Listen, would you mind very much if I killed him?"

Liz: "You keep asking me that. What did he do now?"

Me: "Nothing, he didn't do a damned thing, but he's been in one of those cranky moods of his for a week. I've about had it."

Liz: "I know, I know. Why do you think I don't call him for months sometimes? It's a whole lot of fun, you know, to call him up and tell him you're feeling kind of down because you've gotten some kind of scary notice from the IRS, and he says, 'Well, I guess they're going to get you, then.' So you say, 'I'm hoping some more money will come in from the Dalkon Shield settlement so we can pay them if we have to.' And he says, 'Ah, they'll never pay, they'll take bankruptcy first.' So you say, 'Goodbye, nice talking to you,' and you don't call again. I mean, who needs this?"

Me: "The funny thing is, at the same time he's also developed this sweet streak, sudden glints of warmth and humor out of nowhere." I am thinking of what we had while his eyes were healing and how it still occasionally crops up; too seldom, but unmistakable when it does.

"Yeah, well, knowing him, he's going to lure you into getting all mushy about him and then he's going to croak. Didn't you say he's gotten even thinner than when I saw him?"

He had. I was feeding him up as best I could, but it wasn't making much difference.

"That's what happened with Bernardine," Liz says. "She just shriveled up all of a sudden, and then that was it." This was an elderly cousin of our mother whom Liz had grown close to, living near her in Los Angeles for the last few years of Bernardine's life. "You watch; he'll get you all sentimental about him, and then he'll curl up and die and leave you feeling like shit."

Prophetic words—but they were less about me and Pop than about him and someone else.

Fear of Falling

I should ask him, I know I should. In the middle of one of those foul moods of his I should say, Pop, what's really on your mind? What's bothering you?

Of course I know the answers will all be about things I can't help: Bibi won't eat, the prevailing winds blow exhaust smells in at the window, the kids still run over the roof of his apartment. And I'll have nothing to say but Aw, Pop, it's not that bad, come on, relax. Since I can't fix any of it, I'll end up feeling frustrated and sorry I asked, and I won't ask again. I can see it all playing out into the future just as it has in the past, so I don't even start.

But I should. I should say, How are you? What hurts today? Do you feel like complaining, do you want to cry? Can I do anything? So he can tell me, eventually, about something I can't do anything about, and there I'll be again.

Many people know just what this is about. So many of us, people my age and younger, are dealing with it in an elderly parent.

A friend said to me that she offered to take her own old dad in when he couldn't look after himself any more, and he had refused emphatically. He said he remembered his grandfather moving in when he was a boy, and how his mother had struggled for years, unaided, to cope with the additional and inexorably increasing burdens he presented.

He said to her, "You go find me a decent place, and I'll go there. Old people's homes are a blessing."

My own grandmother, Nana, used to say, "Suzy darling, don't you ever put me in one of those places. I'd rather be dead."

Nana thought the cancer hospital at the corner of 107th Street and Central Park West, almost next door to her building, was an old folks' home; accordingly, so did I. On sunny afternoons I used to look up with superstitious dread at the absolutely motionless patients in their chairs on the high, broad balcony of that looming sandstone fortress, and feel sorry for the poor old folks taking the watery sun in lonely silence, abandoned by their families.

"Don't you ever," Nana said; "promise me, Suzela."

Her heart killed her in the end, slowly, one attack after another, while she pleaded with the doctors to stop bringing her back each time and just let her go.

THE SWEET red Doberman pup, Katie, was as willing and anxious to please as any creature in the world. She slept curled up in a wicker lawn chair in the atrium, with an old blue blanket wrapped around and over her so that only her nose showed. We all loved her for her attentiveness and intelligence and generally ladylike manners.

But only Steve and I walked her now.

Robin after eighty was a different man, or rather the same man whose afflictions had begun to reach critical mass. His voice was so faint that I was always asking him to repeat things, which annoyed him very much. He inched around the grocery store when we went shopping together, and he had no stamina at all.

Alarmed, Steve began urging me to have Pop come eat with us more often, so we could be sure he was all right, keep a closer eye on him.

The doctor prescribed zinc oxide ointment and diuretics. He told me Pop had a heart condition (this caused the ankle swelling, which was contributing to the skin rash) and emphysema (the shortness of breath) and *must*, at long last, really stop smoking.

And was I thinking about a "residential situation" for him? I said no, surely it wasn't time for that yet!

But I felt things closing in, and I saw that there was going to be a lot of thinking and planning to do. For the first time ever, I wrote to Irving's widow.

I began with a breezy update about my family as if Frances and I had been corresponding for years, with emphasis on my two grandchildren. Then I got to my real subject.

SEPTEMBER 7, 1991

At the other end of the age scale, my news is sadder. Robin, who was 80 years old last February, has grown very thin and frail and totters around most alarmingly these days. He has been put on medication to strengthen the performance of his heart and drive the accumulated water out of his ankles, which had gotten pretty swollen. He seems to be getting better, though very slowly.

But he's having a heck of a time remembering what day of

the week it is, and has begun forgetting to feed the cats. This is scary, since he is as deeply attached to the animals here (two cats and a dog) as he is to anything, so I can't help but be concerned.

I don't know the state of your feelings about him, but let me just say that if you care to drop him a line, you can always send mail to him here at my address since he lives now in an apartment adjoining our house His phone number is 505-842-1830.

Mind you (and this is important: I mean it), I am not *expecting* you to get in touch with him, and he's not expecting it either (in fact he never speaks of his family at all unless I bring up the subject). But if you do have any impulse to contact him, this might be a good time to do it. I don't think he's exactly at death's door, but you never know; and watching him deteriorate lately has made me more conscious than I was, I guess, of his ultimate mortality drawing nearer as time passes . . .

Part of the problem was that Pop kept catching his feet on the projecting corners of crooked bricks in the paved floor of his apartment, and he no longer had enough motor control of the muscles in his legs to compensate for sudden shifts in balance.

I had the floor carpeted. He caught his feet anyway, because he dragged them instead of lifting the soles of his shoes clear of the ground when he walked. Sometimes sheer friction bound his shoe sole an instant too long, and over he went. The dragging shuffle of his gait was explained to me by his doctor as an old person's way of trying to minimize the risk of falling. It was a lousy strategy. Robin ended up tripping on anything slightly higher than dead level.

I had noticed back on Fourth Street that his shoes (which I took in periodically to the shoemaker to be mended) wore in an odd pattern, the heels driven thin on the inside edges so that he was almost walking on his inner ankle bones. At some point I remembered that there had been problems with my own feet when I was little, and my mother had briefly considered a doctor's suggestion of corrective shoes for me. But my pediatrician uncle had dissuaded her and my feet had fixed themselves, except for a tendency to turn my ankles that has dogged me all my life.

So Pop's walking problems may have started with some weakness or even mild deformity in his foot structure. (Why hadn't I noticed this sooner? You don't notice what you don't want to notice.) Add to this the inevitable weakening of his leg muscles because of sitting or lying down for hours and hours every day, and the outcome was a foregone conclusion. All our efforts—the dogs, the sessions at the pool—came to nothing in the end; as all such efforts, eventually, must, whatever we tell ourselves in the meantime.

Which is why we have that saying about the journey being the important part, not the destination. It had better be.

OCTOBER 3, 1991
Dear Aunt Frances,

Robin is doing better since I confiscated his cigarettes. His voice has come back (it was almost gone, from lack of breath to support it), and the doctor says he probably won't have to lug an oxygen tank on wheels around with him the way so many older smokers do here. Pop still suffers from a bad drying and scaling of the skin, and I have to nag him all the time to keep using the moisturizing lotion the doctors have prescribed, particularly since going to the pool a couple of times a week seems to dry his skin out even more.

I'm glad you wrote to him. He seemed agreeably surprised to hear from you, and as I was taking down dictation of his reply (his handwriting is so shaky that he wouldn't even try to write on his own) a small mystery got solved, maybe.

You remember when Irving called to tell Robin he was leaving him some money, and Robin said no? At the time I asked why, and he said, "I don't WANT it!" and I had to let it go at that.

This morning he said he was surprised to get a letter from you because the last time you two had spoken, he'd come away thinking you were mad at him (although he can't recall why). My theory is that he has remembered for all those years some ancient argument or a remark of yours that he took as criticism. So when Irving called that night, Robin refused the legacy so he could be sure of not rousing up an old annoyance with him on your part that he thought he remembered.

You may recall that this is a man who will do anything to avoid being disturbed in any way. Even where there is no problem, if he imagines that there is one he will back away from the whole situation rather than try to deal with it on any level. He now seems very pleased that apparently you are not mad at him after all. He is clearly (a) relieved that you're not nursing some old grudge and (b) rather puzzled about why he ever thought you were. So I'm delighted that you decided to write. My father is sometimes an awful idiot.

He's doing well so far, for someone who never took the slightest care of his health ...

The swelling in his ankles would not go down, and the rash, stretching from midshin to instep, persisted no matter what I got from the drugstore for him to try, no matter how often I swiped his socks for laundering. I took him to a podiatrist and discovered that with age the nails thicken and twist, and Pop didn't have the strength in his fingers to cut his toenails any longer even if he could have reached them easily, which he could not; his physical flexibility was much diminished. The jagged projections of horn, unchecked, were what had been ripping through his socks and chewing out the toe-seams of his shoes.

The podiatrist gave him a swirly footbath, trimmed his toenails, and pointed out that the rash was now totally out of control and posed a danger of breaking down that delicate Celtic skin irretrievably.

We went to a skin specialist: more ointment.

I WROTE THE FOLLOWING to a friend in the autumn of 1991 (much of my correspondence at this time elicited similar stories from others in my age cohort):

A roughish Autumn this year—my old dad, who lives next door to me, has been going through a rather steep decline for the past six months or so. Turns out he has emphysema and was smoking a pack a day, which was why he lost a ton of weight and became very weak and slow. I played the tyrant and took away his smokes. He doesn't even seem to miss them, it's absolutely infuriating—he did this entirely to himself over something he doesn't even care about!

I've been working with him on some skin problems and ankle-swelling brought on by poor circulation and heart trouble. There's been one bad fall lately, which fortunately didn't break anything though he landed smack on his face, but the frame of his glasses gashed the bridge of his nose pretty dramatically. God knows what the nurses at the walk-in clinic thought when I brought him in with a great big crusted bruise between his eyes!

I am settling down to a new routine that requires me to give him a lot closer supervision and support than previously, which frets me some but not unbearably. Our neighbor, an M.D. who sees him walking outside to pick up the mail sometimes, says my dad is 'a very old eighty.'

And how.

FROM ROBIN'S JOURNALS, 1960:
The trouble with getting drunk is, you smoke too much.

THEY ASKED HIM not to come to the pool any more. He wouldn't tell me why, but Jackie called and leveled with me: it was the rash, which was starting to suppurate on his ankles and had begun to appear on his arms as well. The other old people in the class were afraid they would catch it, and I could see why they might be concerned. It looked worse and worse, and no wonder, since once he put the ointment on, if he moved at all his clothing just rubbed the stuff off again.

And, he admitted reluctantly, he didn't want to go to the pool any more anyway. He was having trouble with his bladder, he said. He was having incidents of incontinence.

LIZ SAYS he's been grousing to her on the phone. "It's just because you haven't been traveling lately," she says. I haven't been traveling because I've been trying to finish a new book, and because I've been uneasy about leaving Pop for any length of time.

"Usually he gets to moan and groan about how you're gone again, you never tell him, you just vanish without saying a word to him about where you're going or when you'll be back."

Me: "Jesus, you should see all the stuff I put on his calendar, the lists and notes I always leave with him! I've been doing it that way for *years*, Liz!"

Liz: "Oh, he just likes to give me this song and dance about how you travel all the time, as if it was evidence that you were insane. I tell him, you know, Robin, some people like to get up and go outside their house sometimes, it makes them feel good, like not living in a prison cell."

Me: "I'm sure you convince him."

Liz: "Oh, he knows. When I lose my temper and start yelling, he laughs, you know that evil little chuckle of his. He knows he's being an idiot. Only now that you've been staying put more he's got none of that to whine about, and he doesn't want to tell me about wetting his pants and falling down in case I tell you—"

Me: "Me, who hasn't noticed a thing, of course!"

Liz: "—So he's kind of at a loss, you know?"

Me, grim: "In more ways than one. Shit. I hate it that he had to give up the pool class. He got to see other people there, so his whole social interaction wasn't limited to me. But now that's over."

Liz: "He said he really liked it. I think they hurt his feelings, throwing him out like that."

Me, with a sigh: "Liz, you can't blame them. *I* wouldn't get in a pool with him; his ankles look positively leprous. I think the doctor's really worried. You know that damn skin we both got from Pop, it's thinner than tracing paper."

Liza: "Do you suppose he hates to move just because it hurts? I mean, he's eighty-one, he must have a lot of aches and pains even without the ankle thing."

It's not something you think of, not when your own body is still relatively young, relatively ache-less. It's not something I thought of, anyway.

Liz has worked for doctors and with doctors in various medical offices and has had a lifelong interest in medicine. She says, "Did that doctor tell you that swollen ankles like that are a symptom of heart disease?"

Me, taking a deep breath: "Yes. That's why the water-exercise class was important. That's why I haven't been pushing him to come shopping with me any more."

"Good."

"You know he watches the soaps with the sound off? He was telling me the whole story again today of one of these idiot shows, and I asked him why he didn't want to turn the sound up so he could hear it. 'Oh no,' he says; 'I never listen.'"

"That's him," Liz says, "that's our father."

"You know what this says about daytime television, don't you?" I say. "It's really a form of dance. For him, anyway; the old bastard; he sits there watching the screen with about as much attention as his cat gives to it, but his brain is buzzing along the whole time, thinking up ways to make trouble."

We are abusing him to each other this way to make ourselves feel better; whistling in the dark.

THE ANKLES were impossible: they scared him enough for him to hike up his pant-legs one day when I dropped in and show me how bad things were. The swelling was gross, the skin bright pink where it showed between yellowish scales and crusts of pus.

I took him to a new doctor, a geriatric specialist. Dr. Frame said briskly, get him on Home Health Care, which sends visiting nurses. Robin needed help with that rash, and the diuretics for the swollen ankles were at least a part of the incontinence problem. Dr. Frame's staff helped arrange for nurses to come several times a week.

Rob liked the extra attention. I heard him joking with the nurses. I thought, We've got it covered, we're going to lick this.

O**NE** M**ORNING** in late October I found Robin lying on the floor of his apartment. He'd been tapping on the lowest glass panes of the French doors to try to get my attention as I passed back and forth through the atrium, on my usual errands. He was in his underwear and wrapped in the blanket he had dragged off his bed to roll up in, because he had pissed himself and was wet and chilled. He'd been there since about four a.m., when he had fallen, and he'd been calling; but his voice had not been strong enough for me to hear him through the doors.

I nearly fell over too, levering him back up onto his bed, dragging him by both his big hands and trying to use my own weight as a counterbalance to raise him. It was not something I could be sure of doing again. He was too tall and too heavy for me, and too weak in his legs to help. I knew that day that he was going to need more than I could do for him at home, but I didn't want to admit it out loud any more than I wanted to hear it from anyone else.

In November he fell again in the middle of the night; Steve happened to be coming in very late from work, heard him crash down, and got him back up and into the bathroom, where he had been headed, and then back into bed.

We went to Dr. Frame. He said, "The skin on his ankles is starting to break down. If it isn't stopped, you get infection, and if that won't heal, amputation. Steps have to be taken immediately.

Home nursing visits obviously aren't going to do it; he must go into some kind of nursing hospital, and soon. You'd better start looking. There are a lot of decent places in town. You can judge their quality by the demeanor of the residents."

I said, "This really can't be handled at home?"

The doctor gave me an impatient look. "Of course not. He needs a nursing home, and after that, once the ankles are healed up, probably some sort of permanent institutional care. He should have gone in long ago."

TIME OUT for a little social commentary; and if some of it sounds bitter, that's because dealing with this situation made me feel that way, as I suspect it makes most people feel when they have to face it. That's part of the experience—guilt, anger, and a furious resentment that this rich, technically capable, and inventive society deals so meanly and so poorly with the problems of providing for our own aged parents.

Not that there was ever a "Golden Age" in these matters from which we have declined. You get the impression, from what the media serve up on the subject, of impoverished and abandoned old people living on the streets or nearly, and buying dog food to share with the scraggly pet that is their only company. Or else there's the distant, wealthy father in his mansion with servants to push his wheelchair around and maybe abuse him when nobody's looking, because he's abandoned, too, in his own way (We are big on this abandonment issue, so long as we don't have to pay anything to deal with it. Guilt is cheaper, apparently, than action.)

In between there's not much, except a vague notion of the fortunate elder who has raised her children right and lives with them in a nice house in a nice town in the nice sunshine, or who lives in a condo and plays slow but satisfying golf with a set of good-humored friends whose lives have been infinitely enhanced by estrogen replacement therapy and Viagra.

For most of us, it's not like this.

The parents (or surviving parent) live in their own home until the awful day when the pan forgotten on the stove sets fire to the kitchen or there's the fall, that dreaded, hip-breaking fall, that puts an end to the pretense of able-bodied home-ownership and proud—more likely, terrified pretense of—independence.

And you discover the limits of the resources at your command, and the narrow choice of possibilities that they will buy. You are faced with the fact that you have already earmarked your savings for your own old age, as your culture suggests you had damned well better do because otherwise you're out on the street in rags, pal. And here you are in your fifties, and your dad is over eighty, and no way can you pour your meager wealth, hoarded up in fear of precisely this loss of autonomy and health in your own later years, down the black hole of this old man's indeterminate and open-endedly devouring future, such as it is.

Maybe some folks can. Given who Robin and I were, and our past together and apart, I couldn't.

But when I measured that harsh reality against the ideal in my mind, I saw myself at first as a monster of selfishness. What else could I see?

We have in our heads this notion of the "olden days" of "family values," when people kept their oldsters home to die in bed, whatever it took. We mostly do not have firsthand knowledge of just what that meant.

In the first place, there were few nursing homes as we know them, and they were for the rich (the poor died at home or in the street or in the county hospital). Because medicine offered little but care and comfort, without antibiotics and oxygen feeds and all the modern panoply of actual amelioration of pain and disintegration, there wasn't much to choose between a nursing home and a family home anyway.

And then there was the expense; there are no "olden days" in which as many of us as now were as comparatively rich as we are. Middle-class people made a living, not a fortune, and good custodial care was never inexpensive.

But for the modest cost of room and board you could, if you had the usual, extended family of many members and many married couples, attract some unmarried female cousin or auntie to come do the nursing for you, freeing up the rest of your household to go to work or tend the farm (the same pattern let you keep invalid or handicapped family members home rather than institutionalizing them).

Check relevant fiction and diaries and letters from the past for evidence: your family caregiver would be a cousin, widowed or a spinster, with nursing experience. People got seriously sick a lot in those days—from viruses, as always; from bacteria, bad food, and spoiled drink; from dust and pollutants and accidents on the job. Most women past adolescence had nursing experience, often at the deathbeds of their own parents, children, or husbands.

So Aunt Polly, too old to marry again, or Cousin Emily, too homely or neurotic or otherwise unattractive to marry at all, would come live with you in order to care for mother or father in the last years, and not always with tenderness; sometimes with the spitefulness of frustration, with carelessness, with resentment or disgust or outright hostility and abuse.

But it was cheap, and at best it was loving, and nobody missed out on any special advantages of having medical caretakers at hand because there was little that the doctor or nurse could offer that Aunt Polly or Cousin Emily didn't know too.

As a matter of fact, it is clear now that my father, as the youngest of four brothers and the only one formally unattached at the time, had been put into exactly Aunt Polly's position when he was selected (by his brothers, I assume) to go and live with his mother for her final eight years. I have a feeling he wasn't very good at it.

MAINTAINING your old mom or dad in a standard quality nursing home in my western American city—with oxygen tanks for circulation and breathing assist, regular medication and checkups, special diets and pneumonia shots and flu shots and cream for skin that's breaking down—costs upwards of five thousand dollars a month. Pharmaceutical bills and payments for ambulance trips to the hospital are extra.

If you decide instead to hire full-time, in-home help for your aged parent, you will find yourself paying an attendant's yearly salary for an eight-hour shift, five days a week: at least twenty-five thousand a year. For that kind of help round the clock *seven* days a week—given an elder who has to get up four times a night to pee and who stumbles and falls in the dark on his way to the bathroom—you can at least double that figure; you'll be paying *two* yearly salaries, plus weekend help to relieve the regular personnel.

That's for aides who are forbidden, by law, to pick up your dad if he falls on the floor and lies there, unable to claw his own way upright (which is, of course, a major reason why you need the help in the first place). The aide's job is to phone for an ambulance to come take Dad to the hospital and make sure he hasn't broken anything. The ambulance costs sixty dollars a trip and up; the hospital cost depends on how long they decide to hang onto your parent for tests, and what tests they choose.

For the luxury of picking-up-off-the-floor service on-site you need someone with a nursing degree or higher. They must be qualified to check that your mom has not broken bones in the fall and that picking her up won't cause additional problems that could lead to lawsuits. The services of people with nursing degrees come at a higher rate, as indeed they should.

My father had some worn-out clothing and beat-up old books, a lot of fine paint brushes, and a ratty gray cat to his name: he would qualify as indigent because he was, by his own choice—that money from Irving that he had refused. We could get Medicaid to pay for keeping him in a nursing home, but nothing to help keep him in his own apartment.

My task was to get Pop on Medicaid and find him a nursing home bed until the ankles healed. After that, some sort of shelter placement would have to be arranged at our expense, leading eventually, in all probability, back to a nursing home again, this time for good.

The one place he could never live again was home; home was where there was no one able to pick him up off the floor around the clock, or do the kind of care that would heal the terrible ankles; not without paying a fortune, and we didn't have a fortune. Home was out.

I didn't tell him. I couldn't. I just started looking.

FROM ROBIN'S JOURNALS, OCTOBER 1968:

Got organized—shaved, etc.—went up again, again, to Maxine's.... Dinner. Maxine, Carol, Steve, Suzy, Jaime [a friend and revolutionary old Castroite] *... Hungarian goulash.... Still a lousy cook....*

Yak, yak—10 o'clock, f'chrissakes. But—got away and sober. Came home to find—sniff—<u>radiators</u> quite warm! Heat <u>before</u> Oct. 15? <u>Incroyable</u> (if it means what we think it means).

The jernt is comfy. (Funny, how you can <u>smell</u> steam heat.) (Even when it's been gone a half hour.) The heat's up—from 9 am to 6 pm, no heat now (11 pm)—we've had 4–5 wines, and are into 1 final Irish. . . . Comfortable, happy, listening to WBAI.

Vista de la Muerte

Maggie Pacheco at New Mexico Human Services furnished a clear discussion of options for the ankle problem (a nursing home) and a list of "shelter cares" (ongoing picking-up services) for afterward, along with information on applying, fast, for Medicaid for Pop from the state's Income Support Division.

He had to go on Medicaid. We could either pay the entire cost of a nursing home stay, or contribute nothing and have Medicaid pay for minimal service; there was no middle ground. He either has funds or he doesn't. If he has access to any money at all, Medicaid will pay nothing. If he is considered indigent, Medicaid will pay for basic care: no private room, no frills—no cat, that's for sure.

As an author of books that often require supporting research, I'm a quick study, and I have a certain amount of discretion about how I use my time; I spent some learning about nursing homes, for starters. They all had a certain number of Medicaid beds, by law; to get one you usually had to sign onto a waiting list and hope somebody else's old mom or dad kicked the bucket soon to make room for yours.

I must have looked at every nursing home in town. Using residents' "demeanor" as a criterion, as suggested by Doctor Frame, turned out to be a bad joke. Most of these people *had* no demeanor: they lay doped by drugs or TV or slept sitting up in their wheelchairs, or wandered about muttering or crying or calling out in response to nothing anyone else could see or hear.

The demeanor of staff people, though, gave me some idea of whether a place was understaffed and working everyone to a frazzle or not, and, as at any workplace, the staff turnover rate told something about the general atmosphere. I came to think that evidence of lots of visitors, of people taking their old folks out for meals and visits home and holidays, was a good indication that an institution was not just a dumping ground, or so grim that relatives were scared to set foot in the place.

I had noticed too that some nursing homes had their allotted number of "Medicaid beds" on a particular floor, or in a particular wing, which usually meant more people were fitted into each room on that floor or in that wing. You can't avoid seeing the temptation to create a "poor wing" for Medicaid residents and treat them differently from the patients who pay their own way.

The best I found seemed to be (let's call it) Vista Linda, which means "pretty view"; it's the sort of name you find when you check the Albuquerque yellow pages for nursing homes and rehab centers. It was a one-story place with several wings in which paying and Medicaid patients were mixed. There were big windows, letting in lots of light, and cheerful staff people. They said they actually *had* a bed, though they couldn't hold it long. Was I interested?

Interested? I hovered in a frenzy of reluctance, indecision, and eagerness—to have at least this stage of things settled, to take a stab at stopping Robin's slide down the slippery slope, to have some real help with a situation I hadn't been dealing with well, I realized now, for some time. I was out of my depth and drowning, and Pop was drowning with me, and/or vice versa.

Because while I drove around looking in on these places (including the ones that stank of urine and the one made out of an old adobe church with dark little cubby-rooms and a door locked at all times to keep the residents from "wandering off"), while I talked with staff people, while I dithered and considered and worried, Robin rapidly declined and fell. He was going to have to go somewhere, and soon.

FROM MY OWN DIARY, DECEMBER 15, 1991:

Thanks to refinancing our mortgage at a lower rate, we can manage about $300 a month tops for Robin; Ian says he thinks he can pick up some of the rest, and Rob's own Social Security payments, now about $385 per month, will round it out. Looks like after the ankles are taken care of in a nursing home, we can lodge Pop in some kind of sheltered living situation, reasonably comfortable and independent.

The odd part is doing all this without telling Robin about it. Liz said, don't tell him this for *Christmas*, for Christ's sake, the holidays are hard enough when you're depressed, which he naturally is; I agree. Of course his birthday is in February, so we'd have to wait till what, March?

He's being very good, now that I've taped up his thermostat so that he can't totally bust me on heating bills. Ian came and spent an evening, and I vented a bit, about this and other things. Since then, Rob has become very meek and sweet (though he sits around in his underwear and a bathrobe all the time, which cannot be a good sign). Maybe Ian said something firm to him . . .

I'm cooking for him now because there's nothing "fast" he can make for himself that's both low-salt and high enough in calories to keep his weight up; and nothing more complex than "fast" that he will make for himself, period. So I'm suddenly a real hausfrau, hustling every morning to make sure he has his sandwich at lunch and something hot for dinner (in case I'm out later), which he often doesn't bother with anyway (that is, it's in the fridge and he doesn't disturb himself to heat it up for ten minutes in a pot). The nice thing is that I can cope fine with this, and after visits to so many nursing homes I am well aware of how much worse it could be.

The not-nice things are that (a) I resent the extra work, (b) I get the feeling that I am sort of training him to be in a nursing home by not demanding anything more of him—but I am tired to death of nagging him, to tell the truth, and can't bring myself to do it to no further purpose. And (c), I feel in a false position when he says, after coming over to feed the dog and cat at my place, "Well, I'm going home now," and goes back to his apartment—which I'm in the secret process of cutting out from under him.

It's wearing me out, all of it, the cooking too. It doesn't help that he simply accepts everything I do as if it were his due, not a word toward volunteering to do any part of it for himself. It's amazing, really. The result is that sometimes I can hardly wait to get rid of him, because I resent being taken for granted as some kind of unpaid nurse/housemaid. The occasional grunted "Thank you" now and again doesn't do it, though it probably should. And if he and I had a different kind of relationship, maybe it would.

Well, it's not forever; I'd better enjoy what I can of this while we've got it, because after this, everything changes and will never change back. The sticking point of course will be his cat. If I can get a shelter situation to take the damn cat too, for as long as he can take care of it, there will be lots less of a problem; or so I tell myself.

Been looking into the shelter care and assisted living situations, for the long term (after the ankles heal): found one where he could keep his cat, a small cluster of apartments with lots of supervision and a nurse-owner. They promise outings, good food (much of it "Mexican," which Pop hates, unfortunately). He'd have his own apartment, and there are only ten or twelve people in the complex at a time. $1,300 a month, on top of his Social Security income.

Another, a "full-service retirement rental," but you don't have to plunk down a huge initial fee to "buy" your space (with monthly upkeep charges additional, as with Julie at Gracious Gardens). Individual apartment, "suite with bath," continental breakfast, maid service, lunch tickets for the dining room: $1,800 a month on top of his Social Security.

The place on Grove Street offers a small studio apartment, tacky construction and low ceilings for a man who is still tall, but near our house; smell of bad food from the dining room, dinge everywhere. But it's nearby. And the little grocery on the corner right across the street, he could go buy things for himself as many of those folks do: $800 plus, after Social Security. That's manageable, if we all kick in; and it's close.

Only trouble is, none of these places have doctors on duty or even on call. If something goes wrong, the staff people call an ambulance and take Pop to the emergency room, just as with Julie at the Gardens. Not ideal, but I've got to get started lining up some place for him to live after the nursing home stay; waiting lists are long for all the good ones.

I still find Rob charming when he wants to be (in his own inimitable way). Hope he can be stimulated in a new situation to take an interest in the closing years of his own life, instead of more or less sleeping through them with his eyes open.

At that time, I thought he had years.

I WRITE to Aunt Frances about the book I've been trying to sell, a young adult fantasy novel about magic. I use the opportunity to tell her about Pop, too (but not everything):

Robin is feeling quite a bit better, I think, since they took him off the diuretic pills that were supposed to reduce the swelling of his feet and ankles. We've had to stop the pool exercise class, though, because apart from everything else he had developed an allergy to chemicals in the water that were irritating his skin. It didn't help that he was also pulling on a woolen sweater without a cotton shirt under it, mainly because he has trouble dealing with buttons and didn't want to be bothered doing up the buttons of a cotton shirt first. We have had long discussions about this, and he now wears no wool on his skin and has conquered the itchy rash he had developed on his arms and elbows due to the woolen sleeves rubbing there. His ankles are still a real problem.

He reads a bit, if I bring him a book about art and painters and so on, or a good British mystery novel. He and I have similar taste in such things. But mostly he watches TV and shakes his head over how boring, brainless, and repetitive it is; but he keeps watching.

She doesn't write back any more—holding a pen and getting a legible line out of it is too much for her these days, her hands shake so, and she never learned to type, she says in her last note to me. She doesn't call (there may be some hearing problems), and I don't want to intrude on her by phoning because there's so little common ground between us; so I have no idea how she's taking any of this, and I don't want to distress her with truer tales of our floundering efforts to settle Pop somehow.

Frances struck me as a smart woman when I met her on that one visit to Sacramento. I have no doubt that she can figure out for herself how steep and sudden his decline has been.

I TOOK HIM BACK to Dr. Frame because his ankles were weeping again. When we got home, he said he didn't feel like dinner, he just wanted to go "lie flat on my back."

Which was where I found him when I walked in, later that evening, so upset and angry and frustrated that I just said straight out, "You can see where all this is leading, Pop: to a stay in a nursing home."

"Yeah," he said, staring up at the ceiling, "I figured."

"It's just getting beyond me," I said, sitting down in the blue deck chair. "I can't handle it any more."

"Me neither," he said faintly.

I was grateful for that, relieved that we weren't going to have an argument about this, and moved by pity, and I reached over and patted his hand. His fingers were hot with life. It's amazing how hot the skin of the old is; you expect them to be already cooling, body temperature dropping along with competence and energy levels, but it isn't so.

"Well, we'll do the best we can for you, anyway," I said. "See you in the morning, okay? And use the phone if you need me."

Leaving, I saw the shine of tears sliding back into his hair from under his closed eyelids.

DR. FRAME recommends going to see a urologist, to find out whether there might be something surgical to be done about the urinary incontinence, which has persisted even though Rob is off the diuretics. Prostate surgery might be indicated (although that sometimes makes an incontinence problem worse). This has become an urgent priority, all of a sudden.

I have discovered with a shock ("No bedbound, and no incontinence, that's our rules—if they get incontinent, they got to go into a nursing home right away") that no assisted-living or shelter-care situation will accept residents who are incontinent.

At the urologist's, I'm in the hallway having a drink of water from the fountain, and the door to the examining room is open. I overhear a little of the conversation: the doctor has asked about the incontinence problem, and Pop says glumly that it's pretty bad, and that he gets up often during the night to avoid wetting the bed and sometimes falls getting up. And yes, he's had "the other kind" of incontinence, too, for a long time now, at first sporadically, and lately almost all the time.

This suddenly explains the puzzling disappearance of his under-shorts, no matter how often I buy him new ones. "I don't know what happened to them," he'd say, "the laundry must be ripping them up."

I take our laundry out, and his, to be done at a wash-and-fold laundry service. We have installed a little darkroom setup for Steve in place of the washer and dryer in the Cedar Street house. Now I realize that Rob must be throwing his beshat shorts away instead of sending them to be washed, in an effort to keep this aspect of his elimination problems secret.

When we get home, I insist on talking about this.

"If I can't get to the toilet in time, I just have to let go in my pants," he admits at last, with obvious relief (no more secrecy required in that department, anyway). That's what he means when he explains a delay in getting out of the house by saying he was "caught short." Physical events have required him to change his underwear before leaving the house.

We talk about this now, a little, but not much. There's not a lot to say, except that the situation is lots worse than I thought.

Pop sits in his deck chair all day, barely moving, staring at the TV; speaks in monosyllables; is clearly depressed and exhausted. Now that his cover—of being healthy, in control, independent—is irretrievably blown, he goes slack. His eyes follow me with a moist and muted stare. He pointedly asks no pointed questions.

I keep going over the stubborn facts, trying to make them read differently, but they won't. Medicaid will pay for nursing home care as long as there is a diagnosed medical condition to be treated there (as part of "rehabilitation" services). It will not pay for any kind of intermediate care, at home or in an assisted-living residence, once the ankles are healed. But none of the shelter-care or assisted-living outfits will take him if the incontinence persists, not even if *we* pay for it. And we can't afford to install him permanently in a nursing home like Vista Linda at our own expense.

So when the ankles heal, he will be sent home, where he and I can't manage his life and I can't afford to hire in the kind of supplemental care he'll need. Then, when eventually he's diagnosed again with something needing long-term treatment, he'll have to be requalified all over again for admission to a nursing home under Medicaid. When that round of treatment is completed, Medicaid stops paying and he comes home again.

I can hardly contemplate the situation without drowning in tides of helpless rage. My father's interests and mine, thanks to this "system," are now opposed. I need him to be sick enough and stay sick enough to be declared by his doctor to be in need of permanent nursing home care so that he can stay for good at Vista Linda, paid for by Medicaid and his Social Security payments. He wants to get his ankles healed fast and come home, where I can go broke trying to buy him the services he needs to continue to live with us.

I can't discuss this with him, in case he does not know, guess, understand, in case it would come as news—horrible, unacceptable news—to him. The prospect of suddenly having to deal, in a pressure situation (in which *something* has to be done, and soon), with appeals, attacks, defenses from him is more than I can face.

So I keep quiet. I trudge ahead, keeping just the immediate goal in view: a stay of indeterminate length in a nursing home, for the ankles. Afterward will just have to hang up in the air for now.

I don't offer to take him with me to look at any of the places I'm still checking out, and he doesn't ask to come. It's understood between us, I think, that it would be too upsetting for both of us.

FROM MY DIARY, DECEMBER 17, 1991:

What am I going to do with that toothless, rat-tailed, insistent cat of his while he's away? What will she do without him, with no warm, stinky old man to curl up against to sleep?

The urologist called to tell me that he had some drugs to try that might help with the incontinence, but that the condition might also stem from an old injury to the brain. Had Robin had any head injuries from serious falls that I knew of?

We fenced around this for a while until I understood that he was asking if my father had ever been a falling-down drunk.

I said I thought maybe he had, in his much younger days, but that he was no longer a drinker, not for many years now. The doctor thought a scan of the brain could tell whether there was a surgically correctable injury resulting from those "old days" that might be contributing to the incontinence problem now; but that would be for Dr. Frame to set up, so we should go back to him.

Meanwhile, we would proceed with the process of getting Pop admitted to Vista Linda temporarily as a Medicaid patient on the basis of care for his ankles being urgently needed.

FROM ROBIN'S JOURNAL, 1968:

Drank a few and one too many—got home and abed somehow. (Bruises— we fell . . .)

FROM MY DIARY, DECEMBER 19, 1991:

We will get a medical assessment by Dr. Frame tomorrow a.m., his decision tomorrow p.m., packing this weekend, off to Vista Linda Monday a.m., and a merry Xmas to you, too. I've spoken to Ian and to Liz.

I had a spell of tears yesterday in the car. Free-Form played a song, very soft and more spoken than sung, about an old Dutchman being taken care of by a girl named Margaret while his mind wandered and he thought he was in Rotterdam, catching glimpses of her from time to time in the present—sweet and sad, and too much to the point. Killer lines, something like, "Once I was a young man, many years ago; and Margaret remembers that for me."

Well, I cried, driving: not because it has much to do with our present situation. I was sorry not to be a participant in the loving, tender story of that song, but in a much more acrid, rocky story in which I did not and have not and probably will not exhibit that kind of sweetness, and neither has nor will Rob. Maybe it could have been different if I had pushed him for memories before, insisted on spending more time with him right from the beginning—but he was never responsive to that kind of approach, and I'm not overly patient, either. So here we are, and soon that hidden emotional life of his will withdraw even more from being known by any of us, his kids and family.

So I was crying for what we weren't and hadn't been to each other since I guess I was a baby, fresh chance or no fresh chance. Some mistakes can't be corrected. They just sit there, being what they are, and all the waters of your life have to curve and flow around that damned big rock of a mistake ever after, being shaped and formed by it.

Was all our joking around, the puns and the outrageous remarks and the insults, our way of avoiding close ties, or of expressing them? Strange, and ridiculous in a way, to feel guilt and loss from measuring our reality, Pop's and mine, against this song's idyllic vision, which is mostly baloney and very rare and even then much tempered with other, less romantic elements. It simply isn't applicable to us.

I just wish it were.

AFTER THE OFFICE VISIT—the "assessment"—on Friday, December 20, Dr. Frame said (as we had already discussed) that Robin should go into residential nursing care immediately, on the basis of his deteriorating feet and ankles as well as the incontinence problem, which we were still investigating.

"He's ready for admission as he stands," the doctor said briskly to me, and said he would authorize it. I could pick up the paperwork from him on the following Monday, on the way to Vista Linda with Robin. In the meantime, Dr. Frame would arrange an appointment for Pop to have a magnetic resonance brain scan as soon as possible, looking for lesions that might be operable, as suggested by the urologist. If we could get the incontinence cured, when the ankles healed we could move Robin on into one of the shelter-care situations that we could afford, maybe even one that allowed cats.

So the time had come.

I went up to Vista Linda again to prepare the ground. The administrator I spoke with was gracious, kind, and encouraging, a nice woman in a tailored suit occupying a small but tasteful front office, separated by a bend in the hallway from the actual residential floor.

The space they could offer Pop was in a room with two other men, a tidy row of three mechanical-looking hospital beds with curtains in between to set off each nightstand, each little set of shelves and drawers, each reading lamp, from the two others. The space was minuscule, and the floor was surfaced with cold, tan plastic tile that wouldn't soak up leaks and spills. His bed would be the middle one, between the man at the window and the man at the door.

I hated it. I knew Rob would hate it, and would think of nothing but getting better fast so he could come home. I had to hope that he would stay sick enough to have to stay at Vista Linda for the rest of his life.

SO I WALK into Rob's apartment on the morning of Saturday, December 21, to tell him what's going to happen after the weekend, on Monday, the day before Christmas.

He listens, head down. He mutters, "I wonder what the rooms are like."

I nerve myself up enough to explain that he'll be sharing a room, but at least it's not an open ward. He doesn't say anything.

I tell him that at Vista Linda they think they can take care of the skin problem, and maybe the incontinence and the falling down too, and the place looks pretty good, and I'll take care of Bibi for him in the meantime.

He asks how long he has to stay there.

I tell him I don't know, it depends on how fast he gets better.

He says, "What about the place where they said I could take Bibi?"

I told him about that, back at the beginning, to try to cheer him up.

Now I take a deep breath. "Pop, I'm going to say this just once and then I'll never bring it up again; so listen, all right? If you had accepted that money from Irving, it could have bought you a place where Bibi could come with you, now or any time in the future when you might need it. I could have invested that money for you then, and by now there would probably be enough so that we could afford to hire help to come here to you and stay with you and you wouldn't have to leave at all.

"But you refused the money, in spite of everything I could think of to say to you. And here we are, and I have to tell you, on my own I can't afford to do any of those things. I've done the best I can with what we have to work with, and if it's not what you wanted, I'm sorry; but we did talk about it at the time, and you made your decision. And now we all have to live with it."

In a low, bitter voice he says, "I know."

And we never mention the subject again.

DID I ENJOY telling him "I told you so"? Damn straight; if I said otherwise, that would be a lie. I was royally pissed off, as well as distressed by the situation he had brought on himself and us by his stubbornness about that damned money.

He could have made a gift after all to the kids he had left decades before: a gift of his own good comfort and cheer and ease in his last years, without guilt or debt on anyone's part. Maybe this would have spared me having to go looking for the best of a bad lot of choices for him, and having to put him there, and having to hope he could stay there instead of coming home to an inadequate situation. That hope, directly counter to my father's own hopes and desires, I could only see as traitorous and cruel. It made me feel like shit, and it was unavoidable, and it was, maddeningly, his own doing.

I wouldn't have minded being spared, a little. I wouldn't have minded us both being spared.

It's also only fair to point out that even if he had accepted it,

the money might have been invested unwisely, by us or by him—
or he might have spent it all, given it away, or run off to Brazil,
who knows?—and we might have ended up in the same place anyway. But that's not something that occurred to me until long afterward, and anyway, what does it change?

The best I could do, under the circumstances, was to say what
I'd said and stop there, to turn off the rest of the tirade and not
rub his nose in the ramifications, now becoming apparent, of his
decision not to accept the legacy from Irving. There was nothing I
could have said that he couldn't figure out for himself anyway, if
he wasn't actually way ahead of me already, wandering the prov-
inces of Terror and Despond.

So I got up and said, "I'll let you be now, and come back later to
help you pack some things to take with you."

ON SUNDAY we pack a suitcase to take to Vista Linda the next
day. He makes another musing comment about what "his room"
will be like.

I don't reply, and he doesn't ask again. His meekness is killing
me, as it is no doubt designed to do. I don't volunteer anything. I
know what the damned room looks like, and I know that if he saw
it beforehand he'd refuse to go. And he could do that, he could refuse. He is not being committed: he is being admitted.

Although he has signed a power of attorney, so that I can attend
to the Medicaid matter and other financial questions, it would
take another whole procedure, long and unbearable, to obtain the
authority to commit him against his will, even for a limited period
of nursing care. That I will not do.

He *has* to agree. But he can always say no.

FROM ROBIN'S JOURNALS, 1961

How gaily, how joyously
we do EVERYTHING—until our fiftieth year;
and then, how carefully, how inchingly,
we halfdo a few things, and those by ear . . .

Let Me Pop You in
My Sack, Says Death

FROM MY DIARY, DECEMBER 23, 1991:

Monday morning I walked in and found Pop sitting in the deck chair, waiting for me. He had on his good gray pants, his hair was washed, and he bravely wore his navy blue blazer (for social occasions) with a white hanky neatly folded in the breast pocket, and a light dusting of dandruff on the collar and shoulders; and the polished black dress loafers. By his standards, he was dolled up and ready to make a good appearance in a setting that he declared, by his act of sartorial faith, to be the sort of place that values such efforts. Driving over to Vista Linda he put a good face on things, joking with me.

Going in he walked rapidly and with some strength, using the walker I'd had to get for him, but only just: demonstrating that he didn't really belong here, he's fine. It was a performance of dignified rebellion, something I've never thought of before in connection with my father.

The entrance and foyer are angled sharply to the main body of the building, so you don't look right down into the long main hallway with its wheelchaired occupants, who drowse in the sunlight that shines through the tall windows, or who watch anxiously for the arrival of someone to talk to, complain to, beg help from. I know what's coming, Pop doesn't; not yet.

We stop at the administrator's office and sign papers. I write a check for the first month's costs at Vista Linda, which I am assured will be reimbursed when Medicaid kicks in. Ian has contributed to the initial outlay. It's all orchestrated like clockwork and runs smoothly. So far.

A nurse comes to take Rob back to his room; I stay behind in the administrative office because there are more papers, and because I absolutely cannot bring myself to be present when he gets his first look at "his room."

Besides, there's the matter of the "Do Not Resuscitate" release to discuss first. We now enter this territory of custodianship, where vital matters of Robin's life and its conduct are reserved for exploration and decision-making between me and strangers. Terri, the administrator, explains to me in a sympathetic voice: sometimes they get pneumonia, or the heart just stops beating. The usual procedure then is to fly into action, pumping and thumping and pummeling the life back into the moribund old body.

It hurts them, she says; thin, brittle bones break, people end up with a few more weeks of life won at the cost of spending them tubed up and in pain in a strange hospital bed, followed by a slightly postponed and often more painful death. At this age—Pop is eighty-one—it's as much an assault as assistance. Do I think he would agree to sign a waiver so that the staff will be released from having to put him through all that if his heart stops beating?

I say I'll ask. I sign more papers. I am given the Patients' Bill of Rights to read, and the house rules (he has a right to complain, to privacy, to decent food, and so on, and a duty to behave).

Robin is admitted as a "full resident," on "full public aid," meaning Medicaid, although the assistance we have applied for has not yet been confirmed. Nobody has any doubt that he'll be accepted into the Medicaid assistance program for the length of his stay here. They tell me that Maggie Pacheco is good at what she does, and if she says he's got a good claim, everything should be all right.

However you say it, I'm putting my father in a modern version of what my grandmother used to call the poorhouse. At least it's not the workhouse, I tell myself. But I get a sharp twinge of shame, knowing that he's not here on my nickel; I am turning him over, for now temporarily (but permanently, I have to hope), to the support of the state.

The administrator reads my expression; she's had a lot of practice. She says, "None of our floor staff know which residents are on Medicaid. We take great pride in treating everyone equally and with dignity. Don't worry."

I don't worry, we're way past that. I understood all this when they said they mixed up the Medicaid beds with the paying ones. But I still feel raw about it. I still feel strange.

How Pop feels I am about to find out, as much as we can ever really find out such a thing about another *in extremis*.

When I go back to Rob's room—not the exact one I had originally been shown, but its twin in every respect, because all these cells are basically alike—he's sitting in the one chair by his bed, the middle bed, in a dark niche between the brightness of the outside window at one end of the long, narrow room and the dimmer bustle of the hallway at the inner end.

His eyes are wide and glaring, his face pale. An attendant is kneeling at his feet, taking off his shoes and socks to expose the puffy flesh in its strained casing of reddened, scaly skin. The ankles are like inflamed sausages, horrible to look at . . . he who had beautiful ankles and high-arched feet, like a tall white wading bird.

She says brightly to me that Dr. Frame has ordered a footbath right away, and application of a stronger ointment; they're to get to work at once on that rash.

I agree that that it sounds like a good idea to me, going along with the pretense that I am happy with the prospect that the sooner they get him fixed up, the sooner he can get out of here. I busy myself helping another attendant unpack and tuck Pop's clothes away, putting his books on the shelf and laying out his bathroom stuff, talking the whole time as if this were not the poorhouse but a resort hotel, while they are taking his blood pressure and getting him ready for his footbath.

I hated to see his try at jaunty respectability stripped off him so easily and matter-of-factly, but their businesslike attention to the real, immediate problem—the ankles—both impressed me and released me from some of the guilt. These people had things to do for him that could only be done here, and they seemed to know precisely how to do them.

In a flat, clipped tone he answered the formal list of questions put to him by the nurse, Darlene. Every answer sounded to me like, "There is no problem, I am a perfectly healthy man being shanghaied into the poorhouse"; and every answer was, pretty much, true: shortness of breath? No, not since he quit smoking. Pain? No.

"Do you know why you're here?" she said.

"No," he said, glaring at me. "Why am I here?"

So I said, and harshly too because I resented this challenge after I'd worked so hard to get him the help he needs, the help these women in white uniforms are about to begin to provide, "You're here because your feet are disintegrating and you're incontinent and you fall over a lot and I can't pick you up."

He has no answer to this, which we both know to be the simple truth. So when they ask him in my presence, as they must, "You're here of your own free will, Mr. McKee, is that right? You're staying with us by your own choice?" he stares at the floor and says in a small, acid voice, "Yes."

My God. What a world of bitter acceptance in that one syllable! What a world of defeat. I can't help wondering what goes on here when furious oldsters cry, "No! I've been tricked, no one told me it would be like this! I can't stay here, take me home!" Or do they all, or almost all, bow their heads and acquiesce as Robin does, because they know there really is no other choice?

It's horrible no matter how you look at it; I don't see any way that it could not be horrible, or that it could be avoided; and our circumstances are far from the worst I can imagine.

His blue, shadowed eyes are dark when he looks at me, their color deepened with accusation, rage, hurt, betrayal. He knows that one way or another the old life is over, that I and circumstances have closed it down. He doesn't say anything now. There's nothing to say.

They have to get his pants, his pressed gray pants off him so they can do the footbath. I excuse myself out of respect for his privacy—which doesn't really exist for the staff here, no matter how much they have to pretend it does, so it seems all the more important that I honor the privacies between parent and child. And because I've had all I can take for now.

No doubt he's had all he can take too; but some options are closed off for good for arrivals at the poorhouse.

I tell him I'll be back in the evening, and I go, I escape, past the man shouting in the next room, and the TVs blaring in every room (the pervasive deafness of residents means that the place is noisy with the sound of competing TVs at all hours of the day and evening), and the wild-eyed, haggard stranger trying to tell me something really urgent in a stroke-distorted voice that I can't understand.

WHEN I GET HOME I find a notice in the mail that Robin's Social Security payments are now diverted directly to Vista Linda, an increased value of four hundred dollars a month for them, with thirty reserved for his "personal expenses."

What personal expenses, for Christ's sake? There's no place within walking distance of Vista Linda—which sits on the edge of a complex of medical offices around an uptown branch of a downtown hospital—to buy anything, even if you can walk, which at the moment Pop can barely do.

I come back three times that first day, speaking to staff people, bringing things from home. He forgot his shampoo (surprise, surprise).

He signs the "Do Not Resuscitate" waiver, after asking, "You're not trying to get rid of me, are ya?" Feeble and sour, but a joke, by God. Maybe we'll be all right.

I hang around for a couple of hours, talking about the latest adventures and tribulations of Liza, about Bibi, about getting Rob's TV that we've brought from home installed here properly (there is something wrong with the hookup, but the institution's handyman is scheduled to take another look soon). When I leave that time, the attendant on duty stops me in the hall and hands me a wad of bills: "He had this in his shirt pocket. He really shouldn't have this kind of money here."

I mention the locking drawer by his bed.

She says, "That's for eyeglasses, dentures, petty cash. Not this kind of money. And you need to mark his clothes with his name, so things won't get lost in the laundry, or borrowed and not returned."

From long experience of Julie's life at Gracious Gardens, I know many tales of theft committed by high-turnover, badly paid nursing home staff, and how some institutionalized old people become kleptomaniacs out of boredom or dementia or both and go around stealing from their fellow residents.

Nine hundred dollars. I never dreamed that Pop had squirreled this money away. I go back and ask him if it's okay if I put it in a bank for him. He says sure, he doesn't care. Maybe in the place he had created in his imagination he would have had a use for that money, but now he knows this is not a hotel for superannuated gamblers and swells, not a minimall for the aged.

This is his real, personal disconnection from the capitalist money economy altogether and in good earnest, at long last.

The laundry I've run home to do for him, including his bed quilt, I bring in that night. They have bathed and "scaled" his feet, removing dead skin that encourages infection, but by nightfall he has a bloody sore on one big toe that he bumped on the foot of a chair. I am concerned, but nobody will attempt anything at all for this without doctors' orders.

I sit a long time with him that evening, he morose and silent, me writing his name industriously on all his collars, cuffs, and waistbands with indelible ink. He can't put his own name on his things; his hand is too shaky, his signature reduced to a bug-track.

Out in the dining room (which doubles as an entertainment and activities room) I find the couple I was told about with such pride by the administrator back when she was still convincing me that Vista Linda was the place I was looking for: he's a retired professional pianist, and he's playing for his wife (no one else is there). She sits slumped in her wheelchair while he works away at something that might be "Smoke Gets in Your Eyes," it's impossible to tell. He keeps trying to correct the wrong notes by starting over. I escape, leaving my wounded dad behind in the hands of the enemy, his gentle enemies, his patient enemies.

THE NEXT MORNING I call and explain to Darlene, the duty nurse, about using ointment or cream after the footbath, which the doctor has neglected to indicate in his orders. She checks with Dr. Frame, and he agrees and says to use zinc oxide.

The other thing I've learned from Julie's life at Gracious Gardens is that the relatives outside have to keep a sharp eye on everything going on inside because, for all the various reasons connected with warehousing the old in sizable institutions instead of in smaller setups that would allow for more personal supervision, despite best intentions nobody else will.

I use Pop's nine hundred dollars to open the "burial account" of up to fifteen hundred dollars that Medicaid allows an indigent to have without whipping support out from under him and getting him thrown out in the street for not being indigent *enough*.

FROM MY DIARY ENTRY, TUESDAY, DECEMBER 24, 1991:

He was lying on his bed, looking small and gray and exhausted when I visited him today. Said the food was terrible, and in tiny portions (Darlene says they get plenty to eat, but they don't like it because it's not seasoned the way they're used to at home; low salt and none on the tables, doctors' orders).

I brought cookies, banana, an orange. Terri had come and talked to Robin because I had spoken to her yesterday morning about Tony, whose bed is on the inside wall of the shared room. He was playing his damned harmonica (flat and loud) and singing at the top of his lungs after dinner last night, apparently in order to drive Mr. Schoen (in the bed by the window) and his visitors out of the room and into the public area; as soon as they left the room, Tony quit playing.

Terri laughs and says yes, those two hate each other, but it's not such a bad thing—it gives Pop an intrigue to interest him immediately. I'm inclined to agree, but that's partly because I want to be able to agree: I want the intolerable to at least have a positive dimension to it. I know that for me, having to put up with that insane harmonica racket would drive me to suicide, and I know from whom I have inherited my sensitive hearing.

Pop says he couldn't sleep last night because of the sound of Schoen's TV, which is turned up high (the man is deaf). Robin didn't ask him to turn the sound down, of course.

In a new shirt and fresh pants this afternoon he looks alert and alive, but sits in the dark with the TV on, inaudibly (Schoen's is on too, on the other side of the space-dividing curtain, very loudly). He won't walk to the front to see Kate, whom I've brought in the car. He says he's afraid to leave the vicinity of the bathroom, pisses his pants too easily and with too little warning. His main concern seems to be that having to share the single bathroom with two other old men makes him worry about not making it in there in time when he needs to.

(I've spoken about this to Terri—diaper time? She says they don't want to invade his dignity, so maybe he has to ask for diapers; I must find out, because he won't.)

I brought him his Christmas presents last night, stacked them up on his shelves, suggested he open them this morning and I'd see him in the afternoon (giving him time to sneer and snarl about how inadequate it all was, and then maybe be pleasant when I got to see him; some hope).

When I showed up and admired his haul, he said, "Two books about Picasso!" and laughed despairingly. Oh well.

Already he asks very little about Bibi—he will abandon her before she forgets him. Is it a good idea to put her into the cat-carrying case and bring her to visit? I'm not sure now that it is. At home in his apartment, she sleeps in his chair, or on his bed; comes talking and winding maddeningly under my feet when I step into the empty apartment to feed her and pick her up to cuddle a little.

Last night she came into our living room (I had left the doors open, and both Kate and my cat Sixtus were locked away so they could not chase her out again). She walked around rubbing her scent onto everything, over theirs, and spitting crazily into the air, out of fear that Sixtus was lurking someplace and would launch a surprise attack.

I related all this to Rob; he laughed, but watched his nearly soundless TV the whole time that I was there. He says there's no point turning the sound up, what with demented people yelling in the hallways and staff crashing carts and equipment around (I am amazed at how noisy the place is, at all daylight hours anyway).

He says they bathed him very thoroughly and left him feeling sore all over. I'll bet. It's the first time I've seen him looking really clean in years. Terri reported that he showed "some reluctance" about bathing, but part of that could be because it hurts him when they do his feet; and many of the old folks are unwilling about baths, she says—about getting chilled, about modesty.

I have brought him his drool-rag, that he sleeps with under his cheek to keep his pillow dry. I have forgotten to write his name on it, but am not too worried about the horrible thing getting stolen. Every few minutes he jabs at his nose with a tissue, saying angrily, "I wish everything would just stop *running*."

His TV picture isn't sharp; he complains, comparing the reception with that of some of the smaller sets he sees in passing other rooms on his way to the dining hall. Maybe, he said, I should take some of his money and buy a little set for him.

I fiddle with the adjustments, minimally; Oh, he says, that's much better. It just never occurred to him to try to do anything about it himself. He'd rather blow a bunch of money—

his, mine, who cares—than lift one aristocratic-looking finger to improve his situation for himself.

Like the ice cream, a snack available every afternoon. "They gave me vanilla," he said, with disgust.

"Ask for another flavor," I suggested. "They told me they have chocolate, vanilla, and strawberry."

"No," he said, "I'll just wait and see what they do."

See if they'll read his mind and offer him what he wants, he means. It's amazing.

Liza has agreed, it's better not to get him a phone (the rooms don't have them); I'd been thinking about a cellular unit, but the cost is high and Terri says a cell phone would be likely to "disappear" anyway. Rob can use the phone at the nurses' station, and I have no doubt he will—to grouse and make trouble and play us off against each other, the way he used to complain to Liz that I was freezing him to death, et cetera.

Yesterday he said the food was terrible and the portions small. Today he says it's okay (though the turkey slices fell apart "in a funny way" under the fork). He says they're mostly crazy in here, which is probably true if you define senile dementia and Alzheimer's disease as "crazy."

He says, with some satisfaction, that Schoen is worse off than he is, and that Tony, the guy with the harmonica, is completely nuts (for some reason Robin is convinced that Tony is an Italian—because Italians are "musical"? I don't think he is; Italian, I mean).

Tony himself came in while we were talking, returned in his wheelchair from having been taken to lunch by his large and noisy family. As soon as they left, Tony threw up, loudly and odorously, on the floor beside his bed. Then came a huge wave of excremental stink, and he rolled his chair to the door and hollered "Help!" down the corridor.

"He has shit himself," Pop says darkly; and we talk while Tony waits, muttering and groaning in his chair, for about five minutes before help comes. They are beginning to change him when I leave.

I was hugging Kate just now, thinking, the dog invites love and accepts it happily. Rob invites nothing and rejects much of what is offered. His hands are still beautiful; I have hands like his, and mine will probably look much the same when I am old. Will I be like him, body, mind and spirit, when that time comes? Do I fend off love when it's offered? Jesus, I hope not.

At least neither of us is like the revolting Tony. Yet.

There are still tiny gray flakes of skin from Pop's ankles scattered on the carpeting in his apartment. I went in tonight, looked through some papers of his I found in a box—found some old horse-drawings of mine, from when I was a little kid, that he'd saved, and some cartoon roughs of his own with our old address on them, 6 West 102nd Street, telephone Academy 2 something or other, I can't remember now. And all his black notebooks full of tiny writing: it's exhausting just looking at them.

Cleaned out his icebox, found some old meals I had prepared for him to reheat, moldering in their plastic containers. Ice cream for Bibi. In the cupboard, packets of dried soup mix, scribbled recipes on envelopes, boxes of Earl Grey teabags, three different brands. Olive oil. Soap. The drainboard was still full of dishes, some his (mainly plastic plates from frozen dinners), some mine (a thick yellow plate for sandwiches, a bowl I had put noodles in). So this is where my missing teaspoon went.

No tears. I felt like it a bit at first, then thought, what would he be doing here now that he isn't doing there? He sits in his cubicle with the light off and watches the damned TV; all that's different is the quiet and the cat. By next week, if I don't bring her by, I bet he won't even ask about her. It's too much trouble, just like everything else.

The foot of his bed there is tilted up. The edema is already going away, permitting the ankles to start healing. I think the doctor was wrong, and Darlene is right: there's no infection to cure, it's just the salts in the taut-stretched skin that were making the problem. The skin needed cleansing and then lubrication with oily lotions, as they're doing now.

Now I worry that Pop will get better fast and come right home and then in six months we'll have to go through it all again for some other medical emergency; or that the wrong reports will be made, and Medicaid will turn him down, and we'll get landed with a huge bill from Vista Linda for his stay there.

I worry that I chose in too much of a rush, that Vista Linda isn't as good as I could have done for him (he can be moved, of course, given a vast amount of paperwork and fuss, to another institution). I worry that Ian and Cathy will come to visit him and be horrified by what I've done (no, they won't; they'll be damned relieved not to have had to do it themselves). I worry that they will come in six months and find him reduced to a drooling idiot, and blame me.

The lady at the yarn store said, "You'd be surprised at how fast they go down mentally once they go in there; but it can't

be helped." She is speaking from the recent experience of having institutionalized her mother.

I don't worry about coming home and finding Robin lying
on the floor, leaking piss onto the sodden rug, too weak to
even help me help him up.

FROM ROBIN'S JOURNALS, 1968:

*Occasionally, we see one remnant of the old G. Village: Joe Kling [?].
Remember? He had a musty, rundown bookshop on 8th St. ee cummings
used to show his paintings there. We bought a pirated copy of "Ulysses" from
him, around 1933 ($11).*

*Joe Kling, writer—he had at least 3–4 novels published, by his own
press—"Golden Cock" or "Cockerel"—now: a bum. Occasionally, we see
him, but he always sees us—with a suspicious glare of the finally paranoid.
He can barely get about. His ruined eye is worse, and the other seems
affected.*

We haven't seen him for months.
Joseph Kling, a disciple of Joyce.
You won't find him in the telephone directory.
You won't find him.

The Man with the Cauliflower Brain

FROM MY DIARY, THURSDAY, DECEMBER 26, 1991

So today he asked for ice cream in a different flavor from vanilla, and got it; "They'll give me anything I ask for," he said, scowling. "They're very solicitous; too much so, in fact."

He was sitting in the dining area for a change (not in "his" room), slightly odorous and shaky but up and around, sort of. His roommate Schoen shuffled by us a couple of times, probably waiting to be introduced, but Rob ignored him, so I let it be.

Time to bring Bibi? In a harness, maybe, rather than a box?

More papers to sign and go over with him tomorrow, for his signature—patients' rights, patients' responsibilities. And Admin. wants a copy of his Living Will for their files, which the doctor also has to sign off on. We did it a year or so ago.

I wonder if Pop will cancel it, now that we're actually up against the possibility of its being invoked sometime in the foreseeable future. That is his right.

He signs without a murmur.

With the power stuff—"You have to bathe, you have to dress, you have to take your medicine"—transferred from me to others, it feels as if Robin and I can get back to being father and daughter, at least to some extent. It feels rocky, but good.

SATURDAY, DECEMBER 28, 1991:

Something's wrong with his TV, he says; nothing but ads. There's nothing to watch, he says, no matter what he does to it. He thinks it's a different TV, not the one we brought in with him, the one from his apartment—"Look, the word on the front is different."

I go look, but it's the same Panasonic it was back home. He's having an attack of paranoia so blatant and weird that it rattles me; later I wonder why he said "the word," as if he couldn't actually read what the letters said.

The food portions really *are* small—I was there at mealtime yesterday. I phoned this morning and told the nurse to please make sure that Rob understands that he is free to order a second helping if he wants to; he's a big man and needs nourishment. She says she will.

I wonder if he ever picked Bibi up in his arms; probably not recently, his balance being so poor. Come to think of it, I haven't even seen her in his lap in a long time, only curled behind his knees when he was lying down. I leave the radio on for her in Pop's place, and some heat—the TV was always on before, after all. I suspect that those "spider bites" Pop got every summer were actually flea bites from sleeping with Bibi on the bed. Must put a flea collar on her, or she'll give the damn things to Sixtus and Kate.

The roommate in the window-bed, Mr. Schoen, is, Rob says, the only other resident who reads books. But Robin himself does not read now, it's "too much trouble." When I visit I find him lying on his bed or sitting in his chair with the overhead light turned off and his TV on; or sitting out in the common area, waiting for the next meal of overcooked, underseasoned, lowest-common-denominator institutional food. As a seasoned worker in the kitchens of restaurants of varying quality he has done more than his share in the production of bad food as well as good. Unfortunately for his current circumstances, he knows the difference.

FROM ROBIN'S JOURNALS, 1965–69:

Having worked these three months now in a business which feeds a sub-section of the people—counterman in a short order food-joint—one feels qualified to express certain remarks on the peculiar habits of that subsection. Besides being ignorant of literature, art, politics, the sports industries they lose enormous sums on, and of themselves, the American worker is food-ignorant.

The majority of them will just as soon order the great American hot dog at 9 am (for breakfast!) as a bowl of chili. Now, those among us who have been around know exactly why chili is here used as a demonstration point.

In the food dispensing trade, one discovers that "chili" is a mixture of old hamburgers, all the various greases scraped off the griddle, plus the steel particles scraped with them, plus fragments of emery paper used to polish the griddle, together with a fine garnish of scraps, giblets, bacon fat rinds, and small red peppers "imported" for the purpose (from bars where they are eaten with tequila etc.), plus a dollop of finely chopped raw onion. Cooked to a fine, sizzling, white-hot temperature, this is the stuff sought after by the New Rochelle laborer at 10 am as often as at 8 pm or 1 am.

Junk. Sludge. One would be better off eating a stew of dirt, clay, and leaf mold. These "customers" are the people who talk of television and baseball, of boxing and of automobiles, of money and gadgets; the American people, sir.

As days pass I begin not to be so struck—stricken, actually—by the worst-off of the residents: the women babbling and lolling and working their toothless mouths in huge, mindless grimaces, the men staring dumbly or sitting bent completely over, head on knees. I've started seeing the fairly able-bodied who live there too: the ones sidling outside for a smoke, the three sitting and talking together in wing chairs in the main hall, the two walking in to seat themselves for dinner and greeting each other amiably and lucidly, the couple shuffling outside, arm in arm, for a stroll in the winter sunshine.

There are only a hundred souls here altogether, which feels good to me: not so impersonal as the larger outfits I visited.

But Todd, the activities director who seemed so interested to hear that Pop is an artist, hasn't spoken to Robin himself yet. And so far, they have still not "invaded" Robin's "privacy" to the extent of doing something to offset his incontinence. I can smell him when I sit close by.

Errands continue; I have to find him a clothes-hamper that will fit his small storage space (a laundry bag won't do, they tell me) and bring a pocket knife he has asked for to use for starting an orange peel. He has long nails, relatively strong, but can't seem to break the skin of an orange for himself. Come to think of it, Steve can't either; some kind of male thing? Maybe they just don't like getting the pulp under their fingernails.

"Give me a push," burbles an old guy in a wheelchair to one of the smokers on the patio, who has gone over and asked him what he wanted.

"Can't," the smoker says, straightening as if offended to be asked. "I got a bad back."

Steve acts depressed and irritable, and he hasn't even seen Vista Linda yet. I can't blame him: he's probably just mirroring me. We haven't sent out our Christmas cards this year; they are sitting around in the house someplace, with stamps waiting to be slapped on them, and nobody mentions them.

SUNDAY, DECEMBER 29, 1991

Yesterday was the first day since Pop went in that I didn't go visit (I warned him that I had appointments I had to keep and that I wouldn't be showing up). It felt wonderful: free, unburdened. This isn't only the feeling of being relieved of duty; there's a faint flavor of defiant exultation in it: I don't have to come and see you, you know, so don't take me for granted. When he's probably wondering every morning whether I'll ever appear inside Vista Linda's doors again, for there is nothing to compel me. He knows my life outside is frantic with errands and necessities, just like everybody else's life who lives like a normal human being.

I begin to think that I still harbor old anger at him for disappearing from my childhood. And for the rest of it—the laziness, the unresponsiveness, the doubtless unwitting coldness.

I'd better be careful. I could start taking all that out on him now, by just not showing up, putting it off. Abandoning him. It would be effortless, and I doubt anyone would even blame me. This idea gives me such a queasy, sweaty feeling of disgust that I know I am also attracted by the symmetry, the justice—if that's what it would be—of it; and also that it would be despicable, and that I don't want to let things happen that way (it doesn't feel like something you do, exactly—you'd just procrastinate and let absence happen). But I do think about it sometimes.

When I get up now in the morning, or walk in the front door at home on Cedar Street, I'm conscious of an emptiness in what was his end of the house: nobody here but me and the animals. I miss our morning cup of tea together (which I sometimes found annoying at the time because I had lots else to do), wonder if he does. Wonder what he'll say when Liz phones him at Vista Linda (will he berate me to her?), or Ian; when Ian and Cathy come for his eighty-first birthday.

Big meeting tomorrow; what will that be like? Me, him, the staff—a "case conference." Not the doctor, though (which seems odd, but without some serious medical question to consider, I guess it would be a waste of his time; let the women, the nurses and administrators whose time costs less, handle it, for that's how economics works).

I'm not looking forward to it.

We have this meeting at Vista Linda to draw up a "care plan" for Pop while he's there. The nurses report, administrators administrate, everyone is warm, concerned, and breaking their necks to be helpful, within the confines of their rules and regulations. I am impressed by their goodwill and earnestness.

It's not put on; though Robin is behaving with me exactly as the reading I've done about all this predicts—expressing rage and a sense of betrayal and abandonment through sullenness, constant carping, and deliberately wounding remarks—to the staff he is already a charming, funny, still-handsome man, and they show signs of incipient fondness.

Rob is no fool; he knows, I am sure, that the resident who cracks wise and makes himself agreeable will get a lot more help, attention and sympathy out of the staff than a whiner or snapper. So his expressions of bitterness are saved for me, the traitor. Okay, that's only fair.

I have begged, pleaded, cajoled, and demanded that Robin or else the noise-making moron, Tony, be moved to another room. The administrator explains, wincing, that they are aware of the problem and are just waiting for a bed to be freed up somewhere else. Two days later, Tony is gone, moved elsewhere—maybe to another nursing home, for I don't hear his harmonica blasting away anywhere in the place. Or maybe some other resident or staff person, maddened beyond endurance by the noise, beat him to death with the damned thing.

It turns out that a fair amount of shifting around goes on within and among these institutions, to accommodate changes in people's health status, relocation of family members, and problems like drunkenness, sexual harassment, harmonicas, and personal animosities.

At the meeting, they tell me gravely that if Pop does have to have surgery—either prostate or on, God forbid, his cranial vascular system—Vista Linda will have to formally discharge him to the hospital, and then readmit and requalify him when he returns to recuperate. But they will hold the bed for him while he's in the hospital, so we won't have to worry about there being room for him when he's ready to return. I thank them for that small mercy, which is actually a huge one.

If there is surgery and it works, after he recovers at Vista Linda I can set up meals-on-wheels and home visits and take him back to Cedar Street, they say; for a while, anyway. For the short run. There is, we all are aware, no long run, not for him living at home again.

Everyone in the room understands that I want him to stay at Vista Linda, and that he doesn't want to stay, and that if I take him home it won't be to keep him there long. He is not well, has not been well for years, and is never going to be well again, and we all know it, but no one mentions it. We try to spare each other. Robin we spare by leaving him out of this part of the discussion.

What we are waiting for is the result of the MRI to be done two weeks on, and Dr. Frame's assessment of the prospects for surgery of one kind or another to help with the incontinence and balance problems.

I ASK ROB AGAIN if he would like me to bring Bibi up to see him—we could sit outside on one of the concrete patios, I've asked the staff about it—but he says no, it would just make him feel bad and her too, probably.

"I can't go out anyway," he says.

"Why not?"

"They won't let you go out, here."

Me: "Now wait a minute, that can't be right," and on and on.

It turns out, of course, that the patio doors are not locked but are fitted with alarms to stop the residents with a tendency to wander from walking out and getting lost or hit by traffic on the street. This is a real concern, and I understand it well. One of my aunts wandered away from a nursing home in Israel and was found days later, dead in the desert of dehydration and exposure. That happens here in New Mexico, too, from time to time. Potential wanderers wear plastic alarm bracelets to alert the staff when one of them is trying to leave the building.

"I have to go to work now."

"My brother called, he's meeting me in Gallup."

"Where's Eddie? Where's Eddie?"

There's one old woman who sits in the hallway most days, strapped loosely into her chair to keep her from falling or climbing out of it, saying in a soft, ceaseless voice, "Help. Help. Help." I hear that sometimes too from her room as I pass, but I've stopped reporting it. The aides answered kindly, "Oh, don't worry about that. She always says that." She'd leave if she could, walking her wheelchair forward with tiny, effortful steps of her slippered feet, going to Las Vegas, where her daughter lives.

Anybody else can walk outside, or wheel outside, if they wish to. Other residents drift about on the patio or sit on the stone benches in the bright sunlight of the cool New Mexico winter; you can see them through the windows, sitting and smoking.

Robin resists all my efforts to coax him outside with me. It's one of the ways he indicates how miserable he is. Another is that the books he got for Christmas sit on the shelf, still unread. I find him in the chair by his bed, slack and sullen, his gaze fixed on the TV. Occasionally, he'll be out in the big room in one of the armchairs, listlessly turning over the pages of a magazine.

When I ask if he would like to move to the vacant bed by the door (the one that was Tony's) instead of having the middle bed, he says no.

I get the message: no bed is a good bed, not here.

On January 2 I don't visit because we get up very late in the morning, and it's cold. I call, I wish Pop a Happy New Year and promise to come tomorrow.

Then, I go out and break my leg.

I AM STANDING on a slight rise at the south side of the athletics field, up at the university, where I go every evening to let Kate run with other dogs. While I'm chatting with Annie about an upcoming exhibition of her photographs of cowgirls, out of the dusk two Australian shepherds come racing, the lead dog looking back over his shoulder at his pursuer. The lead dog crashes into me and I fall, spun to one side by the impact, to a soft landing on the grassy turf.

Except that the sole of my right shoe, under the foot on which my weight has pivoted, grips the grass and doesn't let go, and I feel a red thread of heat unspool itself around my shin as I go down and know that my leg is cracked, breaking, broken, the hot, tingling pain shooting right down to my toes.

I let out a yowl and hear it ring loud and clear over Johnson Field. People gather as dusk thickens. The dog-walking friends want to bundle me into a car and drive me to the hospital, just a few blocks away. I decline and ask instead for an ambulance. If I lie still, there's hardly any pain, so lying still it is.

Jack, almost toothless and mostly drunk, the owner of a mutt he's trained to pull weight like a sled dog in competitions, stands guard to make sure the gamboling dogs (including Kate) don't come rollicking all over me now that I've come down on the ground to join them. Annie the photographer goes to call 911.

I lie there on the damp, grassy earth of the athletics field, looking up at the washed-out stars while the dog people stand around talking about what's happened to me. It gets dark. The leg doesn't hurt except for a distant, dullish throbbing and a light stinging sensation low over the ankle.

I feel like an idiot, but a lucky idiot, to be cushioned on grassy, if chilly, ground and among friends, instead of knocked down in the street by a car or fallen on a slick sidewalk. Kate, still dashing excitedly around with her buddies, is caught by Jack and taken to stay in another friend's yard til Steve can collect her. Someone has called

Steve, too—he's working late at the office—and reports back to me that he will meet me shortly at Presbyterian Emergency.

In due course an ambulance rolls cautiously out onto the grass for me, and then there is an emergency room experience, nothing out of the ordinary. A nurse is cajoled into giving me a pain-shot. I am "taken down" for an X-ray.

"I can tell just by looking that there's something wrong with that foot," says the X-ray tech wisely. By then my toes, over which I now have no muscular influence, have rotated outward so that the foot lies almost flat on its outer side, although my knee points straight up. Yup, something wrong, all right.

Steve arrives, comfortingly cheerful and in charge, and we figure out who's to be my doctor on this and make some phone calls. Off we go to another hospital, because the only guy we can reach (it's late Friday night by now) works out of Anna Kaseman Hospital, uptown, not here at Pres, which was closest.

I'm in the hospital for five days with a morphine drip—no joy, just lots of snoozing, and horrendous constipation (from the morphine) when I come out, about which nobody warns you—nor do they take any precautions to stave it off. I guess they feel it's what you deserve to pay for the illicit thrills of morphine, which do not, in this situation, exist. (The cure, by the way, is to have a jar of applesauce smuggled in by a sympathetic friend and to sip from it persistently throughout your hospital stay.)

Liza calls on the second day. I mumble into the phone that I feel okay, but I am outraged that they have put that hack Barbara Cartland in the bed next to me. So I guess the morphine did *something*.

The leg is now immobilized in a huge, heavy plaster cast reaching from foot to thigh. Helpfully, I have told the docs about how Mom died of an embolism and Liza quit using birth control pills because of their tendency to produce blood clots. Therefore, my doctor has decided to forego the usual modern method of screwing the bone together, using a light brace instead of a cast. They worried about screws increasing the chances for blood clots to form and get loose into the bloodstream, with lethal results. That's just what happened to Mom; I am not about to argue.

They have set the foot pointing slightly inward, to compensate for the stretching of my ankle ligaments that occurred when the foot was left to slowly sag outward in the ER before the doc on duty got around to putting a temporary cast on it.

The osteopath, when I am driven over to his office a week later for him to admire his own handiwork, takes out a felt-tipped pen and draws a broken bone on the cast over the actual break, with comic-book lines flying outward to symbolize trauma and pain. It takes me a minute to realize that this is super-bad mojo, though masked as humor. At home, I overdraw his design with green and gold, to indicate health and healing.

It isn't til October that I can walk freely and comfortably again. The leg heals a quarter-inch short, with consequent complications ever after (although lately it seems that a year of Tibetan t'ai chi, or some other influence that I haven't spotted, has at last brought the foot into almost proper congruence and length with its mate).

Given a choice, go with the screws.

ALL THIS MEANT that I was housebound and effectively out of it, so far as visiting Pop was concerned, for six weeks, and not good for much in the way of excursions for a month or two after that. I had gotten him installed at Vista Linda just in time. Steve, whose office was not far from the place, filled in for me as best he could.

Pop phoned me at home five days after the accident to ask me how I was doing. This was unusual, since normally he avoided calling and made me wait ages (when I called him at Vista Linda) before he finally made it to the phone at the nurses' station. I told him about my spiral fracture with gusto, pointing out that it was useless after all to have avoided skiing all my life out of a dislike of cold and the prospect of broken bones: the joke was definitely on me.

I think he appreciated that, under the circumstances.

I did, too; although I was stuck in that gigantic cast and getting jabbed every week by a visiting tech so that my blood-clotting rate could be checked, I was also well aware that I had something to be grateful for:

I had been wondering how to start cutting back on my daily visits to Robin. Driving to Vista Linda every day was exhausting and depressing, and the books I had read on institutionalizing your elders suggested insisting on establishing some mutual independence early on, for the benefit of both parties.

To put it another way, going every day to visit a resentful, sullen man in a bright, cheerful establishment inhabited by the decreasingly capable and the outright moribund had been wearing me down. Being there full time was undoubtedly wearing him down worse, but you know what? He *had* to be there. I didn't, not yet, so I damned well didn't want to be there more than I had to. I had not only the right but an obligation to stay busy in the outside world, where I still lived, while he learned to settle, however well he might, into the inside world where he must do his living now.

The enforced hiatus imposed by my broken leg would make a harsh but useful transition, I thought, to a more workable visiting schedule than every single day.

Most of January I sat up in bed (I had to keep the encased leg elevated to avoid swelling, so sitting in a chair was *verboten*) and maintained connections by phone. We spoke every day. I slept a lot, knocked out by painkillers, stress, and the sheer mental and physical drag of managing the cast and the crutches or the walker I needed to navigate even the short distance to the bathroom.

Meanwhile, Steve stopped in when he could to sit with Pop a little. The two of them had never grown close and did not now; closeness seemed not to be the point, just presence. Steve, harried at work and now doubly laden with this additional demand, did what he could and did it well.

It was Steve who took Pop for the MRI on January 14.

On January 18 Dr. Wells, a neurologist, phoned me with the results.

"There is evidence that there's been long-term, massive damage to the brain," this doctor said. Not Alzheimer's, he was sure, but massive all the same: "It could be the effect of many, many small strokes over the years. There's a lot of scarring, and a good deal of degeneration."

Silence, while I tried to think about this.

Finally I said, "Are you saying that he can't manage at all any more on his own? I mean, that he has to be institutionalized permanently?"

"Oh, that should have been done a long time ago," the neurologist said. "I don't think you understand the severity of his condition. I don't know why this man isn't in a wheelchair."

"But how long do you think he's been—in this state?"

"It looks like a number of years of accumulated damage here, going back some time," he said. "It's pretty bad at this point."

"Oh, this can't be right," I objected. "He reads mystery novels from the library and tells me which are the good ones."

"Well," the doctor said, "that's remarkable, but it can't last. Listen, my radiologist misplaced his pictures, that's why we were a little slow with the results. They were looking all over for them when one of the techs came running down the hall waving some negatives and hollering 'Have you seen these? This guy must be a total vegetable!' It was your father's scans. Crucial areas of the brain, large ones, are completely burned out. He shouldn't even be able to talk."

I am stunned: this really means that Pop *has* to stay at Vista Linda. I am off the hook. I am immensely glad, and, of course, deeply guilty. But above all I'm awed: my father has been functioning, or faking it, for what the doc thinks is years, on the mere fossilized imprint of a brain.

ME: "So our dad has been walking, talking, and reading books on half a mind. Just think what he could have done if he'd ever bothered to really use the damned thing when it was whole."

Liza (she too has been speaking regularly with him by phone at Vista Linda): "He just hates that place, Suzy. Does this mean he's going to have to stay there for good?"

Me: "Yes. The doctor made it very clear that Rob should have been set up there a year ago, maybe longer. I started to feel a little guilty about having been so late about it, actually. But who knew? Mentally he seemed fine."

"He says he hates the food."

Me: "He's got a cauliflower for a brain, for Chrissakes, and he's *still* calling you up to complain?"

"How are you going to tell him? He thinks he's going home."

I don't know how I'm going to tell him; but in my heart I know that when he lets himself see the situation clearly, he knows already how things are going to be. With a whole brain or without one, Pop was never stupid.

from robin's journals, 1953, new rochelle:

The matter of age and senility, the latter especially, fascinates us. Why, for instance, is a man like W. Sanger [painter husband of Mary Sanger] obviously in his dotage, that is. Hands trembling, mouth drooling a little, inattentive, he found it hard to think and to talk, and when he talked, it was with difficulty. On the other hand, men like Matisse, Picasso, Rouault, Braque, et al, all of them seventy years old or more, are still vigorous, still in working order, still keen and rational, talkative, excitable, alive and even, on occasion, guilty of posturing.

It is a case, we feel, of an artist gradually losing his interest, his motive, his love for painting. It is this loss that ages him and makes him soft. And the loss, the reason for it? He had little or nothing of his own to contribute. The Impressionists managed to keep going right up to the last. Monet, Renoir painted until the end! The love, the idea, progressive steps, stages, development lured them on: Renoir with his wooden hands. Who can conceive of <u>him</u> as ever having been senile?

Life Sentence

I telephone. "Hiya, Pop. What's going on?"

"Same old thing; not much."

"Listen, do you want Steve to bring your radio up there?"

"No. You can't listen to music here, there's too much racket all the time. How's Bibi? She must miss me, living in my place by herself."

Robin is really asking whether I have completed my betrayal of him by having Bibi put down, whether we have closed up his apartment and obliterated his presence at home—whether he is really in Vista Linda for good. He always leaps unerringly to the worst possible conclusions anyway. I almost prefer this to the possibility that he still thinks he's coming home as soon as his ankles heal. Whatever he thinks or knows, I am sure he has his hopeful moments, like any condemned person.

Steve says Pop's ankles look a lot better. I don't talk about the ankles when I call. Robin doesn't either. He needs more underwear, and a pair of Dockers to replace a pair of slacks that have been lost in the Vista Linda laundry.

I describe learning how to use my crutches without throwing all my weight on my armpits (which gives you shoulder problems, not to mention really sore armpits) but by leaning on the hand grips. It's an incredible luxury, I think, to have something real of my own to complain about.

Late in January, I make the most of telling him about the resetting of the leg. I'm immensely pleased to have a shorter cast, only knee to foot now. This means that to take a bath I no longer have to pull on this gigantic condom in bright yellow rubber that went over the whole leg, toes to groin. Not having to use that is an improvement of colossal proportions.

The leg is also newly sore and swollen (well, they had to break it again to reset it, supposedly straight this time). I figure it's in a good cause.

Then Dr. Frame calls to tell me more news: they've discovered that part of Pop's incontinence problem, according to the urologist, is a big kidney stone lodged near the ureter and pressing on it; plus the degree of swelling that comes with the very slow prostate cancer that any man past eighty is likely to have. We could do both problems in one operation, he says; some risk of death on the table, then a week in the hospital, no guarantee of any improvement, limited activity afterward.

What I am hearing is, a nasty mess for a possible tiny improvement in the incontinence problem, and some permanent degradation of mobility and general life quality along with it. Medicaid/Medicare would pay.

I think about it for a couple of days. Given the MRI, incontinence is no longer a make-or-break qualifier one way or another; the issue of Robin's future residential arrangements is effectively settled. It's all over but the official decision: he's in Vista Linda for good, where incontinence is, as it were, a way of life and *all* the men have enlarged prostates.

I say no to the operation. The doctor clearly approves.

I get notices from Human Services every couple of weeks saying that Robin has been dropped from their income support program. Maggie Pacheco says, pay no attention, it's just the computers. Thinking about the impact of that notice that I only know I'm supposed to ignore because she tells me so, I'm glad I don't have a weak heart.

AT THE END of January, Darlene tells me that Robin has caught a cold. They call me and inform me whenever he has a fall (three or four times since he's been admitted, no damage done). I know some of the staff now by name on the phone and chat with them. He recovers quickly.

In February Ian is in town and, with his wife, makes his first visit to the nursing home. They pile me into Ian's enormous rented car, and we pick up some Chinese food for a birthday dinner and drive to Vista Linda. It's the first time I've seen Pop since I broke my leg.

I can't wear pants over my cast, and I have acquired a long, gray woolen skirt for my rare excursions out into winter. Rob hasn't seen me in a skirt in ages. He remarks, approvingly, that I don't look too bad.

He looks thin but clean, resigned, depressed but no longer actively angry (of course, there are no singing waiters here).

With Ian and his wife along on their first visit, I am reminded that Vista Linda sometimes stinks. This is less because of the widespread problem among the residents of urinary incontinence than because many of the medications they take increase the stench of the old people's piss no matter where it falls, on floors, in beds, toilets, diapers, cushions. The corridors are always occupied by attendants pushing cleanup carts, or supply carts, or medication carts from doorway to doorway.

They always knock on each door and then walk in, calling the name of the resident they have come to see. It's a nicely judged compromise between the privacy rule in the Patient's Bill of Rights and the staff's responsibilities and time constraints.

I like and admire the staff people. From what I observe, they work hard for low pay, and many really seem to care. Most are women of color. Their patience and concern amaze me: who are these helpless, leaking, crazy, cranky, mostly white or Hispanic old folk to them?

Ian gets over his initial recoil-response quickly, and he becomes hearty with what I read as relief that Pop has not wound up in some hellhole. Rob and I have a sort of race to the dining room, each of us clumping along on our walkers. I win, but not by much. He wolfs down his fried rice, speaks little.

There are even things he has come to like about the place, if you can pry the information out of him: that they cut his toenails for him, for one thing. That he can wear slippers all the time now instead of struggling with shoes (although the need for struggle is gone now, with the swelling).

A lot of old age sometimes seems to be about feet, or the lack thereof.

I ask him what I ought to do with all the stuff left in his place—particularly the black notebooks, all fat and warped with interleavings of letters and clippings, that I have boxed up and put in the closet for now.

"Ah, throw it all out," he says, not meeting my eyes. He takes another mouthful of shrimp with lobster sauce while the dining room attendant looks on frowningly (we had to clear the meal with them first, and they were not happy about the salt content of the Chinese food). Around us other oldies slowly pack away a meal of spaghetti and meatballs. I see them look enviously at our table, their nostrils flared for a scent of the delicious, salty stuff in its sloppy cardboard cartons. Good, I think; I hope he's enjoying being envied.

Ian goes home heartened and relieved. I go home very, very tired and achey (the leg feels hot and bloated when I've been sitting where I can't prop it up, like for rides in the car). But I feel vindicated, too; this was a better birthday, in a lot of ways, than the last one. I haven't done so badly, my half-brother has not reproached me, my dad has not made a scene. He is eighty-one, and people qualified to do so are looking after him, while I try to look after my temporarily crippled self.

SHORTLY BEFORE the accident I bought a laptop computer. Now, forbidden to work at my desk for a quarter of a year, I learn to use the thing. It is a large, heavy black rectangle that I rest on a pillow on my lap. The heat from the case quickly seeps through to my thighs but is welcome; the weather has turned colder.

By the middle of February, I can actually work the damn machine. Unable to jump in the car and drive off for a cup of coffee on a whim, I suddenly discover that I can write the new book, the

difficult one, the one about outright war between remnant popula-
tions of men and women. I work like a fiend, with pages of scribbled notes fanned out on the quilt around me.

I plan major convention travels for the early summer, my professional income having taken a small upswing. The doctor says it's
probably going to be okay, if I take it easy.

My own life doesn't even slow down, let alone stop, while I deal
with my dad and my accident. Fine with me. I can hardly wait to
get moving again, I am champing at the bit. The house, where I
spend most of my time these days alone and cooped up, feels
empty and dull, when I notice it that is. Most of the time, I'm im-
mersed in the raw, brutal world of my book. It's when I break the
surface and come up for air that I feel restless.

The two cats, mine and Bibi, squabble sporadically over who
gets to lie on my legs. I still miss Pop's presence in the house. I do
not miss jerking my head up at every unidentifiable sound, wondering if that was Robin hitting the floor.

He sounds cheerful on the phone. He makes terrible puns.

On March 2, I start seriously—if slowly and awkwardly—
cleaning out Pop's apartment.

The next week, I attend my first convention since the broken
leg, Wiscon, the only feminist science fiction convention in the
world, in Madison, Wisconsin. Friends roll me from panel to
panel in a wheelchair and write and draw on my cast. The laughter
is wonderful. I feel like the belle of the ball.

The short cast comes off just after that (an awful, skinny leg is
exposed, with crinkled, fish-white skin, a pickled-looking leg that
horrifies me) and is replaced with a brace, a Darth Vader concoc-
tion of wide black velcro straps and metal struts. I call it Robo-
foot, and I hobble around delighted with my new mobility,
assisted still by the walker.

Midway into March I begin to drive a little, very cautiously (having no flexibility in my right ankle, it's a pretty clunky business). Early in April I drive up to Vista Linda to see Pop for the first time since our Chinese takeout birthday party, over a month before.

I find him thin, shockingly bony about the shoulders and chest. Hugging him (gingerly, because that's how it's always been with him), I am reminded of the last time I hugged my uncle, who died of Alzheimer's disease. Uncle Barney's torso felt as if it was made of wire hangers. Pop feels much the same to me now.

At last the staff and I have the necessary case-management meeting about the results of the MRI, a meeting that was postponed when I broke my leg. It only confirms what we all have known for months: Robin is officially designated a permanent resident, on full Medicaid support. Everyone kindly avoids remarking on my ill-disguised relief. I doubt it's the first time they've seen this reaction. These people are experienced with the family dynamics of the institutionalized old.

I tell Pop: he has to stay for good, doctor's orders.

He doesn't say anything. But when I ask if he wants me to bring Bibi to visit in the cat carrier now that I can get around on my own again, he says, "No. It's better for her to forget me."

I sit with Bibi in my lap that night and pet her and cry some. Robin is not someone I cry over much, but that night I do, for him and for her. She is bony of frame, like him. She purrs, though. Maybe if I petted him, if I insisted on touching more, he would purr too. But he has never invited or offered affectionate touch, and he is still angry with me; it feels like an intrusion, the idea of insisting on touching him without invitation. He has so little scope for decisions left: I can't bring myself to just override his thoroughly justified rage with sentimental gestures.

Maybe this is a mistake. Maybe he is longing for me to touch him, pat him, enfold him.

What crap. He just wants to tell me how bad his TV is—although he speaks approvingly now of Mr. Schoen, who has many visitors (or many visits from the same people), and who is a gentleman, it seems, of parts, as such things go in this grim territory.

It feels to me as if Pop and I are working blind, doing the best we can figure out to do in a bad situation that we somehow neglected to prepare for. It might all be easier, if I had known Robin better when I was a child and he was a young man (of course it would also be much harder, what with deep-rooted love and shared memories to deal with).

We seem to be at a place where nothing is clear-cut, there are no absolutes and no obvious answers. Everything is a balancing act. I should be doing better at this, then; I'm a Libra, aren't I? (This is a joke.)

Another joke ensues: typing on the laptop, I somehow hit the keyboard wrong, hear a funny little snapping noise, and find that the top joint of the middle finger on my right hand now flops forward at a right angle to the rest of the finger, without any control of mine and totally without pain. I hobble off to the emergency room again and find that I have torn the tiny ligament that runs along the top of the finger and attaches at the base of the fingernail and that draws and holds the finger's end up straight.

On goes a little plastic brace that my finger slots into, holding the finger rigid so that I am continually catching it on things, while the damage heals over a period of weeks. When I do the dishes, I have to wear something to keep the braced, bandaged finger dry. The best fit is a condom, sealed at the neck (if that's the right word) with a rubber band.

I'm back in a sheath again. Pop laughs.

Vista Linda doesn't change. I'm getting used to it; I even know some of the residents by name, although you tend not to get cosy with the elderly relatives of others there. The emotional drain of trying to cheer up the one who belongs to you is more than sufficient.

Señora D. is still asking all and sundry to give her a cup of coffee, incessantly, in loud Spanish. The woman who always wants to go out is at one of the doors, pawing without strength at the push-bar. She is trying to walk to a store and buy cigarettes, they tell me.

The woman who picks at scabs on her face is always in the big room, vacant-faced. Her wrists are loosely tied to the arms of her wheelchair with white gauze strips. It looks like cruelty, but what is cruelty, here? How do you define it? It has to be case by case, person by person, with full knowledge of what's happening with each.

A woman in a tan sweater and beige slacks and beige shoes walks up and down the hallways leaning on the railings that run along the walls: up and down, grimly hanging onto her mobility, nursing it along, determinedly cheerful in greeting. A man who wears a cloth cap strolls in and out for his smokes. He is visibly smug about his superior youth and strength, compared to almost everybody else here. There's a truly young man, too, in a wheelchair, recovering from a car crash. He won't be here long. His dark eyes are feverish, his voice vibrates with eagerness when he talks to visiting family.

Pop says, "Why can't I have a wheelchair? It would make it a lot easier to get around."

I tell him the doctor wants him perambulating on his own two feet, for the benefit of his circulation. He mutters, "Oh, sure, yeah," glaring balefully at me.

It's okay. I have come to prefer the acidic growling of his anger to the sullen silence of his despair.

Liza says she calls him as often as she can, but the nurses come back to the phone and tell her, "Mr. McKee doesn't want to get out of bed."

The rest of Pop's stuff—clothes, furniture, the extra pots and pans I gave him, his blankets and a few books—is picked up by a Goodwill truck. You don't realize beforehand how much has to be left behind when entering a nursing home. Quarters are tight, unless you pay a supplement for a private room, which we could not do and retain his Medicaid status. Even then, accumulation is not encouraged. For one thing, there's that problem of theft.

I give his brushes to the university's fine arts department. They are fine brushes, heavy headed and full, if stained. The fine arts staff person seems baffled by the gift, by the idea of really fine old brushes being valued enough to be passed on instead of junked. I think of Pop telling me a million times, you never put a brush away hairs down, never, and wonder if anybody will bother telling the art students that. Brushes are cheap now, made of synthetics to be used with synthetic paints and then discarded, and computer art courses are hot.

Later that spring I start seeing a physical therapist, trying to get back some mobility in my right ankle. Listening to the groans of a lean, dark man who is there to learn how to move his arm again after recovering from a shoulder separation makes me feel lucky again.

Steve is less lucky. His mother, now ninety, is giving out signals suggesting that she must move from her situation of relative independence—her apartment at Gracious Gardens—into smaller quarters in the nursing section of the place. She has been seeing soldiers, female soldiers in uniformed ranks, marching through her apartment. She has been falling down.

FROM ROBIN'S JOURNALS, 1951–52:

One never supposes it quite possible, especially of oneself—no job, no prospects, no money at all and the rent due in four days. It is now that one is most deeply depressed, anxiety-ridden and empty, one recognizes certain impulses to acts which furnish reading matter for newspaper obituary columns.

How fortunate (if that is the word) that one is not a Romantic who, in such a situation, becomes a victim to his own Romanticism and commits that final Romantic act out of a desire to impose, by the act, some logical design, some reason, on what otherwise seems senseless and horribly cruel.

Late in May, Robin calls to ask me to buy and bring him some new clothes: shirt, a pair of Dockers, socks, underwear.

I come to deliver them and find him sitting in the outer lobby waiting for me, a look of expectancy in his face. He has someone with him, a small, pale woman wearing white and pink, in a wheelchair (she's only got one leg—diabetes? You don't ask). She has the kind of fine-honed, fair beauty that makes me curse my square-jawed central European genes that decree dewlaps when you get past fifty.

This is Jane; she has been transferred here from Louisville to be close to family in New Mexico. Robin introduces her with shy courtliness.

I see that now he has stopped fighting when they want to wash his hair; it shines clean and full, in this way station of balding pates stained with age spots and scabs. He looks alert, defiant even, sitting up straight in pressed, clean jeans and the red-and-white checked western shirt that he wears now, in Vista Linda, because he has regular help with the pearl-faced snaps.

He clearly expects—what? Disapproval? Ridicule? What, for God's sake, with that challenging stare?

I shake Jane's small, hot hand and tell her how glad I am to meet her, and I have never meant anything as fervently in my life.

FROM ROBIN'S JOURNALS, 1968–69:

What do archaeologists dig up—besides shards?—bones. That's what endures. The skeleton. Today,—as yesterday—sex "is what it's all about." But is it?—Bones. Which seems to imply (SEEMS) that sex is an illusion (delusion). A guy who has a penis like a lamp-post may be a helluva figure in his lifetime. Dug up, a millenium later, none can guess at his penis-size: it hath no bone. He's dead. Like the rest of us. Death is the ultimate conformity no youth can demonstrate against. Sex is flesh. Blood. Reality is bones.

That chick, over there, is something quick and rare—I feel it in my bones . . . which philosophize, as flesh and blood take over.

But—who the Hell cares, as, who am I?

I care.

Jane, Jane, Jane!

August 19, 1992

Dear Aunt Frances,

Well, I never thought my next letter to you would be a cheerful one, but believe it or not, things are going very well. My broken leg has more or less healed (actually it was healed up fine a month ago, and then I went to the local co-op supermarket to shop and slipped on some lettuce on the floor. I wrenched the scar tissue around the break pretty badly and ended up back at the physical therapist's for another month or so). Steve's big case has been settled out of court, so he can breathe freely again and get on to other things such as living like a human being, I hope. I have revised and sold one new novel (it will be out next spring, title still not chosen), and am finishing another this month.

And your brother-in-law, Robinson McKee, is in love.

A couple of months ago I went to see him and couldn't find him. He wasn't in his room, or in the big activities room, or out in the front lobby. I was alarmed and asked the nurse where he was—had they had to rush him to a hospital or something?

She smiled and said airily, "Oh, he's probably in Jane Lestrade's room. He spends all his time in there now."

Sure enough, there he was, sitting beside the bed of a new resident who has one leg and hails from Louisville. He was sitting in her wheelchair and holding her hand.

I had been wondering why he had suddenly begun refusing to take his daily medications, complaining that the drugs make him sleepy. Now I understood: he has found somebody whose company he values, so he doesn't want to waste his daylight hours snoozing (which is very good, as he had begun developing a bedsore on his right hip from lying on his side all day, drowsing and watching the TV by his bed). They changed the medication to something less soporific, and he takes it now without protest.

Last week I found him alone in the dining room, having come out early for his food (and that's new, too—till now he did nothing but complain about the food at Vista Linda, give the nurses grief over finishing his portions, and just sulk in his room). He said, "Did you see Jane?"

In fact I had naturally gone first to her room but she was alone, and sleeping, so I'd come out again to look for him. I told him so.

He gave me a defiant look. "We're in love," he said.

I said, "I know you are, Pop, and I think it's great."

He glared at me and snarled, "I'm not *kidding!*"

I had to reassure him that I wasn't kidding either, that I wasn't teasing or humoring him but meant what I'd said.

Now when I go visit I head right for Jane's room, where I usually find her in her bed with Rob sitting there, in her wheelchair, looking out her window at the trees and the grass in the central patio (she also shares a room but has the outside wall, with a big, bright window). He's always spruced up and well-groomed these days, with a serene look on his face that I don't think I've ever seen there before.

Everybody told me, you put him in one of those places and in a couple of months you'll see a steep decline and then he'll die.

On the contrary, thanks to Jane, I am seeing instead a wonderful relaxation and mellowing in my crusty old dad. I can't tell you how happy it makes me, that somehow it was completely right to get him a place here, where he was, it seems, fated to find Jane.

Last time I went, my half-brother Ian came with me, eager to meet this lady, who is now famous in our family. Robin was sitting in her room with her as usual, and we asked, in that inane way you do when trying to make conversation in the gap of another conversation that you have obviously interrupted, what they'd been talking about.

Pop grinned at us and said, "We're planning how to break out of this joint."

I said they couldn't do it because they had only one wheelchair between them, and they both burst out laughing at that. Ian was so amazed and delighted by the way it's turned out that he said he would come visit again, which is a big deal for him, I think—he was really leery of the nursing home and I think he only set foot in it on Rob's birthday, last winter, because I persuaded him into it. I suppose he hasn't had all the "opportunity" I've had to get used to places like this.

Robin said yes, he wouldn't mind if I brought him a mechanical pencil and a pad and eraser (he's always said no when I offered, till now). I think he wants to draw Jane. I hope he wants to draw Jane.

I'm absolutely thrilled and delighted by the whole thing, and the nursing staff are pleased as punch—it gives them a lift too, after all, to see a couple of their patients happy for a change!

I hope you're doing well yourself; thinking of you, Suzy.

Jane shared a room with only one other woman, a room at the coveted far end of a corridor, relatively quiet and isolated. Jane's bed looked out on the grounds of Vista Linda, which meant a good-sized slope of grass with some small trees, and then the wall of the parking lot of a medical building next door.

A woman often visited her, her much younger sister, Iris. We would chat in the corridor—Iris was very glad to have moved Jane here and as pleased as I was that her widowed sister had found not just a friend but a devoted admirer in, of all places, a nursing home. We shared our pleasure in coming to visit and finding the two of them sitting together side by side out in the lobby with calm, dreamy looks on their faces, holding hands.

Meanwhile there was the election campaign to attend to, and the unseating of the unspeakable George Bush (but I think all Republicans are unspeakable, so don't mind me). When I talked politics with Jane—she was a staunch Democrat, thank God—Pop would look out the window and ignore the pair of us.

With Rob, Jane didn't seem to need much talk. She was not the chatty type—I found her rather laconic and even acerbic in conversation, when I came to know her better—and he was never exactly a bubbling spring of chat himself. But this felt different; a matter of peace, rather than irritation, or weariness, or abstraction. I would come in and see him sitting by her bed and watching her sleep, or staring out the window while she gazed silently at his profile.

He was noticeably cheerful these days, and I would find myself patting him on the arm, or kissing his clean, thick hair lightly when I left after a visit, because it was a pleasure to do so; something more that I owe to Jane.

And then there was the morning in September when he came rolling down the hall to meet me in Jane's wheelchair and I told him to get up and walk on his own two feet: did he want the circulation to die completely in his legs and end up losing more limbs than Jane had lost? I had to tell the nurses to please discourage him from using her wheelchair if the doctor concurred with my sense of this situation, which it turned out of course that he did. When I talked to Jane about it, she too agreed, with spirit and firmness, that Robin needed prodding to make the most of what strength he had left. I don't think she had many illusions about him.

She had a patrician profile: narrow, arched nose, strong brow and jaw, and the deep-set blue eyes of a Gibson girl. I thought sometimes that Pop had returned, in age, to the ideals of his youth. Perhaps his first wife had looked something like this, a Wasp beauty. I know that Irving married a woman on a similar model (though I had only seen her in age, on that one visit I'd made to Sacramento after Irving's death).

"A great beauty" almost always means a cool, porcelain-skinned blonde with "classical" features that wouldn't be out of place on a fine cameo or marble bust. My mother had had a broad-faced, European type of beauty, and a bohemian style of gaiety that seems to spring not from the martini glass but directly from a warm, excitable soul. She was an exotic, I realized, to look at as well as to live with, to someone coming from Robin's background.

Pop, West Coast white-bread and descended from an "old family," on one side at any rate, had come to New York and had done something like "going native" in marrying Maxine, with her immigrant family who spoke German and Yiddish at home, and her name that honored a famous actress of the time, Maxine Elliot (the story is that in her youth my grandmother made hats and corsets for a number of prominent theatrical women).

I felt a little resentment, a touch of disapproval, of this current circling back of my father's toward his original cultural fold—the Wasp beauty, I mean, represented by Jane—at the end of his life. There was the faintest flavor of betrayal of my mother about it; entirely in my own mind, of course, and I knew it and derided myself for feeling it.

What could be more appropriate? Hadn't Pop's excursion into my mother's heated world been a disaster all around? And if it's true that Mom had thrown him out, there was nothing left for him to betray, was there?

But this is upon reflection after the fact. At the time, I was just so glad to see Robin with a companion, to catch him smiling sometimes (even the awful teeth looked better, more natural; he was probably cleaning them now).

Jane's voice had a bit of a flat twang that made her sound sarcastic even when she didn't intend sarcasm, although often she did. She was sharply critical of those around her, not a drooping, sweet, old lady no matter how delicate and even ethereal she might appear; a good match for Pop, I thought. She always looked me in the eye and spoke up crisply, except for those occasions when she was clearly focused elsewhere and seemed not to hear what was said to her. She seemed older than Rob to me, but that may have been the effects on him of being in love: it made him younger.

I thought they were beautiful together.

I asked Darlene about them recently, when I went back to have a memory-refreshing look at Vista Linda: I wanted to know, how often did it happen like that, in a place like this?

They had expanded, adding beds in the midnineties. She said, "We have one couple now that have bonded like that."

Just one couple, out of over a hundred residents.

Pop, unlucky all his life at cards and in love and in so much else, was lucky at last.

FROM ROBIN'S JOURNALS, 1948:

Again and again it happens: one sees beauty and no doubt frankly goggles; and one gets a smile, one is even followed, but something intervenes, crosses one up; and the immanence of meeting is lost, lost, lost.

November 7, 1992

Dear Aunt Frances,

Well, would you believe it—Robin's friend Jane got him to register and to vote, for the first time in about forty years! Apparently everyone at the nursing home cast an absentee ballot, according to Robin and Jane. Everybody was involved and interested because of the various candidates' positions on Medicare and Medicaid, and they all watched the returns on Election Eve on their TV sets. So mark up another score for love! Robin hasn't been this engaged in the life of the world since I've known him, I think. *I* could never get him to vote, though God knows I tried. It's just amazing, and very gratifying.

Not that he's physically any better off. He has a lot of trouble walking, and every once in a while they call to tell me he's had a fall. The last time, he missed the wheelchair when he was sitting down by Jane's bed, and he landed on the floor—no harm done, he never breaks anything, thank God.

Did I tell you that I am picking out some of his art work for a public exhibition next month? The activities director at Vista Linda is very keen on the arts, and he was excited to find out that Robin was a painter. He has arranged for a show of work by residents, there and at one other local nursing home, to be hung in the main library downtown in December, and he wants to "feature" work by Robin, the only professional artist he's got among the lot of them. He wants five or six framed pieces, and as Rob insists that he doesn't want to bother, the selection is up to me (the few pictures he brought with him from New York are stored in my place anyway, so it's no problem). Who'd have guessed that someone living in a nursing home would have so much going on in his life!

Too much, sometimes. Last week one of his roommates started hitting him, for no reason that anyone can figure out. But no damage was done, the problem vanished, and he seems to have forgotten all about it himself.

Also, he asked me for some art supplies. I think Jane had convinced him to try to do some drawing again. I got him some, but the first batch he left lying around until it "disappeared." The second batch he says he hasn't used because he can't start anything without people buzzing around asking what he's doing, and he hates the bother of that. I noticed a wobbly sort of sketch tacked up on Jane's wall with Robin's name printed under it, and when I mentioned it to him he got angry and said he never did that lousy drawing, it must have been somebody else; and I see that it's been taken down since.

I think he did try to use the materials I brought him, but found that his hand is just too shaky these days for him to do work to a standard that gives him any pleasure, so he's backed off the whole idea. It's too bad; I thought the sketch was pretty good.

But on the whole things roll along well for him. We're close to the first anniversary of his move into Vista Linda, and he's lively and alert and has Jane to spend his time with, and the staff there all know and seem to like him, so I feel that our luck has turned out to be very, very good! Imagine, Robin voting! Quintessential cynic that he is.

I was delighted and relieved to learn from your last letter that you have your nephew keeping tabs on you now, and some live-in help too. I hope your health is holding up and the McKee luck is working as well for you as it seems to be working for Pop.

FROM ROBIN'S JOURNALS, MID-1940S:

In Aesopus' animalist terms, the meaning of government is that most of the sheep must be fed to keep the wolves fat, all of the sheep must be kept happy by means of mirrors, and there must always be enough sheep to go around: simply, government is control of the wolves and distribution of the sheep.

It was working unbelievably well, in fact. Iris even took "Bob" to her house, with Jane, for Thanksgiving that fall, which was a considerable undertaking since he walked with great difficulty and was still fighting off the necessity of diapers. Steve and I had Juliet to go and feast with at Gracious Gardens as always, and I would not have separated Robin from Jane in any case, so everyone was happy with this arrangement.

I was more than happy; I was delighted. Why shouldn't he have an important piece of his life, now that one was happening, out of my view? He must have fretted sometimes, living first under my eye, and now under the eyes of the Vista Linda staff. So I was glad for him to be bundled into Iris's car along with Jane and her folded chair and whisked off to someone else's festive board, a guest rather than a ward.

Jane's sister was with her frequently when I came to see Pop, bringing in the laundry that she took away to do herself, nice blouses and underthings that were thus not subjected to the indignities of the communal washing machines downstairs at Vista Linda. Commenting to me years later, Darlene and the supervising nurse (both still working there) agreed that Jane had been "a challenge" to look after.

She'd been a socialite in Louisville, they said, married to a prominent businessman, with a childless household. She'd had a long marriage and a long widowhood, and had come to Vista Linda with the heavy blow of her crippling still fresh and smarting. That must have been horrible for a woman used to being independent and admired, an avid golfer, a person with the appetites and habits of country-club social life.

She'd had money and servants in her old life, apparently, and now the Vista Linda staff found her "hard to take care of," "very demanding," all of which I read to mean she was angry and impatient about her demotion to dependency and contemptuous of primitive New Mexico, compared with civilized Louisville.

"She wanted everything done right now," Darlene said, without rancor.

I asked them how the lovers had met in the first place. Apparently Jane was seated at Robin's table one day at lunch and they began talking, which was a victory for the staff, since Jane had refused to speak to any of the other residents up till then. Several staff members said to me, "He was very good for Jane."

In other words, she was spoiled and sulky, finding herself so much reduced after many years of comfort and indulgence, and having a handsome, intelligent man like Pop dote on her cheered her up and made her feel human again. She was very particular about her appearance, especially after she started "bonding," as the nurses put it, with Rob. She fussed impatiently about the proper shade of lipstick and the fixing of her hair. They put up with it all in good part, feeling it was a positive thing, a sign of life: bonding beats brooding every time.

I like to think about how the admiration of a man in his eighties buoyed Jane's spirits and calmed some of her resentment of her fallen state. And oh, how well I can imagine the interior sense of that anger: I don't suffer fools—or foolishness in myself—gladly as it is, and I foresee trouble dealing with my own temper in old age (well, why not, since it's a terrible pain in the ass to me now as it is). We middle-class white American women are likely to be long-lived these days and well cared for in our dotage, but not as we would care for ourselves in ways that only we can see or value.

It's not something I could talk about with Jane at the time, but now I wish I had. We are perhaps too circumspect with the old about our own pains and fears, in terror of being overwhelmed by their unhappiness, or of just looking stupid by comparison with their need to deal with fears much more pressing and proximate than ours.

I asked her once about her past. She had been, she said, a career civil servant, the first woman in her state to rise to a solid administrative post in the justice system of Kentucky, until she had married her husband. But when I said I'd like to talk with her about her experiences as a woman of unusual local prominence for her time, she turned away and said she didn't really remember much about all that now. I didn't press the point.

Darlene, who was in charge of their hallway at the time, later told me that Jane had been a secretary before she married and had worked afterward managing her husband's office.

I don't know the rights of it. I don't care. Whoever and whatever she had been, she made my old dad happy, or something damned close to happy (and who knows what he told her, and her sister's family, about his own background and career!). As far as I was concerned, she was an angel straight from heaven (in which I do not believe, but what the hell).

As to religion, Jane believed, or at least she kept to the forms. To my everlasting astonishment, I heard from the staff that Robin had begun attending Sunday services at Vista Linda with Jane. I never said anything to him about this: it felt most distinctly like something intimate involving the two of them alone—well, the two of them and Death, who loomed close to them in an obvious way that was not (so far as I knew, anyway) true for me.

It all felt like none of my damn business, and I managed to keep my questions bottled up. If Pop had to give up his independence and his own place and every shred of his privacy to be taken care of properly at Vista Linda, I could accept my role there as an outsider, a visitor, with no right (except for reasons relating directly to his health) to shove my nose into whatever life he was managing to make for himself. It was bad enough that I had spies there whether I wanted them or not, in that the nursing and administrative staff felt obliged, quite properly, to fill me in on their observations of what went on with my dad.

I hope they kept some secrets from me.

Now when I got up to leave them, Jane would demand a good-bye kiss, too, and I would gladly bend down and give it. Because of her, my curmudgeon of a father was transformed before my eyes, before all eyes, into a romantic. This softening enabled me to glimpse him as the young man he had once been, susceptible to the longings and trances of love.

Besides, Jane was so beautiful, so vital, so imperious! Who could have refused her a kiss? Such feverish skin avid for touch, such brilliance in her big, sunken, crepe-lidded eyes! Her eyes, when not faded into visions of the past or glazed with dozing, were always wide open, as if not willing to miss a second, a flash of what there was to see, at least while Pop was there. I hoped, without much optimism, that the two elderly lovers could if they wished find a quiet corner somewhere for a real kiss, a cuddle, whatever they were up to and desired.

But what I observed was two people who simply basked in each other's company, soaking up life-force from each other, passing awareness of each other back and forth between themselves without even the necessity of words.

When it became possible—because I was extraneous, because they were so involved in each other—for me to come in and sit and say (beyond a word of greeting) nothing while they said nothing, I felt privileged. And I didn't stay long. Glad as Jane always seemed to be to see me—in Robin gladness was more difficult to discern—I didn't like to linger. Their time alone together, found so late, had to be painfully precious to them both.

However, if indeed Robin had been a man of property, my feelings might have been tinged with fears that he would insist on marrying Jane and diverting his wealth to her heirs instead of his. His poverty did this one good thing (for I doubt that I would have been immune to such materialistic interests): it freed me to be a wholehearted partisan of his late-life affair and let me see with relative clarity what was open to my observation, undistorted by financial self-interest.

I felt that the whole portion of Robin's life that had begun with his marriage to my mother and extended, after a break, into the seventeen years in New Mexico with Steve and me, was over at last. Something else, something that burned with a kind of slow, banked urgency, was transpiring now: a whole different lifetime compressed into a few months, blazing away before my eyes but basically indifferent to my gaze, almost oblivious, in fact, to my existence.

I didn't mind. I'd had all I could have wished to have of being near my father, thanks to his "alcohol poisoning of the eyes." That period, I could now see, had ended in a way much more decisive than I could ever have imagined when I got him admitted to Vista Linda. He knew people there (others besides Jane were now sometimes mentioned, like his new roommate, Shorty) whom I didn't know at all, and they knew him as I never had done and never could do.

They all called him Bob—he had finally gotten rid of that damned name that he had hated all his life, that he said "sounds like a bird."

Strangers who saw me as an outsider now took care of his bodily needs in much more intimate ways than I had ever done. It seemed to me that our second chance for intimacy had come and gone, with full amplitude, and we had made of it what it was in the two of us to make, no less (I hope) and no more.

Now it was right for someone else to have a chance with what-

ever time he had left. If she had him going to church, after all these years, as well as voting, of all things, more power to her.

FROM ROBIN'S JOURNALS, 1945:

The Bible does not mention the artist—let alone the painter—thus the painter owes theology nothing; what did Christ know of art? Probably what he liked.

FROM MY DIARY, DECEMBER 28, 1992:

The art show is mounted—they had an opening, and the artists and their friends from the nursing homes were carted down to the library in the van for it, but I missed the event, traveling on business that had been arranged the previous spring. I went to see the show as soon as I got home. It was a pathetic huddle of small works, most of them from well back in their makers' lives and careers when eyes and hands still functioned, all pinned up with care on a collection of free-standing panels in the big, open exhibition space up front.

Good thing I went, too. The first thing Jane asked me when I stopped at Vista Linda after coming home was, had I seen the show, and wasn't it wonderful?

The things we say for those we love, the things we say to keep our own spirits up—Isn't it wonderful? Or maybe it's just that she's not very sophisticated about art, for all her beauty and background.

Or, she's right: staff people at Vista Linda did what was re-quired to get those works out there to be seen, and that is wonderful. And; or.

I shouldn't be so negative, but boy it's hard—part of this is menopause, of course, now that I finally understand that "mood swings" means depression and restless, unfocused

anxiety, just as "hot flashes" means drenching sweats and a fiery face, in public if possible. The things your elders don't spell out for you are omitted for a reason.

I'm glad the show is up. I hope Pop is glad, or at least proud to have made Jane proud. I don't ask. Jane has a lot of rather prickly dignity; it reaches out and shields him as well. I hope this is a good thing. It doesn't matter whether it's a good thing or not, it's how things are, how adding a love affair to the parent-child equation alters our situation and the ways he and I interact.

In some respects it's a huge burden off my shoulders: I've always sensed a problem in the fact that his blanket exclusion of others meant that all his emotional needs had no one to look to for response but me. Now there's Jane, may her God bless her. If it also means the closing off of a deeper intimacy between Robin and me that might otherwise have come at this stage of his life (unless I barge in somehow to claim it, which I won't), so be it.

There is no good thing without its cost, and this late-life romance in a place that could never be home was, in my estimation, a good thing beyond price.

FROM ROBIN'S JOURNALS, 1952:

I am in love again; and I have a cold: two ailments for which nothing can be done—today, at least.

And Then You Die

FROM MY DIARY, JANUARY 13, 1993:

Robin is sick. Iris called from Vista Linda last night to say she was worried about him. She passed his doorway on her way out after visiting Jane—the door was open, and she heard him saying quietly, "Help, help, help." When she stepped in to see what was wrong, he didn't know who she was. She says he seemed very weak. She told the nurses he was calling for help; they said it was nothing, he was just doing that because he wasn't feeling well.

I thanked her, explaining that Steve and I have been away visiting the kids in California and that I was planning to go to Vista Linda next day. Last week before we left town I'd seen Rob and he'd complained of a runny nose, but had seemed otherwise fine. I guess the problem escalated while I was gone.

I went up there today and found him lying on his back in bed wearing a blue shirt and his jeans, his eyes closed, whispering, "Help. Help." When I spoke to him he opened his eyes and clearly knew me, but could not tell me, when I asked, just what kind of help he wanted. So I sat with him a while, correcting the galley proofs I had brought with me. He lay on his side and mumbled. Sometimes I would say, "What? What did you say, Pop?" and he'd answer irritably, "Nothing. I'm just saying 'oh.'"

He kept coughing this wet, gooey cough. I asked him how he was feeling.

"Rotten." He scowled at me and wrinkled his nose. "You've been eating garlic again."

I didn't stay long. It's just a cold, they tell me; they are staying on top of it.

JANUARY 14, 1993

Stopped to see Rob, but he was asleep although it was only midafternoon. Talked to Jane. She says "they" haven't told her anything or let her go see him. "It's closed in there," she said. Later she said that it had been reported to her that he didn't want her to visit now, and had said so to a nurse: "I don't want her to see me like this." She wouldn't go in his room until he asked for her, she told me.

I went back and sat with him a while longer. He was still sleeping.

In the hall again, on my way out, I looked back and saw someone in a wheelchair roll into his room. I thought at first it was a demented woman he has complained about before, who was always "bothering him," so I went in to ease her out again if I could.

But it was Jane, wheeling toward his bed, calling out, "Hello, Bob."

Robin, on his back, opened his eyes and said, "Hi."

I went away without disturbing them.

JANUARY 17, 1993

Robin stopped breathing this morning. I was talking on the phone with the doctor—who said Pop was getting stronger but was still sick—when a nurse from Vista Linda called me on the other line. She said Robin had gotten up for breakfast (he's been having his breakfast in bed while fighting this cold) but had wanted to go back to bed afterward.

The nurse, Mary, went to get help getting him into bed— he makes heavy going of it so the nurses assist him, two at a time because he's so tall and so weak and it's not an easy task. She came back (alone, no help available) and found him collapsed on the bed with no breath in his body.

She told me proudly how she pounded him on the breastbone, and he began breathing again, seemed none the worse off, but she warned me he could still "pass on" at any time. I wondered what the hell had happened to the "Do Not Resuscitate" order, thinking of that frail old body being bullied back into life just when it had found a quiet moment to finish, simply and fast. But whether or not the nurse knew about it (she's new on the staff), her training would probably have pushed her to do what she did anyway.

I showered quickly and drove up there. He was in bed dozing, didn't say anything about the morning's drama, or much of anything at all. I didn't bring it up; why frighten him with it, if he didn't remember? What if he panicked and said, "All right, gimme the life-support machines next time"? I'd have to say okay, and if he gets sicker we could drag along here for ages with him languishing in bed, slowly forming bedsores in that translucent, Celtic skin. I don't know how well I could stand that. I don't know how well he could.

They say you're supposed to talk about this kind of thing with aged parents. Easy to say that, when you're not right up against it. Maybe I should have had a serious discussion about all this when he went into Vista Linda; but he was so angry at first, and then he was so happy about Jane. What would have been the right moment to talk with him about dying? Maybe I've just been a coward about it.

I read once in a book about the death of aged parents that the process is often not as opaque and ambiguous as it sometimes seems. With some people you get clear signals. "When they're ready to go, they'll let you know. Your task then is to let them."

Is stopping breathing a signal? It seems so obvious. But I find I'm half afraid to know what I know, in this situation, if that's even the situation this is. We have a friend whose partner, an older man, stopped breathing in bed next to her one morning three years ago. She clawed him back into life and into a hospital, and they've gone right on living comfortably together since.

Today Pop seemed to be hazy and sleepy, not up for deep talk about death or anything else, since for the most part I could barely understand what he said when he did speak and I doubt that he understood me. I think he was hallucinating some of the time.

I feel tired tonight but okay; spent all day up there, watching him slip in and out of sleep. He mutters words with so little breath in them that I can't hear even when he's awake. He coughs awful, rolling, wet coughs, and his beard is smeared with yellow mucus which he doesn't seem to know is there.

I keep circling around because this next part is so—well, it's the answer to my question above, I think, about the signal; and that's hard to look at straight on.

He whispered something this morning, while he was drowsing: "I see a path."

I leaned closer: his eyes were closed, but who was he talking to if not me? To a phantasm of Jane, maybe? I said, "What, Pop? What kind of path?"

"Just a path. There's light on it."

I dropped my papers, thinking, Jesus, is this it? The tunnel, the light that people say they see as they head for death, dead relatives waiting? Awed, excited, I said, "What else, Pop? Can you tell me more?"

I stared and stared at him, trying to see into his mind, holding my breath. I felt as if I'd been let behind the curtain, if only a little way. In my own mind I saw a meandering trail in a forest, sun-dappled brown earth leading on away through lush greenery.

"I can hear things," he murmured, barely audibly. "All kinds of things . . ."

"What things?" I said. "What do you hear, Pop?"

"Things . . ." he sighed, and slept.

So that's how come I'm thinking, this is it: no machines, no hubbub about holding onto him for dear life. He's ready, and he's going, and he as good as told me so. Mostly I think it's my job to help that happen with the least amount of friction, but without explaining, because who will understand, who'll believe that I've been given the signal? And what about Jane? What can I say to her?

I talked with the nurses about the morning's event of stopped breath. Darlene knew quite well that Rob is officially DNR, but she was on break at the time it happened, so someone else (Mary) took care of things. I went and talked with Terri, the administrator, and I managed to say what I needed to say: that I understood that this illness was more than a cold, that it might be a terminal situation, and that I just wanted Robin kept comfortable and his strength kept up as best we could, in case he bounced back after all and needed it to heal with after.

She said they were getting some food into him and keeping his fluids up and staying in touch with the doctor about him. I said that sounded fine.

I didn't visit Jane today. There's only so much I can handle at a time.

JANUARY 19, 1993

I was up there again yesterday, Monday. He was in bed wearing a white t-shirt top and some kind of diaper-thing; uncomfortable, coughing, complaining of pains in his legs.

"Here?" I said, "in the calf?" I felt his calf-muscle for knots, having some experience rubbing out the occasional charley horse in Steve's legs.

"No, the calf, the calf," Robin said, panting a little and shifting minutely on the bed.

"Here, you mean?"

"No, no!" he exclaimed with escalating force and irritation. "That's not the calf. The calf is the *thin* part of the leg!"

I think it's the first time I've ever known him to be wrong

on a simple, factual matter, and I suppose for that reason it shook me. I didn't argue; I just made sure I had the pain located, and went off to tell the hall nurse about it. I said I thought he might be suffering from phlebitis in his legs (recalled this from the time Tricky Dick Nixon was in the hospital with phlebitis years ago).

She said she would tell the doctor, and hurried on about other business. Maybe she passed on my comment, maybe not; I never saw Rob's doctor up there, but was told that he kept in touch by phone.

I went back to Robin. He was jumpy and distressed, and when I sat down carefully on the end of his bed he complained that I had sat on his feet, which I hadn't. Apparently he was feeling even the lightest touch as heavy and mistook the pull of the sheet, drawn by my weight, for the actual pressure of my hip. I asked if he'd like the light quilt taken off, and when he said yes, he was feeling warm, I folded it and stowed it on a shelf.

My being there, of little use but unable to keep from trying to help, plainly irritated him. It made my heart thump painfully to see him churning around so slowly and feebly, trying to get comfortable. He muttered continuously, breathlessly, and all but inaudibly, and I didn't know what to answer (assuming he was addressing me at all). If I said, "What did you say, Pop? I can't hear you," he got angrier and gabbled loudly at me again, furious that I refused to understand him.

I would say, "Can I do something? Should I move this out of your way? What can I do?"

No, he said; leave the table by the bed alone; don't let the foot of the wheelchair (I was sitting in the one they kept there for him now) hit the bed, the jarring was bothersome;

don't try to adjust the pillows more evenly under his heavy head.

Finally he said fiercely, "Go away, go home, will ya?"

I met Mary, she who had delivered that saving thump to his chest, in the hall outside his room. She said with emphatic cheerfulness that she was hanging onto him, she wasn't going to let him slip away. She told me that he was always asking to have fewer pillows, to put his head down lower so that he could sleep, but that made him choke up with mucus and start coughing so they had to refuse.

She went in to wrestle him into the bathroom, something she was proud of having done on her own the day before. Standing outside, I couldn't hear his voice but I heard her declare in no uncertain terms that she wasn't going to let him just lie there and mess himself so somebody else would have to "clean up yo' *crap.*"

This was a nurse that Rob and Jane had both complained about, saying she was too rough with them. Sounded to me as if she had Pop's number just right.

Out in the foyer, on my rather despondent way toward the exit after having been essentially ejected by my father, I ran into Iris, heading in.

"We're very worried about Bob," she said. "He's not eating hardly at all. Have you talked with the doctor about intravenous feeding?"

"No," I said, "he hates being bothered with what they're doing for him as it is, and Mary says she's getting food into him and keeping his fluids up. She's having pretty good luck with soup, juice, mashed potatoes and so on, and I think the interaction with people over food is better for him than just hooking and unhooking a tube."

"Well, maybe," she said doubtfully.

"Besides, with his skin, you don't want to go sticking things in that stay there if you don't have to. I had a drip when I was in the hospital last spring and it took months for my hand to heal, and I've got skin just like his. Anyway, the doctor hasn't suggested it."

She looked anxiously into my face and asked me how I thought Robin was doing.

I thought about this for a minute, and then I just blurted out the truth: "I think he's dying."

"I think so, too," she said.

I went back in with her to see Jane, and Jane asked the same question. I gave the same answer. Jane said, "I think so, too."

She wanted to know just what was wrong with him, why he was having such a hard time. She said they wouldn't tell her anything.

I said they probably weren't sure what I would or wouldn't want said to nonfamily members, so they'd left it for me to tell her what they'd told me: "With the emphysema and the congestive heart failure he's been living with for so many years, you could say he has what they used to call a weak chest. Now he's sick with this cold he can't shake off, and that's where it's hitting him hardest."

Jane suggested sending him to the hospital. Her eyes were intent on me, very bright and piercing.

I said the doctor had recommended against this; there was nothing (short of invasive "heroic" measures that we had agreed to avoid) that they could do for Robin in a hospital that wasn't being done at Vista Linda. It would not help to subject him to a sudden and stressful move to an alien place where nobody knew him, away from his friends and from Jane herself; leaving aside the possibility of scaring him to death by this confirmation that he was indeed seriously ill.

In fact he was not that sick in the sense of fighting an infection; he just had a cold that wouldn't quit, not quite pneumonia (or anyway no one had used that word to me), and his body was not fighting it well.

I assured Jane that I spoke to the doctor every day, which was a lie; we spoke when we caught up with each other by phone, and even then there was nothing much to say. When Jane asked what the "DNR" sign on Rob's door meant, I lied again and said I didn't know, and she didn't press it. She must have sensed the barriers going up. She loved him, but she was not his family, and this was family territory.

It must have been very hard for her. Both she and Iris were extremely delicate in their comments to me, their expressions of anxiety and concern. They were pleading with me to do more, to get Pop more help, to save him, but tactfully, knowing that they had no official standing, as it were, in the situation.

I was as gentle as I could be in return, assuring them that he was getting all the help he could use, but making it clear that if this was indeed Robin's death, I was not going to intervene in it with painful, stressful, and ultimately vain measures unless I had a doctor's assurance that intervention could change the outcome.

I begin to get some sense of what it must be like to have an entire family clamoring for heroic measures, and to see how lucky I am not to be besieged by relatives each with their own opinion, their own emotional stake in the situation.

My emotional stake at present is simply unavailable to me in any coherent form, all such considerations being overwhelmed in the immediacy of what's happening. I feel that my part is to stay alert, to keep the way clear, to be attuned to what Robin wants and needs, and what he does not want and need, without his telling me—or needing to tell me—anything in words one way or the other. I need to concentrate, I need not to be distracted from the work in hand. His work, great work, and my small part in it.

Besides, I feel a little under the weather myself—a touch of rawness at the back of the throat, a hypersensitivity of the skin, and tiredness of course: strain. Or maybe I am just picking up echoes of Robin's own feelings and trying them on, in a distanced, attenuated way.

I have my moments of doubt—maybe I should insist on a hospital, on special feeding, more medications, more *something*. But I haven't the heart to maul the last days of an old man for no certain return but a feeling of my own virtue. If these are his last days.

I sometimes still doubt that he really is dying; but I never doubt it very deeply. There is such a feeling in his room of hard effort, of forging ahead with a difficult project, of the absorption of his attention in accomplishing it.

Or is that just me, projecting my own feelings on him?

When have I ever seen my father press a job of work through to its conclusion?

FROM ROBIN'S JOURNALS, 1948–52:

Witnessing the way in which one's father died, one questions the fear of death. His attitude, all his life, was that we come from nature's organisms and we return to enrich them: just what he did. Dying, he knew it, his sole concern being that his wife know where to lay her hands on money, bonds, etc. for her own future subsistence; and these facts he told her quickly, a soft "goodbye," then silence. No fear, oh, ye churchmen!

FROM MY DIARY, JANUARY 19, 1993

I went today in the early afternoon, although I was feeling really crappy myself—sniffly and exhausted. Just allergies, I hope—it's been a warm winter, and that always brings the pollens out and the sneezes on early.

Robin looked terrible. He wore a hospital gown and a diaper, and his hair stuck out in greasy-looking tufts. But he still had his teeth in, by God; good for him!

He lay on his right side with his eyes closed, holding onto the guardrails of the bed and panting. I sat for a bit, watching him and thinking, he could stop breathing any minute, and then what would I do? Would I have the guts to just sit there and wait for someone else to come in and confirm that it was all over, or would I run for help after all, or start thumping his chest myself?

When he started grimacing, struggling to roll over (complaining that his back and his right leg pained him), I got up to go get him some help. I was afraid I would tumble him out of that narrow bed if I tried to reposition his weight by myself. I was also a little afraid to touch him.

He yelled faintly into his pillow, "That's right, run away, that's what you always do!"

Shocked and hurt, I stammered that I wasn't running away, I was just going to get some help for him, and that I would be right back. When I brought a nurse back with me, Robin said he didn't want to turn over any more (he was settled on his right side again). The nurse brought the suction machine they had used to clear his bronchial passages once already (he could speak and breathe without bubbling so badly now, though he was still venting gobs of yellow mucus from his mouth which I wiped off his beard with a tissue).

She helped him hold the suction tube for himself and put it in his own mouth this time, which calmed him—he had been afraid she would apply it (much more intrusively but also more effectively no doubt) for him. He had said that he didn't want to be "suctioned" again. I could well imagine what it felt like to have that plastic tube stuck down your throat.

I went out into the hall with the nurse. She said he wasn't eating much, but they were keeping after him with soups and such.

I went to Jane's room. I knocked on the half-open door and she said come in, so I did, and found her sitting on her porto-pot by the bed. She was obviously upset—her eyelids were red and swollen, and her whole face looked strained and pale—but was making an effort to bear up. She didn't say much. I said I would stop and see her each time I came, to keep her posted on any developments.

Doubts again: but what would be the point of suddenly going for more aggressive treatment? A few extra days, maybe, in discomfort and fearfulness, for Jane? Now that I think of it I remember seeing him last week, before all this started, sitting out in the lobby by himself and idly turning the pages of a paperback book, a western of all things. I'd asked him where Jane was, and he'd said she would come down later from her room, but he'd sounded detached, uninterested. I'd thought he seemed depressed, grunting his answers, looking sideways at me in a rather dull, oddly furtive manner (of course I was sitting next to him on the couch, so he had to look sideways to see me, but still, there was something—). He seemed to be running at a very slow idle all the way through, and I remember wondering if he was just let down after the opening of the art show down at the library, or if he was even "off" Jane for some reason.

Anyway, today: I went back to his room and sat a while with my galley proofs in my lap, watching him talk and twitch in his sleep. I sketched him on the backs of a couple of the galley sheets, in pencil. His sleep was restless and active: his mouth would quirk and curl almost independently of the rest of his face so that it looked like a peculiar mechanical movement, no expressiveness to it. His hands jerked in his sleep, his long hands so fine and slender even now, except for that one knuckle, the middle finger on the right hand, that's been swollen and stiff with painless arthritis for years.

Sometimes he would open his eyes, very dark, huge pupils with pale blue around them, and I'd say, "I'm here," and feel foolish because wouldn't he think I was an idiot, saying I was there when I was sitting a foot away where he could see me for himself? He never answered or acknowledged that he had heard, but I said it anyway.

I did something a friend—a longtime student of the occult—had told me about once: I thought about golden light, hovering in the air over the bed, and then falling gently like bright mist and sinking into Robin's form, and then more, and then more: an energy feed, a love token. There was no visible effect, but it made me feel better and gave me something to do, something I could tell myself might do some good and was surely, at least, harmless.

After a while he opened his eyes and complained that the

air in the room was too hot (to me it felt just pleasantly warm), and how hot and heavy the blanket was across his legs. I told him there was no blanket, only the sheet, but I don't think he believed me.

"Take it off, take it off me," he insisted, pushing ineffectually at the sheet where it lay over his shoulder. "Go ahead, I'm not modest."

Then he began fighting with the hospital gown, so I untied the strings behind his neck and drew the cloth down his chest a bit (I couldn't get it off all the way because his arms were through the armholes of the short sleeves). His skin felt not hot to my touch but normally warm. I didn't think he had a fever; they'd had him on antibiotics for days.

But he said, "I've been lying here panting all day, it's so hot."

I took the big ring-bound calendar from the side-table and fanned him with it a while, mostly on his bare back and the side of his face.

The separator curtain around his bed was partly drawn for privacy; maybe that cut down on the circulation of the air in the room. Neither of his roommates was there. I wonder if they chose to be absent for these distressing hours, or whether it was just policy to keep them busy elsewhere so that Pop might sleep more easily. The room seemed very quiet, so empty of all but us two and without the burble of Schoen's TV.

I asked Pop if the fanning made him feel better.

"Yeah."

"Feels good?"

"Yeah."

"Okay, I'll keep doing it."

His legs looked as elongated and finely shaped as those of

some El Greco saint. There was no swelling in his ankles any more, probably because he is so seldom on his feet now that gravity has no chance to pull fluids down there against the weak pumping action of his heart. My God, he was beautiful, his skin pale and unmarked, no rib-bones or anything poking out in spite of his ethereal slimness, and even the diaper wasn't incongruous. He looked perfectly proportioned and natural, like some desert saint in a painting, lying nearly naked on his side.

After a while he said he wanted to get up, he wanted to stand. To go to the bathroom? I asked, willing to try to help him get up on my own, but not, out of daughterly squeamishness, to take him into the bathroom and help him there.

"Maybe," he said. "I just want to stand up."

So I went for the nurse. She got him on his feet and seemed set on heading him into the bathroom while she had the opportunity, so I decided to go.

That was my last sight of him today, standing a little crookedly on the far side of his bed with the nurse supporting him, his hospital gown hanging off his arms, his hair wild, his eyes all big black pupils, his face stark and outraged-looking.

"Pop," I said. "I'm going to go now, I'm not feeling so hot myself. Allergies, probably. I'll go take some aspirin and stuff. I'll see you tomorrow."

"Yeah."

"So long, Pop."

"Yeah, so long."

Outside I met Mary coming in for her shift. She said he'd almost "gone" on her a couple of times, but she was working on keeping him around. "He's fightin'," she said. "He's fightin'. I cut his hair a little for him yesterday, did you see? He let me do that."

She also said I might as well take that TV out of there (I noticed that Pop's TV had been off, unplugged, on Monday and Tuesday). "He don't want to see it. I asked him, Bob, you want to look at TV? No, he says. Radio? No."

I said I'd rather leave the TV because he might read our taking it away as a sign that we had all given up on him. She agreed that that made sense, and told me to get on home because I didn't look so good myself. And she told me not to worry too much about my daddy, since he might be okay after all, him being so grouchy and all.

But I know what I was doing sitting by that bed. It was a death-watch, which is what families used to do—taking turns sitting up with a dying family member. I never really understood what it was for—so the dying person wouldn't be alone? But there's surely nothing you do in your life that's as alone as your dying, no matter who's in the room. To be a witness that so-and-so is dead and gone, and how, exactly, it happened, for historical and maybe legal reasons? Probably originally just to pray for the departing soul.

And what the hell was I doing, imagining gifts of golden light, if it wasn't a kind of prayer? But that's a form of concentrated attention that doesn't ask for anything or say thanks for anything either, so I guess it doesn't qualify after all.

Anyway, he has others keeping watch over him now—his friends there, the staff who know him and who seem fond of him and definitely in his corner in his struggles; Shorty the roommate, who helped me plug the TV back in just in case Rob decides he wants to look at it after all. And Jane, of course, who says she won't go in unless he asks for her but goes in anyway, as I saw; good.

Mary was right, I'm not well (which is why I'm brooding over this stuff, I guess). It's seven o'clock and I can't keep my eyes open; I'm in bed with what I am now pretty sure is the start of a big, fat cold or flu attack, choked up and sneezing my brains out and aching all over. It's probably Robin's damn cold, that I've caught sitting by his bed while he coughed and bubbled germs all over the place. Steve says he'll go look in on Robin tomorrow for me.

JANUARY 20, 1993

Inauguration Day. I slept through all of the TV hoopla this morning, too sick and beat to keep my eyes open. When awake, I fought off distressing fantasies—that Rob would pull through just so he could blame me for not getting him to a hospital and turning on the heroics, full speed ahead. Or he would come back the way my cat might have come back from severe illness, the vet had said, with his character changed— and not for the better—by suffering. I mean, as far as character goes, there was not a lot of wiggle room there for Robin. Or, I thought miserably, what if he's bored with Jane, or has fallen out of love with her, and he'll come back and have to work that one out; poor Jane!

Are we starving him? Would he recover if we got him on intravenous feeding? What if we did, how would that prevent him from dying next week? Well, for Jane's sake, then. But his sake comes first, and wouldn't he come out of this knowing perfectly well that it's just going to happen again and he'll have to go through it again, trying to get the job of dying done?

I fell asleep again thinking, He didn't look happy when I saw him in the lobby last week with that silly book in his hands; he was finished, he was ready to go then. No, no, he's a stubborn old coot and as soon as I get better I'll find him sitting out there in his Dockers and that plaid western shirt with the snaps and he'll be demanding irritably to know where I've been . . .

I woke up with bright sun coming in the window at 3:45 p.m., and one minute later, while I was still rolling over and groaning with the soreness of my achey joints, the phone rang.

FROM ROBIN'S JOURNALS, 1946–51:

In studying people, the most salient feature seems to be their needs, continual and enormously complex in their ramifications. In contrast, one cannot imagine how even so integrated a dead system as a mineral crystal can be said to have needs. But to turn about, one can—and does—imagine how a human being can conceive the wonderful integration in and of a mineral crystal, and cast about him for ways and means by which to impose this order on life: for if the order can be imposed on life, and the result is beautiful (feelings of complete security?), why then life itself is not meaningless, but can be ordered, beautiful. Simple, hah? (You ask what art is—well?)

Who Was That
Masked Man?

FROM ROBIN'S JOURNALS, 1952–59:

Think of the dog races—that's it. And what's up there that everybody's chasing? A mechanical rabbit, brother—mechanical. Well, <u>this</u> dog has stopped running, for the moon has come up and needs a little howling to . . .

"Is this Mrs.—Chainas? This is Ruth, the duty nurse at Vista Linda. I just went to look in on your father, and found that he had expired."

"Oh," I said. I felt a vague, interior jolt, nothing more. "Oh, gosh." Surely there was something more articulate and expressive that I was supposed to say? But what, when this news felt so anticlimactic?

She was telling me how he had been sleeping most of the day, and she had just gone to make sure he'd taken his afternoon meds, and he was lying in bed not breathing. I thanked her for calling me, and told her that Steve was in fact on his way there for a visit and should arrive shortly. He'd told me he would drop by Vista Linda in my place at four.

Did I want to come and see the body? asked Nurse Ruth.

I knew I should go, but in fact I had no choice in the matter since I was so woozy from illness, sleep, and medication that I had no business driving up there to look at Robin or anything else. I said no. The nurse asked about a funeral home, and I said I'd have to let her know. I hoped they would make sure he had those damned false teeth in before Steve looked in on him, since Rob had always been so adamant about not being seen without them.

It was clearly time to call the people at the Sunrise Society, the local cremation outfit that I had signed not only Steve and me up with but Pop as well. I got up and shambled stupidly around in my office, looking for their form in my files. Finally I found it and got on the phone with a steady-sounding woman who drew me into an easy, calming conversation on a very matter-of-fact level; although, drugged to the gills as I was, I didn't feel much in need of calming. It was all I could do to keep my eyes open.

I found myself talking more about Jane than about Rob; well, she was alive, he was dead.

The Sunrise Society woman said she had an assistant who'd gone into a nursing home and had two boyfriends die on her there, one after the other. It's tough to go through, she said, but the experience of finding love even in such a dismal setting is ultimately so positive and life-affirming that it's worth it to everybody concerned.

"Were you with him when he died?" she said. "No? Don't let that bother you, you just said you've been with him this past week. Don't let yourself get all guilty about not being right there at the specific moment. You were there when he was aware of you, when he needed the company, and that's what's important."

I wondered how many times, to how many people, she had made that little speech, but I was grateful for it all the same.

"If you change your mind about having a last look at him, call me back in the next fifteen minutes and we'll delay the pickup till you get over there."

I was thinking about how I had seen, this past week, the way Pop slept sometimes the way I often do: on the right side and shoulder with the right arm doubled back, aslant along the left cheek and jaw so that the face is tucked into the crook of the elbow. Strange to see that in him and recognize it as a habitual posture of mine.

Steve called from Vista Linda later: he had found Robin lying on his back, his head to one side a little and his mouth slightly open, as if still sleeping. I suspect they must have done some hasty cleanup on him; I remembered wiping a long shine of mucus off his forearm yesterday, while his vast-pupiled eyes watched me do it, curious as a child's.

"Stevie, you'd better go tell Jane," I said.

He said (when he got back home) that Jane had thanked him sincerely for letting her know and had asked what sort of "service" we were going to have. Oy. If there was one thing Pop hated, it was ceremony. I'd have to explain later, to Steve and to Jane.

I called Liz and told her that Robin was dead. She was quiet a minute. Then she said, "He died in his sleep, right? So it makes no difference whether you were there at the exact minute he stopped breathing or not. And what if you had dragged your feverish butt up there to look at him after he was dead? It would be just the same as when he was alive, only it doesn't move."

I laughed. I must have been giving off guilt vibes a mile a

minute, even by phone, for having missed Pop's Big Moment. She said she was really sorry not to have been able to come and help us with all this, but that maybe her personal chaos would settle down sometime soon and she could come visit again—if she could get someone to house-sit and take care of her dogs and cat and her horse in L.A.—and then we could try to decipher Robin's diaries together. And she'd like a painting of his to take home.

I would be glad to see her: she was the only other person I knew who had any memories of Robin when he was younger, when he was some kind of father to growing children rather than whatever it was that he'd been to us as adults.

My other sister, Patty, suggested trying to track down any copies that we might have of the children's books he illustrated in the days when he was doing that, to keep for the grandkids. Good idea; I had some, I'd put them away safe.

FROM MY DIARY, JANUARY 20,
LATER THE SAME DAY:

I gave him golden light yesterday while he slept; I think in return he gave me the vision that came into my head today while I was sleeping: in my mind I was looking down at my own feet in little-kid shoes at the edge of the rowboat lake in Central Park, where he used to take baby-me to feed bread crusts to the ducks. My feet, in white socks and red shoes with straps and buckles, and the concrete curb of the lake-shore; brown ducks paddling in eager little circles on the brown water, craning and gaping their beaks for bread.

Maybe I was with him in my sleep today, glimpsing a memory of his until he took off, waking just in time for the phone call.

Liz told me she had to have her old dog Wolfie put down

yesterday, and Patty says she lost her little cat to cancer last week. Must be the season, I said. What I meant was, how absolutely fitting it is for Pop to take off in the same skybus with some beloved pets of ours. How completely typical.

JANUARY 21, 1993

From too much love of living,
From hope and fear set free,
We thank with brief thanksgiving
Whatever gods may be
That no life lives forever;
That dead men rise up never;
That even the weariest river
Winds somewhere safe to sea.

Swinburne,
"The Garden of Proserpine"

No, I didn't look this up for the occasion; I just came across it in the middle of a mystery novel from the library; a tale of premonitions and second sight, as it happens. Synchronicity strikes again.

The Sunrise Society lady came and talked to me in person. She says they mill the "cremains" down to coarse ash as a matter of routine, so your loved one doesn't come back to you as disquietingly large chunks of bone. She advised me to specify that I intend "scattering" for the ashes (on their paperwork) because "burial" means you have to get a permit from the county to designate the chosen spot as a grave site. Oh, scattering, I said, in that case definitely scattering. I have dealt with the county before.

She says she likes her work with the Society, though it can be rough: talking to the families of suicides is the worst. In self-defense, she mostly manages to foist those jobs off on the clergyman who started the organization (as an alternative to the extortionate and exploitive practices of many funeral homes).

She needed Robin's mother's name for the death certificate. I wasn't sure what it was, ours having been such a close, open family; plumped at last for "Marcia Frances Doyle." I know I have it written down someplace, but where? Didn't want to hold things up or invite red tape interference by leaving the blank blank, so I took my chances on memory.

Phoned Social Security to tell them he was dead ("What's his name again? What's his number? His name is what?" I wonder if maybe after you're *dead* you get to stop having to deal with idiots all the time). Phoned Maggie Pacheco re Medicaid; she was sympathetic but not sentimental, another together lady, a pleasure to deal with at a time like this. Went to the bank and emptied out the burial account to pay Sunrise, came home and crawled back into bed to continue being miserably sick.

Later: read a copy of Pop's will that Steve had left out for me on my desk. Wouldn't you know it, he left everything to "his children," plural; well, sort of. If we can't agree, then after a year of us growing to hate each other as we quarrel over his vast legacy, I, as executor, get to make a final disposition of Robin's stuff, thereby alienating my siblings forever. Thanks so much, Pop! Luckily, there's nothing to fight about.

When I remember all the times I borrowed a twenty from Robin when we were shopping and I came up short, and he'd hand me a bill and say, "Here, take it, it's all your money anyway." The times he said, "What do I need a will for? I'm just leaving everything to you, whaddaya think?"

So what happened? Three guesses. The lawyer must have said to him, "If you want to actually *disinherit* your other children and give everything to Suzy, you have to say so in the Will." And Robin thought, Somebody might get mad at me, and besides it's too much trouble, so he said, "Never mind, just leave it to all three of them."

I told this to Steve. He said, "I bet that's exactly what happened."

Not that it makes the slightest difference in the long run; it's just exasperating and slightly insulting, like so much about Pop. I explained it to Liz on the phone tonight. She laughed. "Just do whatever you want and don't worry about it. A saint can do no wrong."

This afternoon I dragged myself out of bed again, dressed, and drove up to Vista Linda to collect his paintings that had been returned from the library exhibition (and the thirty dollars left in Rob's personal account up there), not because I felt well enough to be moving around but because I was so depressed and jittery that I needed to get out of the house. (So much for plans to sleep all day and get better. Will have to get better without sleep.)

Saw Jane; the nurses said she was very cut up about Pop, and she did look pretty wrung out. I spent some time with her, even got her to smile. They gave her a photo of Rob from his case file. She had it in an envelope to keep it clean and fresh, and she showed it to me and asked if I wanted it: a harsh, horrible, true picture of him very much as I last saw him (except wearing a shirt instead of the hospital gown): eyes wide, hair on end, face stark and hard, staring straight at death.

I said she should keep it, until I could bring her a better picture. Steve took some excellent ones in the old days, out on Fourth Street. I'll get that really nice one, the profile with the old straw hat on, and frame it for her.

She said he asked her a hundred times to marry her, but she

wasn't going to "get into that" at this stage of her life. "He would sit here for hours," she said. "You know, Suze, many's the time he said to me, 'You make it so hard for me to leave you,' and I said, 'Well, how badly do you want to go?' and he said, 'I don't want to go,' and he stayed another hour.'"

I told her how he'd been a hermit for most of his life, and so her relationship with him in these last months was really extraordinary, and how happy we'd all been about it. That seemed to please her. Then I brought up the matter of having a service. I said we had decided against it because Pop was all his life a pretty aggressive (for him) atheist.

"Oh, really?" she said. "Well, that's strange, because, do you know, he went to Mass with me last time I went."

I refrained from pointing out that that was almost certainly on account of her, not on account of Catholicism, for which (along with all other religions) he had always expressed a robust contempt. I was just glad she didn't make a fuss about it. Told her I've asked kids and relatives to write to me with any memories of Robin that they have, to make a little collection for curious grandchildren to look at. She said she'd write something herself, and I promised to give her a copy of the whole lot once I had gathered it all up.

The nurse out in the hall said that Jane had asked her to watch for the obituary in the local paper and clip it for her. I explained that since Pop knew hardly anyone in New Mexico I was placing an obit in *The New York Times* instead, and would bring Jane a copy of that. Ducked back in to tell Jane so, too.

Tonight, writing notes to everybody I could think of who might be interested—about a dozen all told, beyond members of my mother's family who had known Robin—Jackie at the pool at

St. Joe's, Pauline who does not have Parkinson's, etc.—I did cry a little, mostly for the evident paucity of significant contacts in his life. Maybe somebody in New York will see the obit and get in touch, somebody from the old days at the Lion's Head, or some painter who knew him from that time.

FROM ROBIN'S JOURNALS, 1968:

8/16 (midnight)

Rain. Lovely. It catches the whistling, hooting idiots down in the street. Souses them, we hope. Anyway, it disperses them. Not the traffic. Endless. Noise, the curse of the '60's. How we've preserved our acute hearing is a mystery. (But we rise, ayems, shaking and unsteady—ourself a victim.) Cheer up, Buddy, you're alive! At 57. Is there time? Energy? Will?

Opposite: [clipping about a show of the artist John D. Graham at Museum of Modern Art]—J.D.G. . . . We saw him, once, at Diller's (14th St). Our only memory of him is a bald head and moustache. Said not a word. (Gorky—Arshile—was there, J.J. Sweeney, K. Dreier, Alex Calder, maybe Balcomb Green, dunno). Circa, as they say, 1932–3–4.

Now, we know nobody. Nobody knows us. We don't even know ourself. Nicht.

That's why we're anxious—yes—to get back to THE LION, where we are known, if only as "Bob"! ("Good morning, Bob," says Joel Oppenheimer at 3 pm, when he comes in, lusting for drink).

12:30—Good morning, Bob. Morning, Joel.

Raining like hell . . . outside . . . and rain inside . . .

February 10, 1993

Dear Aunt Frances,

I thought I'd write with some details about Robin. It was all very simple and pretty painless, as far as I could tell. He had the sniffles; then he had a cold; then he began coughing a very wet, congested cough, all in the course of about a week. He was still getting up every morning and going to the dining room for his breakfast. But after about a week and a half, he died. Now they think what he had was the flu. He complained to me that his knees and legs hurt, which is what tipped me off to this, so I asked if it was a possibility and they say yes, it was. It's ironic, because I asked him several times last autumn to have a flu shot, and he refused, saying everybody knows that flu shots *give* you the flu.

Steve brought back Pop's stuff (there was a lot more than I'd thought you could store in his space at the nursing home). The local cremation society took over from there. A week later I took delivery of Robin's ashes in a cardboard box—they told me they used to use a more aesthetically pleasing plastic container, but people objected on environmental grounds!— about 6" cubed; and early next month my half-brother Ian will come by on business, and we'll take the ashes and a bottle of wine out to the old house on Fourth Street, where Rob lived a quiet life next door to me for more than a dozen years, and we'll scatter the ashes there. I don't know enough about the rest of his life—where he was happiest, for instance—to choose anyplace else.

I tell you all this not to be morbid, but because I think it's a pretty good story as death-stories go. And there's a bit more: remember giving me Mary McKee's address years ago when I visited you, and how I told you that I didn't write to her after all because I had no idea what to say to an aunt I never even knew existed? Well, I wrote a letter with the news of Robin's death, and last week I got a call from Houston, from Mary McKee's son, Brian—Robin's nephew.

The funny part is, as far as Brian knew his Uncle Robin, the Greenwich Village artist, was washing dishes at the Lions' Head one day, and the next day—he had vanished into thin air! For all these years none of Robin's back-east relatives have had the slightest idea where he's been, he was just gone without a trace—disappeared! He never told any of them where he was going, or tried to contact them after he got here.

So here I am in this odd position of bringing news that solves a mystery for a family I have never met and do not know; like something out of a novel, don't you think? When I told my sister Liza about it, she laughed. "Well, I'm not surprised. That was him all over."

And it was. But there are people around here who remember him with some fondness, even if he was a hermit. I had a note from Jackie, who ran the water exercise class he took at St. Jo's rehab center for a year or so. She writes that on his application to enter the class there's a question, "What do you hope to gain by taking this class?" Robin had written in answer, "Glory."

And that was just like him, too.

I hope you're well, and send my best wishes as always.

I did not hear anything more from Frances (she died several years later in a nursing home in California). Maybe she *was* mad at him.

For some months I continued to visit Jane at Vista Linda. It was difficult. To tell the truth, I hated the place after Pop died. I hated his absence, and the way life there just closed up behind him, even that pinched, compromised life, and rolled on as if it didn't matter at all that he had come and gone; it was so ruthless. I felt this way in spite of the fact that the staff were very warm toward me, always welcoming, and eager to make comments showing that they remembered Pop, not always fondly but clearly, at least for the six months or so after his death; and in spite of Jane, too.

I brought Jane the good photo of Rob, the obituary from the *Times*, the letters from the kids about how he had been a mysterious presence in their lives, intermittent and opaque but basically benign. She was touchingly glad to get them. But I watched her closing off, shutting everyone out. I'd walk in and greet her—she was always in her room now, as she had been before the connection with Pop—"Hi, Jane, what's doing?"

And she'd say bitterly, "Absolutely nothing," and glare out the window.

I once told Iris, when she thanked me for coming to see Jane after Rob died, that I viewed Jane as family because of how close she had been to him those last six months, and how much that had meant to all of us. So I'd like to say that I kept up the contact for the rest of Jane's life. I could say it, but that wouldn't make it true.

She wouldn't talk. Her despair was palpable in the air, and her fear: she would clutch at me sometimes as I rose to leave and cry in a kind of panic, "Kiss me goodbye!" and I would, but it upset me, that clutching. We want our elders serene and accepting, I think, and that's not what was happening here.

I also felt an obscure guilt over her being left behind while Rob, having had his last romance, had slipped away. It made me feel oddly responsible, as if I should have, could have, forbidden him to go until Jane did. And I resented having to deal with the anguish and turmoil he had left in his wake—again.

In practical terms, I was just too pressed. Between Steve's mother at Gracious Gardens and our old Fourth Street neighbor Pauline (who was nearing eighty herself and had been in a bad car crackup recently), I was still carrying a full load of elders. So in time my visits trailed off, and eventually I stopped going to Vista Linda at all. Jane had her sister, of course, who was very attentive; but I still felt badly for letting Jane down.

She stayed there until her own death in 1997. According to Jane's obituary in the local paper, she was born the same year Pop was.

I AM CURRENTLY TRYING to work out some way that Pauline, who doesn't drive any more, can stay in her own place out on Fourth for as long as possible. She has no relations nearer than Arkansas, is apparently not close to most of even those, and has outlived most of her friends. That was a hard-living, heavy-smoking generation; Pop's generation. The tough ones live long, but their bodies bear the effects of a lot of rough mileage.

I said to Pop once that there was no excuse for keeping on smoking, now that everybody knows that cigarettes kill you. He gave me one of those looks. "Ah, Suzy, we always knew that, everybody knew that. Why do you think we called them 'coffin nails'?"

Steve's mother is ninety-nine and in a wheelchair at the Gardens now. She is still often sharp in her wits, although her attention span is short. The staff up there thank us for being such a supportive family—usually we come to share a meal every weekend. Most of their residents, they say, have no visitors at all, and indeed I seldom see others visiting when we're there.

I wonder about this when I think of the many visitors I saw at Vista Linda, which on the whole housed a poorer class of resident than Gracious Gardens does, economically speaking. I used to run into Walter Johnson, whose small shop took care of servicing my old IBM electric typewriter, when he came to see his father at

Vista Linda. Walter's father was a wheelchair-bound Alzheimer's victim, gaping and bawling unintelligibly and waving his hands around. Walter and his wife and kids visited more than once a week. Even the disgusting Tony had relatives who came often and took him out to eat and drink himself sick on the cheese and chili and beans he wasn't supposed to have.

I keep a copy of that nice profile shot of Pop in the beat-up straw hat in one of our books of family photos. I wish I had a picture of Jane.

FROM ROBIN'S JOURNALS, 1960:

Clipping up ye Bouuerie in search of 7″ brush we'd seen in a hardware store window, we were stopped by a wildly gesticulating little Russky: "You know who you look just like?" he shouted. "No," we shouted back.

"Count Winter! Just like: He was—he was—"

"Yes," says we . . .

"He was the Czar's Secretary of Commerce—You look just like—You too are tall, thin—not just the head alone, but that is exact the Count's! You are thin, like him; your shoulders stoop a little: but your face!"

There have been so many Winters and de Winters in history and fiction. The little guy went right on, gibbering, "He was not like the rest. He tried to make the Czar industrialize, to put the lazy, the hungry to work . . . But . . ."

Well, we left him, feeling no better for resembling a long defunct Count who probably got assassinated for his pains . . . Which Czar? Must have been Nick. This little villain was not 60. Suppose we should have stopped and talked longer, but you cannot chance such things on that street . . .

Visitations

Leafing through Rob's journals, I see flares and flashes of the man who lived next door to me: the scornful cynic with socialist (not to say anarchist) ideals, the disappointed romantic, the idolater of great painters, the scathing grouch, the ponderer, the playful troublemaker, the starving bohemian. It dawns on me that the notebooks turn out to be his shy gift of himself to me, made at long last and in perfect congruence with his nature: at a safe remove, on paper, a one-way communication with no possibility of direct response.

All the painting of today is dramatic, violently beautiful; all the literature dark, violently revolting; and all the poetry richly coiling, squirming violence that leaves a pain in the mind . . . what a sick world it seems to be! . . . What an enormous guerrilla-war for attention there is going on all the time (1960)

Passing a grocery store on 2nd Ave. this a.m., we noticed the sign, large, new, plain red lettering: "A & C, SUPERETTE!!"... super... ette!... Greatest; little! What the hell does it mean? (1969)

If Oedipus' blinding himself is symbolic castration, why didn't he also cut off his <u>nose</u>? (1952)

There is a decided advantage to being a pipe-smoker and a consumer of cigarettes as well: when one is especially low in funds, food, and future, one can always root out numbers of cigarette butts which one has with subconscious genius neglected to throw away. These make not the freshest or most pleasant pipe tobacco, but they do make a base. And one is relieved for another hour, one's stomach is stupefied for half an hour, and one is kept busy by the original inspiration, hunting up more butts between diminishing glasses of tea and cups of coffee... (1952)

With mixed feelings I read that scientists can at long last breed bi-sexual mice; as if there are not enough of them walking around now! (1950)

All the arts for a thousand years were enslaved by the church and the quarreling rich. Art, from the 6th to the 15th centuries, was the art of slaves for masters. The great Impressionist Movement, 1865–1906, was the first really free art, produced by really free men. (1960)

To work at 5 am, must shave. Oy.
*   To the Head by 6. . . . And, like . . . like . . . y'know? . . . y'know? Yinnow, yinnow? Like . . . like . . . yinnow! Y'know? That's conversation, y'know? Wow oh—yinnow? Like—Oh wow* . . . (1968)

Whatever an instrument is operative upon, in time, is operative upon the instrument. The stone will transform the chisel. The old chisel can be beautiful—perhaps it is the chisel which is beautiful, not the statue. (1946)

You cannot convince me that a rose would not be somehow different were it called a klotz. (1948–50)

Love happens; sex you shop around for. (1944)

Naught may come of all our canvases; but we *shall be preoccupied, motivated, alive. Is all that counts; and the best love of all—we love Giotto, Titian, Tintoretto, El Greco, Nick Poussin, Cézanne, and Pinky Ryder: three wops, a Greek, two frogs, and one American.* (1969)

Or rather, this fellow is *like* the man I knew, but more passionate, more desperate, more bitter, more ambitious—altogether more charged and vivid. Robin as I came to know him here in New Mexico was a personality darkened and crusted by a pall of seldom lifted cynicism and gloom; set against that, the loneliness and longing, the edged whimsy, the angst, the playfulness, the unswerving devotion to art and artists that pours off his journal pages comes like cold water dashed in the face.

In the four or so years between when he stopped writing the journals and when he came out West (1969–1973), he seems to have *faded.* He had lost interest, or perhaps was simply overwhelmed and muted by the onset of physical debility much more severe than anyone guessed, even he himself. Although he brought his notebooks out with him, he never (he told me himself) read them, he never looked back. Not surprising, really: "Aw, Suzy, whaddaya want to know for? It was a long time ago."

When he told me in 1973, "I wouldn't mind retiring," I think he meant retiring not just from restaurant work but from the painful struggle to become the recognized artist that he had wanted to be—retiring from all that inner heat and pressure. Maybe the space for him to finally relinquish his goals, fold his tent and steal away was what he needed from me, much more than a refuge from the problems of dwindling eyesight or a place to paint full-time.

Yet he couldn't entirely abandon that introverted but deeply felt past, or else why had he lugged those forty volumes of journals out West with him? That instinct to hang onto the physical evidence of his former life was a true urge: even half-forgotten and entirely unshared, his years as a struggling artist had prepared him for the final love of his life.

Of course he fell in love with Jane Lestrade; she'd been there too, in that postwar, post-Prohibition America he'd lived in when he was fully alive (she was almost exactly the same age he was, after all). Hers was no doubt a white-gloved, comfortable version, the glowing opposite side to the cold, meager coin of his younger years, but it was the same world as Pop's in ways that my world could never be.

And so, despite everything, you could look at it this way: enduring the pain of relentless failure, he stayed with his life until he achieved a great reward at last. Not a perfect reward, and not for very long; but it found him at Vista Linda, a place that he might never have entered at all if things had gone better for him, if he had made more pragmatic choices, more prescient ones.

His one greatest error led him to his last, and perhaps his best, joy. Isn't there hope for the rest of us in that brief and unexpected blooming out of ruin and decay? I wrote "ruin and decay," but that's not all there was, even before Jane. Withdrawn and shrouded as he was, Robin nevertheless *taught* me, in his absence and in his presence and in his death.

Without him, as a child, I think I grew stronger and more self-reliant. Later, when he came to live with us, the irascible, willful, demanding aspects of his nature helped me to become more patient (well, a little), more flexible, and, I hope, less self-centered (writing, like painting, is a very self-centered—and centering—activity). The exigencies of his ending tested him and tested me, and while I'm not proud of everything about the way I handled things, on the whole I think we both did pretty well. That's a strengthening knowledge, and calming in the face of my own aging and that of others around me whom I love.

On a daily level, trying to figure out what was going on in his head and in his life that I needed to know about stretched my empathy and my imagination in ways that are good for any soul, but priceless for someone who is a story-teller by trade.

One other result of having known the outward man (and reading, afterwards, the journals of his inward life) is that lately when I notice an elderly person having coffee at the local café or hobbling out of the public library with an armload of books, I'm inclined to see more than just what my eyes show me. My brain performs an automatic projection of the imagined appearance of that person at sixteen, or twenty, and sketches quick, tentative stories about the shape of the life that youth has since led. I can't see the details of their past, but I can feel its presence and vitality in them.

I don't know anything about the person, but I know there is much to be known; the mysteries of time endured in the world. There is dignity in those mysteries, which I can only infer from present evidence; they are the hallmarks of each seasoned individuality. I see elderly people a little more attentively and (I hope) sympathetically than I did, because of Robin. I get a stronger sense of how generations are divided by unsharable experiences, and also of how I, as I am now, have been divided by my own years of living from myself as I was at earlier times in my life.

Pop brought me up hard against the implacable power of time. That part of a parent's job he did superlatively well, and I'm grateful.

And yet, we have powers, too, we ephemeral beings; we're not just helpless pawns in Time's grip. That's something else that I learned from how we lived together.

True, the ordinary closeness of a father and a little kid growing up could not be revived or reconstructed between us after the fact; actions have consequences, and reversal is seldom an option. But if we couldn't be a "regular" father-daughter pair, still what we *could* be we made of ourselves over nearly two decades of close proximity. I think that was a long lesson in persistence and resilience, as well as in acceptance, however reluctant, of those things that we must recognize as beyond our ability to change.

Except in imagination. In imagination, all things are possible, and gold can be spun out of any quality of dross.

It's not an accident, I believe, that so much of my fiction centers on unlikely bridge-building over yawning gulfs—between humans and animals, between aliens and earthlings, between natural and supernatural beings, between plain men and women, and (in a novel just completed) between estranged parents and their daughter. The solitary man, the alienated intelligence gifted with insight and talent, shows up often in my work—as victim, as predator, as baffled, struggling creature, fascinated and appalled by the frightful power of and necessity for love, the need for the intimacy that expresses our deepest humanity.

How trans-(as it were)parent; looked at that way, it's downright embarrassing.

But where else *should* we find our master themes, we who write and paint and choreograph and compose? They surface from our dreams, which are grown from the seeds of memory, which come from whatever form of family raised us or allowed us to raise ourselves.

So I guess I'm less embarrassed than grateful, really. Robin, whose own artistic efforts sank with barely a trace, gave me the soul of my personal artistic work by allowing himself to be knit back, however clumsily, however late, into our family.

That said, I can't deny that at the time, anyway, I would have preferred having a dad who was a recognized artist with a rising reputation, or a still-struggling artist with a bunch of interesting bohemian friends, or a talkative man with a lifetime of sharply observed Village life to share, or—the range of possibilities expands outward as I think about it. I mean someone more regular, someone easier, someone more sparkling with the vigor of his own interests and achievements.

Instead, I got what I got: the burnt-out shell of a man whose potentialities had been thwarted, ambitions sunk, relationships frozen, his interests narrowed down to a pinpoint of fitful, paranoid attention, glum dissatisfaction, and a close attachment to his cat.

In other words, the person who came to live next door to me was less my father than my father's ghost; the ghost of my father as I had known him and imagined him all my young life. He was also, I suspect, the ghost of the man he himself had set out to be but never became.

Well, I'm a lucky devil: he was a good ghost, an instructive ghost. I owe him for such understanding as I have that even a life that seems (as all lives do from time to time) failed, stunted, scratched at the post, in fact masks depth, strength, and even beauty that are worthy of respect and regard.

I don't presume to know what he learned from me; but I trust that (in some measure that I can't speak for—only Rob could) I gave as good as I got.

. . .

THERE WAS another sighting, of sorts, that I choose to think of as the final one. I had been doing research on the traditions of shamanism for a story I had in mind, and in discussing some of the functions of shamans with an anthropologist, I had come across the spiritual work that he referred to as the function of the "psychopomp." This ancient word describes one who guides the dead, specifically one who enters the lands of Death to aid disembodied souls in finding their way through to their next stage of existence.

The idea of trespassing onto Death's own territory in order to give a helping hand to those who have for some reason been delayed there struck me as peculiarly tender. Most of what I learned about shamanism was far from that, leaning instead toward the grim, deterministic, and somewhat brutal, as befits the toughness of the hunting and herding cultures in which shamanic practice developed. Actually, thinking about it now, I'd lay money that the work of the shaman-as-psychopomp was really meant to urge the dead on their way so that they wouldn't hang around scaring hell out of the living.

In any event, I'd been doing some reading and studying about all this during the autumn before Robin died. I had even gone so far as to take a mental journey to find an animal "spirit helper" as a way of experiencing something of what such a journey might mean to a fictional character who was a believer. Like any sensible person I would have chosen a lion or a hawk as my totemic guide, but what we came up with was—a squirrel, or as my teacher put it, the archetypal squirrel: Squirrel. So much for grandiose ambition. You never refuse an animal that offers its services as a spiritual guide. Squirrel it was.

I didn't use those studies in my writing project of that time after all, but they left their mark all the same.

Three months or so after Robin's death, I dreamed one night that Squirrel came to me and flew with me through a large, white-framed doorway into what looked at first like a deep chunk of dark, starry space. But as soon as we passed through the doorway, I found myself standing just inside the French doors to Robin's dim but airy apartment at Cedar Street. It was daytime, and there was no radio or TV playing.

Rob sat on the side of his bed, bent over, legs braced apart, as he concentrated on the struggle to cut his fingernails with a small scissors. He wore jeans, his black sweatshirt, and that damned Navy watch cap, and he had his warped brown loafers on his feet. He did not look up.

I said, "Hi, Pop."

Still not looking up, he said, "What are you doing here?"

I said, "I've come to help you go where you belong." No response. "What are *you* doing here, Pop?"

"Resting," he said. "What does it look like I'm doing?"

Resting; well, *quelle surprise.*

My instructor in shamanic work had told us that when the newly dead stall out, as it were, between worlds, they mentally create the environment they expect to find "on the other side," or else just something familiar to surround themselves with. There they stay, sometimes for a very long time, parked, stagnant (that sounded made-to-order for Pop). They are often unaware, even, that they have died.

So I said, "You do know you're dead, don't you?"

"Of course I know I'm dead," he growled, still not looking at me. "I've done this a couple of hundred times by now, y'know."

I remember thinking, oh, of course—he's a much older soul

than I am, been around the block quite a few more times; no wonder he was always so tired and so reluctant to bestir himself.

"Well, come on, then," I said. "I'll take you to the light."

"I don't want to," he muttered.

I looked at Squirrel, who sat alertly on the floor nearby with its forepaws tucked against its narrow little chest, and who as my guide was supposed to have all the answers I needed on a shamanic journey. "Is he ready?"

Squirrel said, "Yes."

I turned back to Robin. "Come on, Pop, you know you're ready to move on."

I reached down, took his hands, and pulled him to his feet. There was no weight and no resistance. I turned to go with him in the direction that I knew, without looking, to be the right one.

"Don't walk fast," he said in an angry, anxious tone. "You know I can't walk fast, Suzy."

"We won't walk at all," I assured him. "Just link your arm through mine and Squirrel will do the rest."

We floated gently along like that, side by side and upright as if walking but not moving our legs, not far above the ground (the carpeted floor was gone, and also the apartment itself, melted into a bright outdoors afternoon), until we saw a great, squarish blob of brilliant white light straight ahead of us, just hanging in the blue air.

I checked our progress; I knew it wasn't good for me to go too close. This was Robin's trip, not mine. "There, Pop, there's the light."

"Oh, yeah," he said, straightening up at my side. "I was thinking about that, I was going to go." He turned to face me, and he was tall again, straight and strong-looking. "Come on and give me a kiss; we didn't do that."

Before he died, he meant, at Vista Linda.

I reached up and kissed him beside each corner of his mouth, and with that he turned and walked quickly and easily toward the light. Suddenly he stopped and turned back: "How's Bibi? Are you taking good care of her?"

"She's fine, Pop, she's hanging around in my kitchen as if she owns it, and she's started to eat dry cat food without complaining about it." I was so anxious to relieve any worry he might have about that damned cat that I babbled on like an idiot. "I think she still misses you sometimes, but mostly she seems pretty contented and—"

"Okay," Robin said, and turning away again, he walked into the light.

Then Squirrel and I headed home in the way that you do on these adventures, slowly releasing the focus until you open your eyes once more on what we are pleased to call the real world. I felt calm and satisfied.

Two months later, a tumor under the skin of Bibi's flank rapidly bloomed to the size of a small bunch of grapes, and she began to lick the place raw. Other tumors were already starting elsewhere on her skinny body. On my vet's advice I had her put to sleep. I figure that's a form of taking care, too. It's the last, best care we can offer to animal friends. I haven't seen her in the country-between, where my dreams have so far not ranged again. I think what I had to do there got done.

Except for this last part, which is done now too, as well as I can do it.

FROM ROBIN'S JOURNALS, THE FIRST VOLUME:
While I am alive, I want only a few to know it.
When I am dead, I should like everyone to know
That I was here.

Okay, Pop. Now they know.

About the Author

SUZY CHARNAS, a native of Manhattan transplanted to the Southwest thirty years ago, lives with her husband and two rollicking cats in an Historic District near downtown Albuquerque. A returned Peace Corps volunteer and teacher, she has been writing speculative fiction for over three decades. She is currently at work on her fourteenth novel.